# THE GOOD MORNING AMERICA
## Cut the Calories
### COOKBOOK

# THE GOOD MORNING AMERICA
# Cut the Calories
## COOKBOOK

*120 Delicious Low-Fat, Low-Calorie*

*Recipes from Our Viewers*

*Edited by*

## Sara Moulton with Jean Anderson

*Foreword by Emeril Lagasse*
*Recipes tested by Karen Pickus*

**HYPERION**

NEW YORK

LIBRARY OF CONGRESS CATALOGING-IN-PUBLICATION DATA
The good morning cut the calories cookbook:
120 delicious low-fat, low-calorie recipes from our viewers/
edited by Sara Moulton with Jean Anderson; foreword by Emeril Lagasse;
recipes tested by Karen Pickus. — 1st ed.
        p.    cm.
Includes index.
ISBN: 0-7868-6163-0
1. Cookery, American.    2. Low-fat diet—Recipes.
I. Moulton, Sara.    II. Anderson, Jean.
TX715.G61715      2000
641.5/635/0973—dc21        00-021859
CIP

*Book design by Richard Oriolo*

FIRST EDITION

10  9  8  7  6  5  4  3  2  1

The contributors of individual recipes are listed on pages 282–284.
All recipes are © 2000.

To all the *Good Morning America* viewers who
so generously contributed their recipes.

# CONTENTS

Foreword by Emeril Lagasse ix

Acknowledgments xi

Introduction by Sara Moulton xiii

How to Use This Book xv

## ENTRÉES

### 1. SEAFOOD 3

From Grilled Halibut with Rum Sauce, Great Greens, and Olives to Poached Sea Bass
with Shiitake-Soy Broth . . . from Dill-Crusted Salmon to Southport Seafood Pie . . .
from Stonington Clam Chowder to Cioppino to Red Pepper Soup with Pan-Grilled
Shrimp . . . from Spicy Salmon Salad to Crab Enchiladas

### 2. POULTRY 49

From Oven-Fried Chicken with Andouille Sausage to Feta-Stuffed Chicken with
Cucumber-Dill Sauce . . . from Chicken Breasts and Fresh Tomatoes with Capers to Tasty
Tangerine-Grilled Chicken . . . from Coq au Vin to Cajun Chicken Pasta . . . from Pecos
Chicken-Cornbread Salad to Chicken and Vegetable Enchiladas with Sour Cream and
Scallions . . . from Turkey Salsa Meat Loaf to Labladie's Lite Chili to Cabbage Soup with
Turkey Sausage

### 3. MEAT 107

From Fajitas Richard to Gazpacho Casserole . . . from Veal Stew in the Style of Ossobuco
to Some Kind of Wonderful Venison . . . from Romero Green Chili and Beans to Spicy Asian
Pork Rolls to Pasta e Fagioli

4. MEATLESS ENTRÉES        135

From Sunny Penne Pasta with Seven Vegetables to Risotto-Stuffed Artichokes . . . from Mushroom Veggie Burgers to Quick Tortilla Pizzas to Southwest Couscous Salad . . . from Sweet Potato Burritos to Mexican Black Bean and Quinoa Lasagne with Ancho Chili Sauce . . . from Teresina's Minestrone to Caramelized Onion Soup with Lemon-Corn Chutney

# DESSERTS

5. CHEESECAKES        177

From Caramel Cheesecake with Praline Sauce to Orange Cheesecake . . . from Paul's Chocolate Cheesecake to Double Chocolate Hazelnut Cheesecake . . . from "Not" Cream Cheese Cake to Black Forest Cheesecake

6. PIES AND PUDDINGS        191

From Italian Ricotta Pie to Peach and Almond Custard Tart . . . from Lee's Low-Fat Peanut Butter Pie to Banana Flan with Exotic Sauce . . . from Carol's Tirami Sù to Low-Fat Chocolate–Banana Bread Pudding

7. CAKES AND COOKIES        217

From Plain and Fancy Tea Cake to Spicy Whole-Wheat Angel Food Cake . . . from Nonna's Raw Apple Cake to Chocoholic's Carob Cake with Orange Marmalade and Carob Frosting . . . from Heavenly Chocolate Pudding Cake with Hot Fudge–Kahlúa Sauce to Caramel Apricot Brownies . . . from Energy Cookies to Peanut Butter–Chocolate Chip Cookies to Lemon Meringue Cookies

8. FRUIT DESSERTS        249

From Amaretto-Baked Pears in Pastry to Celestial Fruit Mousse in Meringue Nests with Raspberry Sauce . . . from Balsamic Berries with Vanilla Cream to Blueberry Crisp . . . from Luscious Lemon-Berry Parfait to Heavenly Roasted Fruit and a Bonus Recipe, Skinny Whipped Topping

APPENDIX        277
    A. A Cross-reference of Recipes by Category    277
    B. Recipe Contributors    282
INDEX        285

# FOREWORD

As we approach the new millennium, it has been obvious to me and others just how exciting food and cooking have become to a vast audience: men, women, and children. It has been the most exciting time for all of us to eat in America.

When a group of us at *Good Morning America* decided to see how creative people were cooking, we said, "Let's try to see how America is cutting calories." It wasn't a matter of cutting corners or cutting quality, just plain calories. We established the criteria that each entry in the *Good Morning America* Cut the Calories Cook-Off must be an original recipe, either savory or sweet, and certainly low in fat and low in calories. This would be a challenge. We were shocked by the number of entries. These were all narrowed down to five finalists in each category— Entrées and Desserts—after being screened and tested by *Good Morning America* Food Editor Sara Moulton and her *GMA* team.

The most popular dishes we received were cheesecakes, trifles (layered desserts in footed clear bowls), and chicken recipes. Surprisingly, we had more main dishes than desserts, but nearly everything we saw was creative, thoughtful, moderately priced, delicious but low in calories. Dishes like Turkey Salsa Meat Loaf; Spicy Salmon Salad; Grilled Halibut with Rum Sauce, Great Greens, and Olives; Chicken Cutlets with Roasted Red Peppers, Clelia Style; and of course our entrée winner, Oven-Fried Chicken with Andouille Sausage.

Or how about Luscious Lemon-Berry Parfait, "Not" Cream Cheese Cake, Plain and Fancy Tea Cake, or our dessert winner, Caramel Cheesecake with Praline Sauce?

Under the direction of Chef Michael Lomonaco of New York's Windows on the World, Wolfgang Puck and I judged the ten finalists, the top five entrées and the top five desserts, on the basis of taste (*most important*), originality, and healthiness. Wow, were we surprised by the amount of excitement! ABC's mail room was swamped with over 70,000 written requests for these creations!

So, congratulations to all who sent us entries, to our finalists, and of course to our winners. I, Wolfgang, Sara, and everyone else at *Good Morning America* say, "Enjoy, keep eating, and keep cooking!"

—Emeril Lagasse
*Good Morning America*
Food Correspondent

# ACKNOWLEDGMENTS

We'd like to thank, first and foremost, the thousands of *Good Morning America* viewers who participated in our Cut the Calories Cook-Off. Without them, without their recipes, there would be no cookbook.

Next, we'd like to thank Shelley Ross, executive producer of *Good Morning America (GMA)*, whose brainstorm it was to stage a low-fat, low-calorie recipe contest among *GMA* viewers to cap off a four-month interactive diet challenge; Wendy Roth, former *GMA* senior producer who with Patty Neger and Melissa Morgenweck oversaw the entire *GMA* diet series project; Margo Baumgart, *GMA* food segment producer, who produced the Cut the Calories recipe contest both on-air and off; Debbie Babroski, *GMA* researcher, who assisted Margo with all aspects of the contest; and grocery guru Jimmy Scheuering, who gathers all the food for *GMA*'s cooking segments.

We couldn't have conducted a valid or meaningful diet series without the professional guidance of Dr. Louis Aronne, assistant professor of surgery at Cornell Medical Center in New York, or of Kathy Isoldi, registered dietitian, who assessed the nutritional content of all the recipes entered in our Cut the Calories Cook-Off.

Huge thanks also go to the ABC mail room, which handled the avalanche of entries and recipe requests (70,000 and counting!); to Robin Ormsby, *GMA* promotions producer, who organized the Herculean task of fulfilling those recipe requests; and to ABCNews.com, which posted the top ten Cut the Calories recipes on-line for viewers to download.

Our deepest gratitude goes to Karen Pickus, gifted, good-natured *GMA* food stylist and chef, who not only tested dozens of recipes for the contest and *all* of the recipes for this book but also supplied several of her own. And many thanks to Joanne Lamb Hayes, Ph.D., who computed the nutrient counts for each recipe.

We'd be remiss if we didn't also salute Phyllis McGrady, vice-president in charge of production for *Good Morning America,* whose idea it was to gather all the most creative Cook-Off recipes into a cookbook; also Leslie Wells, executive editor at Hyperion, who so ably shepherded *The* Good Morning America *Cut the Calories Cookbook* from idea to reality, and Leslie's editorial assistant Lauren Weinberg, who manned the phones and fax and logged in the permissions forms and bio questionnaires with efficiency and grace.

A hearty "thank you" goes to the three chefs who picked the winners from the top ten finalists: *GMA* food correspondent Emeril Lagasse, *GMA* chef-contributor Wolfgang Puck, and Michael Lomonaco, executive chef at New York's Windows on the World restaurant, who not only organized the judging but also supplied the venue for the judging and the staff to prepare the top recipe contenders. Additional thanks go to Emeril and his assistants, chef Felicia Willett and Marti Dalton—Emeril wrote the Foreword and also contributed his best low-fat savory and low-fat sweet recipes to the book.

Finally, our gratitude to *GMA* anchors Diane Sawyer and Charles Gibson, who called the winners to bring them the good news, then welcomed them onto the show.

# INTRODUCTION

by Sara Moulton,
*Good Morning America* Food Editor

The *Good Morning America* Cut the Calories Cook-Off was a natural extension of "Lose the weight with *Good Morning America*," a series begun last February and featured once a week by project leaders and ABC news correspondents Sylvia Chase and Cynthia McFadden.

We then decided to give *GMA* viewers an additional challenge: come up with a recipe that was as delicious as it was low calorie and enter it in our Cut the Calories Cook-Off.

I must admit the prospect of such a contest scared me. And when Margo Baumgart, *Good Morning America*'s food segment producer, called to ask how to run the contest (at *Gourmet* magazine, where I'm executive chef, we'd done many recipe contests), I tried to talk her out of it. I knew how much was involved and I knew we'd be overwhelmed by entries. I was right.

I announced the Cut the Calories Cook-Off on air on March 9, 1999, giving the deadline (viewers had one month to submit their entries) and spelling out the rules:

• There were two recipe categories only—entrées and desserts—and only one recipe per category was allowed.

• The recipes submitted must be original.

- The recipes must be low in fat and low in calories.

- Each recipe must be accompanied by a photograph of the finished dish.

The stakes were huge. The two Grand Prize Winners, in addition to being flown to New York for a couple of days (first class all the way including limo service, dinner at a fancy restaurant, and tickets to a Broadway play), would join me on air in preparing their winning entrée or dessert for Charlie Gibson and Diane Sawyer.

Entries avalanched in and we observed some interesting trends: Ostrich meat was big (no pun intended) because several ostrich ranchers submitted recipes using this unusual lean red meat; cheesecakes were far and away the most popular dessert; fish and fowl, even good vegetarian dishes, outnumbered red meat ten to one.

Then the selection process began. We assembled a team of six, including *GMA* food segment producer Margo Baumgart and Karen Pickus, *GMA* food stylist and chef, to review the mountain of recipes. First, we eliminated those entries that failed to follow the rules or didn't sound tasty (my criteria were taste—*first always!*—then originality, freshness of ingredients, and healthfulness, which meant that many recipes filled with highly processed foods fell by the way). Next, nutritionist Kathy Isoldi rejected all remaining recipes with faulty nutritional profiles.

This intense winnowing reduced the number of contenders to about fifty. The next job—the huge task of testing those fifty recipes—landed in the capable hands of my good friend Karen Pickus. From the recipes that tested best, Karen and I then picked the top five entrées and the top five desserts. It was an eating marathon, but I got through it and am pleased to say that my two top picks were also those chosen several weeks later in the final judging by *GMA* food correspondent Emeril Lagasse, *GMA* chef-contributor Wolfgang Puck, and Michael Lomonaco, executive chef at New York's Windows on the World restaurant.

To prolong the suspense, we didn't announce the winners right away. Then one morning, Wolfgang, feeling frisky, decided to phone a few finalists on air. Needless to say, they were surprised and thrilled. Reaching Sandy Greene for her grand-prize-winning entrée (Oven-Fried Chicken with Andouille Sausage) was no problem. But contacting grand prize dessert winner Jan Curry was no piece of cake (make that *cheesecake*, specifically Caramel Cheesecake with Praline Sauce).

She was vacationing at her beach house south of Wilmington, North Carolina, and we practically had to call in the FBI to locate her.

After the winners prepared their recipes on air and after I demonstrated a number of the finalists a week later, Diane Sawyer held up the hastily photocopied top-ten recipes and invited viewers to write in for them.

The response was so tremendous that Phyllis McGrady, vice-president in charge of production for *Good Morning America*, thought we should gather all of these creative recipes together in a cookbook. Next, Rickie Gaffney, *Good Morning America* senior broadcast producer, got the project rolling.

To organize the book and write the text, I enlisted the help of my good friend and mentor Jean Anderson, a prize-winning, best-selling cookbook author; and once again, my good buddy Karen Pickus, to retest each recipe, fine-tuning them wherever necessary and putting them all into a consistent recipe style. For the nutritional breakdown of all recipes, I called in another friend and colleague, Ph.D. and home economist Joanne Lamb Hayes.

Finally, Emeril, Karen, and I have all added a few low-fat, low-calorie sweets and savories of our own to this *GMA* viewer collection of well over one hundred recipes.

The result, I think, is a terrific cookbook full of enticing recipes that should prove, once and for all— *even to nondieting diehards*—that food can be flavorful, satisfying, and healthful all at the same time.

## HOW TO USE THIS BOOK

• Read each recipe before beginning, twice if necessary.

• Do not substitute one ingredient for another in recipes unless substitutes are suggested.

• Use only the casserole and pan sizes recipes call for; they are necessary for the recipe's success.

• Whenever a recipe calls for a nonreactive pan (most often when what goes into the pan is highly acidic), use flameproof glass, enameled metal, or stainless steel. Cooked in nonreactive pans, acidic ingredients won't take on a metallic taste.

- "Cool" means to let something hot come to room temperature.

- "Chill" means to refrigerate.

- Preheat oven 20 minutes before using.

- Preheat broiler 15 minutes.

- A number of recipes in this book call for fresh leeks, which must be washed thoroughly because they grow underground and grit and sand may lurk between the layers. The quickest way to clean a leek is to trim off the root and tough green tops, then to slash the leek lengthwise from just below the green top to the root end. Give the leek a quarter turn and slash again, then two more quarter turns and two more lengthwise slashes. Next, hold the leek under cold running water, separating the layers as needed to flush out all dirt. Pat the leek dry on paper toweling before using as recipes direct.

- Use freshly squeezed lemon, lime, and orange juice only.

- Lemon zest, a term unfamiliar to many, is simply the colored part of the rind. It contains all the aromatic oils; the white pith underneath is bitter. The same holds true for orange, lime, and grapefruit zests.

- Use pure vanilla extract only, not imitation, which has a vulgar perfumey flavor.

- Wherever you see "freshly grated Parmesan cheese" in a recipe, that means *parmigiano reggiano*. This is the best of all Parmesans, imported from Italy, with a mellow nutty flavor that's not too sweet and not too salty. Domestic Parmesans can't compare with the real thing. Buy *parmigiano reggiano* by the pound (its name is stamped on the rind), chunk it, and grate it yourself in a food processor by pulsing quickly. Stored in a tightly capped jar in the refrigerator, it keeps for weeks and even then tastes amazingly fresh—not true of bottled grated Parmesans, which seem stale and taste mainly of salt. All of the above also applies to "freshly grated Romano cheese." Reject bottled domestic romanos and insist upon *pecorino romano*, a sharp, hard sheep's cheese made in the vicinity of Rome. As with *parmigiano reggiano*, buy it by the chunk, grate it yourself, and store in an airtight jar in the refrigerator.

• All nutrient counts are per serving unless otherwise indicated. Here's what the abbreviations mean: g = gram, mg = milligram.

Unless otherwise indicated:

• Black pepper is freshly ground.

• Butter is unsalted.

• Eggs are large.

• Flour is all-purpose flour and, except for amounts measured by table-spoons, is sifted *before* being measured. And that includes flours marked *"presifted"* on the bags.

• Garlic cloves are medium size. TIP: To peel garlic cloves zip-quick, whack them with the broad side of a large chef's knife—the skins will slip right off. And to make garlic mince more neatly and keep it from sticking so tenaciously to the knife, sprinkle your cutting board with a little salt.

• Mushrooms are the common white supermarket variety.

• Nonstick cooking spray is plain or unflavored.

• Olive oil is extra-virgin. For salads and quick sautés, the fruitiness of extra-virgin olive makes all the difference. For slow-simmering soups, stews, and braises, however, a general, less expensive all-purpose olive oil is perfectly acceptable.

• Onions are medium-size yellow onions. NOTE: Yellow onions are bigger than in years past, so you may get as much as ⅔ or ¾ cup chopped onion from a medium-size onion. The standard equivalent 20 or 30 years ago: 1 medium-size onion = ½ cup chopped onion. Small onions yielded ¼ cup chopped (few onions today are *that small!*) and large ones, 1 cup chopped. In testing these recipes, we found that today's large yellow onions yield about 1½ cups chopped, medium-large onions 1 cup chopped.

• Potatoes are medium-size all-purpose (Maine or Eastern) potatoes.

• Bell peppers are medium size.

# THE GOOD MORNING AMERICA
## Cut the Calories
### COOKBOOK

# Entrées

# SEAFOOD

Grilled Halibut with Rum Sauce, Great Greens, and Olives *(Finalist, Entrées)*　　4

Herbed Snapper with Warm Mango Salsa　　7

Cajun Cod Fillet with Melon Salsa　　9

Poached Sea Bass with Shiitake-Soy Broth　　11

Sea Bass with Curried Lentils and Rice　　13

Emeril's Potato-Crusted Fish with a French Green Bean Relish　　15

Baked King Salmon with Red Wine–Mustard Sauce　　18

Dill-Crusted Salmon　　20

Fish Masala　　22

Spicy Salmon Salad *(Finalist, Entrées)*　　24

Southport Seafood Pie　　26

Shrimp in Tasso Cream Sauce with Eggplant Medallions　　29

Chipotle-Beer Shrimp with Pasta　　31

Creamy Shrimp with Rice　　33

Shrimp and Asparagus Casserole　　35

Rebecca's Linguine with White Clam Sauce　　37

Linguine with Crab and a Touch of Lemon　　39

Crab Enchiladas　　41

Cioppino　　43

Red Pepper Soup with Pan-Grilled Shrimp　　45

Stonington Clam Chowder　　47

## JOAN W. CHURCHILL

*Dover, New Hampshire*

Born and brought up in Venezuela and New Jersey and now head of design in the Department of Theatre and Dance at the University of New Hampshire, Joan claims that she conceived her recipe for Grilled Halibut with Rum Sauce, Great Greens, and Olives—a finalist in *Good Morning America*'s Cut the Calories Cook-Off—on the computer. "I sat down at my computer and thought. Then formulated essences that could go together. Then what was low cal. Then what was trendy." Placing among *GMA*'s top five entrées isn't the first time a seafood recipe of Joan's has scored. She won Merv Griffin's "Sexy Seafood" contest.

FINALIST, ENTRÉES

# Grilled Halibut with Rum Sauce, Great Greens, and Olives

*Makes 4 servings*

*If fresh halibut is unavailable, choose another lean white fish such as cod, scrod, or haddock. Most supermarkets now routinely stock fresh mesclun, a mix of baby greens that usually includes radicchio, frisée, and arugula. If it looks crisp and fresh, by all means buy it. Otherwise, use any combination of tender young greens you fancy.*

NOTE: *Make the dressing first so that the flavors mellow and marry while you prepare the fish.*

TIPS: *When making an oil and vinegar (or citrus) dressing, always combine the seasonings with the vinegar (or citrus juice) before adding the oil so that they'll dissolve completely. They dissolve poorly in oil. Also, always use a nonreactive container when making acidic dressings and marinades so that they don't take on metallic tastes. Good nonreactive materials are glass, porcelain, china, even enameled metal pans.*

### DRESSING

1 tablespoon balsamic vinegar

1 tablespoon fresh orange juice

1 teaspoon Dijon mustard

1/8 teaspoon freshly ground black pepper

2 tablespoons olive oil

### MARINADE AND FISH

2 tablespoons dark rum

1 tablespoon fresh lime juice

1 tablespoon fresh orange juice

1 tablespoon peeled and finely minced fresh ginger

1 tablespoon coarsely chopped fresh cilantro

1 tablespoon honey

1 large clove garlic, finely minced

1/4 teaspoon ground cumin

1/4 teaspoon ground allspice

1/4 teaspoon freshly ground black pepper

1 1/4 pounds 1/2-inch-thick halibut steaks, skin and bones removed, then cut into 4 steaks of equal size (see headnote)

### TO COMPLETE DISH

2 cups mesclun or assorted baby salad greens, washed and spun dry

8 whole brine- or oil-cured ripe olives such as Niçoise or Kalamata

PER SERVING

287 calories
....
12 g fat (2 g saturated)
....
45 mg cholesterol
....
240 mg sodium
....

1. *For dressing:* Whisk together all ingredients except olive oil in 2-cup glass measure. Drizzle in oil, whisking briskly. Cover with plastic wrap and set aside.

2. *For marinade and fish:* Combine all ingredients except halibut in 10-inch glass pie plate or shallow nonmetallic bowl. Place halibut in marinade, turn so both sides are well coated, cover with plastic wrap, and refrigerate for 1 hour, turning fish in marinade two to three times.

3. Spray 10-inch ridged cast-iron grill pan with nonstick cooking spray, set over moderately high heat until almost smoking—about 2 minutes.

4. Pour marinade into small nonreactive saucepan and set, uncovered, over lowest heat.

5. Arrange halibut steaks, not touching, on smoking-hot grill pan and grill 2 minutes, basting with hot marinade and giving steaks a quarter turn after 1 minute to create crisscross grill marks. Turn steaks over and grill flip sides exactly as you did the first sides.

6. *To complete dish:* Mound mesclun on large deep platter, whisk dressing until creamy, then drizzle evenly over greens. Arrange halibut on greens and spoon remaining hot marinade over all. Scatter olives on top and serve at once.

RECIPE FROM

*Joan W. Churchill; Dover, New Hampshire*

Jamaica-born and self-taught, this young chef is married to a writer/producer who shares his interest in imaginative cooking. "My wife and I were tossing around ideas," he wrote us, "and she came up with this choice for a low-calorie entrée. It's a simple recipe that takes very little time to perfect. After preparing the snapper and salsa, garnishing it with lemon and mint, and taking photos of the dish, we both devoured the food and licked the plate clean!"

# Herbed Snapper with Warm Mango Salsa

*Makes 4 Servings*

*Try to use fresh herbs for this recipe—most good supermarkets now carry bunches or packets of them all year round. Dried herbs lack their delicate fresh bouquet. If mangoes are unavailable, substitute papaya. Just be sure the one you choose is firm-ripe.*

TIPS: *The easiest way to free a mango of its big, fuzzy, clingy pit is to upend the mango and cut straight down on either side of the pit. Once it's exposed, you can trim away any additional flesh. To dice the mango, score the unpeeled large sections crisscross fashion, making the cuts ½ inch apart, then run the knife flat along the skin, freeing the dice and peeling the fruit in one fell swoop.*

**FISH**

*1 tablespoon chopped fresh thyme (preferably lemon thyme), or ¼ teaspoon dried leaf thyme, crumbled*

*1 tablespoon chopped fresh rosemary, or ¼ teaspoon dried leaf rosemary, crumbled*

*1 tablespoon chopped fresh sage, or ¼ teaspoon dried rubbed sage, crumbled*

*1 tablespoon chopped fresh mint, or ¼ teaspoon mint flakes, crumbled*

*1 tablespoon chopped fresh oregano, or ¼ teaspoon dried leaf oregano, crumbled*

**PER SERVING**

271 calories

....

9 g fat (1 g saturated)

....

42 mg cholesterol

....

78 mg sodium

....

2 tablespoons olive oil

4 (4-ounce) skinned red snapper fillets

SALSA

1 large firm-ripe mango (about 1 pound), pitted, peeled, and cut into $\frac{1}{2}$-inch
dice (2 cups diced mango; see Tips on page 7)

$\frac{1}{2}$ cup finely chopped yellow onion (about 1 small onion)

2 medium-size cloves garlic, finely chopped

$\frac{1}{4}$ cup finely chopped green bell pepper (about $\frac{1}{4}$ large pepper)

$\frac{1}{4}$ cup finely chopped red bell pepper (about $\frac{1}{4}$ large pepper)

1 tablespoon chopped fresh thyme (preferably lemon thyme), or $\frac{1}{4}$ teaspoon
dried leaf thyme, crumbled

1 tablespoon chopped fresh rosemary, or $\frac{1}{4}$ teaspoon dried leaf rosemary,
crumbled

$\frac{1}{4}$ teaspoon ground white pepper

GARNISH

4 lemon wedges

4 sprigs fresh mint

1. *For fish:* Combine thyme, rosemary, sage, mint, and oregano with 1 tablespoon olive oil in large shallow glass bowl or 10-inch pie plate, add snapper, and turn in oil-herb mixture to coat all over. Let marinate at room temperature 10 minutes, turning fish two to three more times.

2. Heat remaining tablespoon olive oil in very large nonstick skillet over moderately high heat until ripples appear on skillet bottom—$1\frac{1}{2}$ to 2 minutes. Arrange fish fillets side by side but not touching in skillet, and sauté until fish is golden brown and almost flakes at touch of fork—about 4 minutes on each side.

3. Lift fish to medium-size heated platter, cover loosely, and keep warm.

4. *For salsa:* Combine all ingredients in skillet and cook and stir over moderately high heat until mixture steams and mango begins to soften—about 2 minutes.

5. Spoon salsa over or around fish, garnish with lemon wedges and mint sprigs, and serve.

RECIPE FROM

"John" Vernon Reid; Santa Monica, California

*Ashburn, Virginia*

After she married an aerospace engineer, executive secretary Shirley Panning decided to become a "domestic engineer." This involved, among other things, learning to enjoy creative cooking—deciding which flavors go well together, inventing new recipes, improving on old ones. Having lost twenty-five pounds and kept the weight off by following her own healthy eating and cooking regimen, she plans someday to write her own low-fat cookbook. Sure to be included is her unusual recipe for Cajun Cod, inspired by her determination to find a topping for fish that would be uniquely different and delicious.

# Cajun Cod Fillet with Melon Salsa

*Makes 4 servings*

*If you can't find fresh cod, good alternatives for this recipe would be haddock, halibut, or other fairly chunky lean white fish—sole and flounder fillets are too thin. Be sure to use fresh melon and pineapple (the frozen or canned just don't cut it). Cajun spice blends are now stocked by most supermarkets, and specialty groceries will carry several different brands. Find one that you like, then use it for this and other Cajun recipes, but be forewarned, most of these are loaded with salt.*

TIP: *If the rice is to be done at the same time as the cod and salsa, you should put it on to cook before you do anything else. The best method? Follow package directions.*

COD

1½ pounds cod fillet, skinned

2 tablespoons Cajun seasoning (see headnote above)

1 tablespoon olive oil

1 tablespoon fresh lime juice

1 cup converted rice cooked according to package
    directions (see Tip)

PER SERVING

401 calories
....
5 g fat (0.8 g saturated)
....
73 mg cholesterol

812 mg sodium
....

SALSA

*1 cup ½-inch dice firm-ripe cantaloupe (about ¼ medium-size melon)*

*1 cup ½-inch dice ripe pineapple (about ⅓ medium-size pineapple)*

*1 cup ¼-inch dice red bell pepper (about 1 medium-size pepper)*

*½ cup thinly sliced scallions, some green tops included (6 to 8 medium-size scallions)*

*1 tablespoon fresh lime juice*

1. Preheat broiler. Also line broiler pan with foil and set aside (this simplifies clean up).

2. *For cod:* Cut cod into 4 pieces of equal size. Quickly combine Cajun seasoning, olive oil, and lime juice in large shallow glass or ceramic bowl, add cod, and turn gently to coat. Let marinate at room temperature while you prepare salsa.

3. *For salsa:* Place all ingredients in large shallow glass or ceramic bowl, toss gently, and set aside while you broil cod.

4. Arrange cod on prepared broiler pan so pieces do not touch, set in broiler 3 inches from heat, and broil until fish almost flakes at touch of fork—10 to 12 minutes. No need to turn cod as it broils.

5. Divide rice among six heated dinner plates, place broiled cod alongside, and top it with melon salsa.

RECIPE FROM

*Shirley J. Panning; Ashburn, Virginia*

## KAREN R. BERNER

*Rhinebeck, New York*

As director of special projects for continuing education at the Culinary Institute of America, Karen understands the importance of healthy cooking, although she admits to a liking for "classical French cuisine—with all the butter and fat!" She traces her culinary talents to her grandmother, "who had a passion for cooking," and credits a Vietnamese chef, Charles Phan, with inspiring this particular recipe. "I took a course with him in San Francisco," she explains, "and was inspired by his use of truly fresh ingredients."

# Poached Sea Bass with Shiitake-Soy Broth

*Makes 4 servings*

*This broth is both light and delicious, in fact it's so good you can serve it with other lean white fish, even thin slices or strips of pork, chicken, or turkey cutlets.*

NOTE 1: *If fresh shiitake mushrooms are unavailable, substitute the more common white "supermarket" variety.*

NOTE 2: *This recipe calls for a nonreactive skillet, which means it's made of something that won't react with the acid in the broth—enameled metal, for example, flameproof glass or porcelain, even stainless steel.*

½ *pound shiitake mushrooms, stemmed and*
    *thinly sliced (see Note 1)*

1½ *teaspoons peeled and minced fresh ginger*

1 *medium-size clove garlic, minced*

2 *tablespoons reduced-sodium soy sauce*

2 *tablespoons rice wine vinegar*

½ *teaspoon hot red pepper flakes*

1 *tablespoon honey*

½ *cup water*

½ *cup dry white wine*

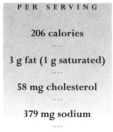

**PER SERVING**

206 calories

····

3 g fat (1 g saturated)

····

58 mg cholesterol

····

379 mg sodium

····

1 medium-size shallot, minced

4 (5-ounce) sea bass fillets, skin removed

¼ teaspoon freshly ground black pepper

¼ cup coarsely chopped fresh cilantro

1. Combine mushrooms, ginger, garlic, soy sauce, vinegar, red pepper flakes, honey, and water in small bowl and set aside.

2. Bring wine and shallot to a boil in very large, heavy, nonreactive skillet over moderately high heat.

3. Add sea bass and black pepper, reduce heat to low, cover, and simmer 4 minutes. Using spatula, carefully turn fish, cover, and simmer just until fish almost flakes at the touch of a fork—about 4 minutes more. Lift fish to large heated platter, cover loosely with foil, and keep warm.

4. Add mushroom mixture to wine mixture in skillet and simmer uncovered over moderate heat, stirring occasionally, until mushrooms have softened—about 5 minutes. Spoon mushrooms over fish and keep warm.

5. Raise heat under skillet mixture to moderately high and boil uncovered until flavors develop fully—1½ to 2 minutes.

6. Stir in cilantro, ladle broth over fish, and serve.

RECIPE FROM

*Karen R. Berner; Rhinebeck, New York*

## CARL FRANCO

*West Chester, Ohio*

The founder and pastor of an interdenominational contemporary church, Carl was born in Brooklyn, New York, and brought up in New Jersey. Although he came from a food-loving family, he considers himself a self-taught cook with a preference for gourmet rather than everyday dishes. "I love the challenge of melding unique flavors to create a new and marvelous taste," he says. "I thought it would be fun to do this while keeping the recipe low in fat—making something that tastes great and is good for you is the ultimate challenge!" The beneficiaries of Carl's creative culinary streak? Friends, wife Jeannine, an administrative assistant, and two young children—Dominic, four, and Marissa, one.

# Sea Bass with Curried Lentils and Rice

*Makes 4 servings*

*Most upscale supermarkets carry basmati, a slender-grained Indian rice of mellow flavor, in their international sections, also red lentils. And both are staples at Asian or Middle Eastern groceries. If unavailable, substitute converted rice and green or brown lentils (these take slightly longer to cook).*

TIP: *Prepare rice according to package directions while the lentils cook so you don't waste time.*

MARINADE AND FISH
*2 tablespoons soy sauce*

*2 tablespoons dry white wine*

*1 tablespoon fresh lime juice*

*1 tablespoon ketchup*

*1 medium-size clove garlic, finely minced*

*1 teaspoon peeled and finely minced fresh ginger*

*⅛ teaspoon ground hot red pepper (cayenne)*

*2 (8-ounce, ½-inch-thick) skinless sea bass fillets, halved crosswise*

*1 tablespoon olive oil*

PER SERVING

436 calories
....
10 g fat (2 g saturated)
....
49 mg cholesterol
....
666 mg sodium
....

LENTILS AND RICE

*1 tablespoon olive oil*

*1 cup finely chopped leek (about 1 large leek)*

*1 medium-size clove garlic, finely minced*

*1 cup red lentils*

*1 tablespoon curry powder*

*1 teaspoon ground cumin*

*1 (14.25-ounce) can reduced-sodium, nonfat chicken broth*

*1 cup cooked basmati rice (see headnote)*

*1 cup coarsely chopped stemmed watercress (about 1 small bunch)*

1. *For marinade and fish:* Combine soy sauce, wine, lime juice, ketchup, garlic, ginger, and cayenne in 10-inch glass pie plate or shallow nonmetallic bowl. Place sea bass in marinade, turn so both sides are well coated, cover with plastic wrap, and refrigerate 1 hour, turning fish in marinade two to three times.

2. *For lentils and rice:* Heat olive oil in medium-size heavy saucepan over moderately high heat until ripples appear on pan bottom—1 to $1^{1}/_{2}$ minutes. Add leek and garlic and sauté, stirring often, until limp—about 5 minutes.

3. Add lentils, curry powder, cumin, and chicken broth and bring to a boil. Adjust heat so mixture bubbles gently, cover, and simmer until lentils are almost tender—about 15 minutes.  Fork in cooked rice, cover, and cook 5 minutes more.

4. Meanwhile, cook fish. Heat olive oil in heavy 10-inch skillet (preferably cast iron) over moderately high heat until ripples appear on skillet bottom—1 to $1^{1}/_{2}$ minutes. Lift fish from marinade; arrange, not touching, in skillet; and sauté until golden brown and cooked through—3 to 4 minutes per side.

5. To serve, divide lentil-rice mixture among four heated plates, then top with fish and chopped watercress, dividing amounts equally.

RECIPE FROM

*Carl Franco; West Chester, Ohio*

Though Emeril and New Orleans are practially synonymous, this medium-tall but definitely dark and handsome forty-year-old chef grew up in Fall River, Massachusetts, of Portuguese–French Canadian heritage. As a boy he worked at a local Portuguese bakery; then when still a teen, he put himself through the culinary program at Johnson & Wales University in Providence, Rhode Island. After honing his culinary skills in Paris and Lyons, Boston, New York, and Philadelphia, Emeril replaced Cajun chef Paul Prudhomme at the legendary New Orleans restaurant Commander's Palace. He remained there seven and a half years; then, in 1990, he opened his own "Big Easy" restaurant, Emeril's. Today he has six restaurants, three in New Orleans, two in Las Vegas, and one in Orlando, Florida. In addition, Emeril has written five best-selling cookbooks, he hosts *Emeril Live*, a daily cooking show on the Food Network, and appears every Friday morning as *Good Morning America*'s food correspondent. Now single, Emeril lives in New Orleans with two grown-up daughters from his first marriage in what he calls "a small French chateau." The kitchen alone measures 1,000 square feet and contains "every possible gadget."

# *Emeril's Potato-Crusted Fish with a French Green Bean Relish*

### *Makes 4 servings*

*The trick here is getting the potato crust to stick to the fish and what helps, Emeril says, is rolling each fish up tight in a damp towel. You could do this half an hour ahead of time, refrigerate the fish, and in the interim get started on the relish. For it, Emeril uses* haricots verts *or tiny French green beans. If you can't find them—entirely possible if you live beyond a big metropolitan area—choose the smallest green beans you can find, babies, if possible.*

NOTE: *Also see Emeril's Roasted Peach Soup with a Peach and Raspberry Sorbet (page 269).*

FISH

4 (4-ounce) skinned flounder or other firm
   white fish fillets

1/8 teaspoon salt

1/8 teaspoon freshly ground black pepper

4 teaspoons Dijon mustard

1 large baking potato, peeled

2 tablespoons olive oil

1/2 teaspoon Creole seasoning

1 tablespoon coarsely chopped fresh Italian (flat-leaf) parsley

RELISH

1/4 pound tiny green beans, tipped (see headnote)

1 teaspoon olive oil

1/4 cup thinly sliced red onion (1 very small onion)

1/2 cup thinly sliced red bell pepper (about 1/2 medium-size pepper)

1/2 cup thinly sliced yellow bell pepper (about 1/2 medium-size pepper)

2 large cloves garlic, minced

1/8 teaspoon salt

1/8 teaspoon freshly ground black pepper

PER SERVING

253 calories
....
10 g fat (2 g saturated)
....
54 mg cholesterol
....
430 mg sodium
....

1. *For fish:* Season fish with salt and pepper, then spread mustard on both sides of each fillet. Using swivel-bladed vegetable peeler, shave thin lengthwise strips from the potato, making them about 3 inches long and 1 to 1½ inches wide. Wrap potato strips around fillets, overlapping as needed, until each fillet is entirely encased in potato. Now tightly wrap each fillet in a damp tea towel.

2. *For relish:* Blanch beans in boiling water 1 minute, drain, and plunge into ice water for 2 to 3 minutes. Drain and set aside.

3. To cook fish, first remove tea towels. Heat oil in very large heavy nonstick skillet over moderately high heat until ripples appear on skillet bottom—1½ to 2 minutes. Add potato-wrapped fish fillets, jiggling skillet a bit to keep them from sticking, and brown until potato is crisp and fish cooked through—about 4 minutes on each side.

4. Meanwhile, finish relish. Heat oil in second very large heavy nonstick skillet over moderately high heat until ripples appear on skillet bottom—$1\frac{1}{2}$ to 2 minutes. Add onion, beans, and red and yellow peppers, and sauté, stirring often, until onion browns lightly and peppers begin to wilt—$2\frac{1}{2}$ to 3 minutes. Add garlic, salt, and black pepper and cook and stir 30 seconds.

5. To serve, place fish on four heated dinner plates, sprinkle with Creole seasoning and parsley, then mound relish on top, dividing total amount equally.

RECIPE FROM

*Emeril Lagasse; New Orleans, Louisiana*

"My mother taught me to cook," says this forty-eight-year-old freelance theater director/actor who is married to an attorney. "She taught me to read directions." Wanda considers main courses her particular favorites—meats with sauces—and adds that she created this salmon recipe while visiting friends in Seattle. "I had never thought of using a red wine sauce with fish before, but they had a recipe book that suggested this. Unfortunately, they had nothing in their kitchen that was in the recipe, so I manufactured it. The most important thing was not to have the red wine sauce overpower the salmon, so I chose a lighter red wine (not a cabernet) and used the spices that my friend had in her cupboard. I wrote down what I had used, and when I returned to Phoenix, I kept playing with the recipe." Wanda adds that it took about six months to perfect but that the salmon she found in Arizona was never as good as that Seattle salmon.

# Baked King Salmon with Red Wine–Mustard Sauce

### Makes 4 servings

*This is such a quick and easy recipe. If you prepare the sauce while the salmon bakes, dinner's on the table in 10 minutes. Just be sure the salmon is fresh, fresh, fresh—the flesh should be "sea-sweet" and evenly moist, not wet.*

TIPS: *To keep the sauce from taking on a metallic taste, use a nonreactive skillet—enameled cast iron, for example, or stainless steel. If shallots are unavailable, substitute one medium-size scallion for the one small shallot this recipe calls for.*

1 pound salmon fillet, skinned and cut into 4 portions
   of equal size

1½ cups Merlot or other fairly light dry red wine

2 tablespoons honey

¼ cup red wine vinegar

| PER SERVING |
| --- |
| 272 calories |
| 8 g fat (1 g saturated) |
| 62 mg cholesterol |
| 250 mg sodium |

*1 small shallot, minced (see headnote)*

*2 tablespoons Dijon mustard*

*⅛ teaspoon freshly ground black pepper*

*2 tablespoons coarsely chopped fresh cilantro*

*1 medium-size bunch fresh arugula, stemmed, washed, and spun dry*

1. Preheat oven to 450°F. Coat 10-inch ovenproof glass pie plate or shallow baking dish with nonstick cooking spray.

2. Arrange salmon pieces, not touching, in prepared baking dish and bake uncovered until firm to the touch and fish almost flakes at touch of a fork—about 10 minutes.

3. Meanwhile, boil wine uncovered in 10-inch nonreactive skillet over moderately high heat until reduced by half—about 6 minutes. Whisk in honey, vinegar, shallot, mustard, and pepper. Return to boiling. Sauce should be consistency of light syrup. If not, continue boiling uncovered 1 to 2 minutes. Remove from heat and stir in cilantro.

4. Divide arugula among four heated dinner plates, arrange salmon on top, and drizzle with sauce.

RECIPE FROM

*Wanda McHatton; Phoenix, Arizona*

## JOSEPH V. SCHNEIDER

*North East, Pennsylvania*

"I wanted to use fresh salmon and fresh dill together in a recipe," explains this retired appraiser of stamps and coins, who learned to cook by watching others. "Starting with a mayonnaise with a nice even taste, I added dill, then bread crumbs to make it a spread without changing the flavor. When I had it all mixed, it was too stiff to spread on the salmon so I thinned it with a little milk. It tasted great the first time—my wife loved it. The secret is keeping it simple and remembering always to use fresh dill!"

# Dill-Crusted Salmon

*Makes 4 servings*

*Fresh dill is the only thing to use for this recipe, and the fresher the better. Not so long ago, finding fresh dill might have been a problem. Not so today with most supermarkets carrying little plastic pouches of it and greenmarkets selling it right through the growing season. Fresh salmon, too, is far easier to come by than it used to be, thanks to jet transport.*

| |
|---|
| 1 (1-pound) salmon fillet cut 1¼ inches thick, skinned, rinsed and patted dry with paper towels |
| 1 tablespoon fresh lemon juice |
| ¼ cup finely chopped fresh dill |
| 2 tablespoons low-fat mayonnaise |
| ¼ cup fine dry unseasoned bread crumbs |
| 2 tablespoons skim milk |

**PER SERVING**

212 calories
....
10 g fat (1 g saturated)
....
65 mg cholesterol
....
159 mg sodium
....

1. Preheat oven to 350°F. Coat a 9 x 9 x 2-inch flameproof baking dish with non-stick cooking spray and set aside.

2. Sprinkle salmon with lemon juice and lay flat in prepared baking dish.

3. Combine dill, mayonnaise, and bread crumbs in small bowl, then mix in milk. Using back of a spoon, smooth mixture over salmon.

4. Bake salmon uncovered 20 minutes, then remove from oven and preheat broiler. Also cover broiler pan with aluminum foil.

5. While broiler heats, very carefully lift salmon from baking dish and place, crust side up, on prepared broiler pan.

6. Position salmon 3 inches from heat and broil until brown and crusty—3 to 5 minutes. Serve at once.

RECIPE FROM

*Joseph V. Schneider; North East, Pennsylvania*

*Southbridge, Massachusetts*

Born in Calcutta and brought up in "almost half the world," Suraiya speaks seven languages and has worked as a United Nations employee, a model, and a film actress. Not surprisingly, she favors an international style of cooking. "I cook for myself and my family and we hardly ever eat out," she explains, "so this is my daily routine; every day I am perfecting my recipes. All of them are low-fat." This last detail may account for Suraiya's success in maintaining a slim 120-pound figure without dieting. Her family's reaction to low-calorie meals? "Happy!" says Suraiya.

# Fish Masala

*Makes 4 servings*

*Masala is a type of curry, and this one usually consists not only of an entrée but also of several side dishes (note that this curry contains no curry powder, only a few of its components—this is the authentic Indian way). The recipe Suraiya sent us actually included five separate recipes: curried salmon, and then separate accompaniments of spinach, broccoli, okra, and rice. To simplify things, we concentrate on the fish, but would suggest that you serve the masala over rice. Suraiya's method is to start with one cup rice (Indian basmati rice is best), then when it's half done, to add two moderately finely chopped medium-size carrots. If you decide to serve the rice—a good idea because there's plenty of delicately flavored sauce—cook according to package directions and add the carrots halfway through. You will also need to increase the per-serving nutrient counts given here by 192 calories, 1 gram fat (0 gram saturated), 0 milligrams cholesterol, and 160 milligrams sodium.*

1 tablespoon vegetable oil

3 cups coarsely chopped yellow onions
    (about 3 medium-large onions)

1 large clove garlic, minced

½ teaspoon ground coriander

| PER SERVING |
| :---: |
| 254 calories |
| .... |
| 11 g fat (1 g saturated) |
| .... |
| 62 mg cholesterol |
| .... |
| 134 mg sodium |
| .... |

*¼ teaspoon ground turmeric*

*⅛ teaspoon salt*

*⅛ teaspoon ground hot red pepper (cayenne)*

*2 medium-size vine-ripe tomatoes, cored and seeded but not peeled, then cut into ½-inch cubes, or 2 cups canned low-sodium crushed tomatoes*

*¼ cup water*

*1 pound skinned salmon fillet, cut into 4 pieces of equal size*

*¼ cup coarsely chopped fresh cilantro*

1. Heat oil in very large heavy skillet over moderately high heat until ripples appear on skillet bottom—1½ to 2 minutes. Add onions and cook, stirring frequently, until uniformly golden brown—about 7 minutes.

2. Add garlic, coriander, turmeric, salt, cayenne, tomatoes, and water and bring to a boil. Adjust heat so mixture bubbles gently, cover, and cook 10 minutes.

3. Add salmon, pushing pieces down under sauce, cover, and cook 5 minutes. Turn salmon over, cover, and cook just until it flakes easily—about 2 minutes more.

4. Ladle vegetables and sauce into a heated deep platter and arrange salmon on top. Sprinkle with cilantro and serve.

RECIPE FROM

*Suraiya Soofi; Southbridge, Massachusetts*

# POOLSIN KRISANANUWATARA

*Houston, Texas*

Poolsin is a native of Thailand now living in Houston with her husband, an electrical engineer, and their two teenagers. "I developed this recipe by using a basic Thai salad dressing and combining it with baked salmon fillet, American style," she explained. "It took me only one try to get it right! My husband, Chaiporn, is my taster and he loves it. It has become one of our favorite recipes because it has a fresh flavor and is full of fresh vegetables."

FINALIST, ENTRÉES

## Spicy Salmon Salad

*Makes 4 servings*

*Be sure the tomato you choose is sun-ripened and bursting with flavor, and be sure, too, to use fresh mint—mint flakes lack the necessary fresh clean flavor.*

NOTE: *If you add dry sherry to the dressing, you will raise the calorie count. But only slightly.*

DRESSING
¼ *cup fresh lime juice*

*2 tablespoons Chinese fish sauce*

*1 tablespoon dry sherry (optional, see note)*

*4 teaspoons light brown sugar*

*2 teaspoons finely chopped, seeded Thai chilies (4 to 5), or 3 tablespoons finely chopped, seeded jalapeño chilies (2 to 3 medium size jalapeños)*

SALAD
*1½ pounds salmon fillet*

*1 teaspoon olive oil*

*1 large, firm ripe tomato, cored, cut into 16 (½-inch) wedges, and 8 of these halved crosswise*

PER SERVING

341 calories
....
13 g fat (2 g saturated)
....
99 mg cholesterol
....
774 mg sodium
....

*2 cups very thinly sliced Bermuda or Spanish onion (about 1 medium-large onion)*

*1 cup fresh mint leaves (measure loosely packed)*

*6 cups 1-inch pieces romaine (about 1 medium-size head)*

1. Preheat oven to 400°F.

2. *For dressing:* Whisk all ingredients together in a small bowl and set aside.

3. *For salad:* Place salmon skin-side down in shallow baking pan and brush evenly with olive oil. Bake uncovered until salmon almost flakes and looks opaque—25 to 30 minutes. Cool salmon 15 minutes.

4. Transfer salmon to large mixing bowl. Carefully remove and discard skin, also any bones the fishmonger may have missed when filleting the fish. Then use a fork to separate fish into 1-inch chunks. Add halved tomato wedges, onion, and half the mint. Whisk dressing, drizzle evenly over salmon mixture, and toss very gently.

5. Line large platter with romaine, top with salmon mixture, then garnish with whole tomato wedges and remaining mint. Serve at once.

RECIPE FROM

*Poolsin Krisananuwatara; Houston, Texas*

# JESSICA GAMBINO

## *Cañon City, Colorado*

When Jessica was just ten years old, she won a Colorado Muffin Contest, and although since then this artist has won several other cooking competitions, including the Mississippi Cattlewoman's Beef Cook-Off, she still prefers baking breads and pastries. Having lost fifty pounds by combining low-fat cooking with a balanced lifestyle, she's constantly looking for alternatives to traditional pie crusts. "After spending time in the Deep South where seafood is fresh and abundant," she told us, "I developed this shellfish pie with a rice crust. It became a favorite for my husband Joseph and me." (Joseph, no slouch himself as a cook, created the recipe for Caramel Apricot Brownies, page 234.)

# *Southport Seafood Pie*

### *Makes 8 servings*

*There are many ways to recycle leftover cooked rice but none more imaginative than this pie crust. If you have no leftover rice, simply cook ¾ cup converted rice according to package directions and you'll end up with 2 cups.*

NOTE: *To keep the sodium content within reason, use fresh crabmeat instead of canned. Lump or backfin is best but also, alas, the most expensive.*

CRUST
2 cups cooked converted white rice

1 tablespoon chopped fresh chives

⅛ teaspoon ground hot red pepper (cayenne)

1 large egg white, whisked until frothy

SEAFOOD FILLING
1 thin slice lean bacon, snipped crosswise into thin strips

¼ cup finely chopped yellow onion (about ½ small onion)

1 large clove garlic, finely minced

| PER SERVING |
| --- |
| 199 calories |
| …. |
| 3 g fat (0.9 g saturated) |
| …. |
| 98 mg cholesterol |
| …. |
| 430 mg sodium |
| …. |

*2 tablespoons flour*

*1 (12-ounce) can evaporated skim milk*

*1 teaspoon finely grated lemon zest*

*½ teaspoon salt*

*⅛ teaspoon freshly ground black pepper*

*⅛ teaspoon ground hot red pepper (cayenne)*

*⅛ teaspoon ground nutmeg (or better yet, freshly grated)*

*1 tablespoon finely chopped fresh basil (no substitute)*

*1 tablespoon minced fresh parsley*

*½ pound shelled and deveined, cooked medium-size shrimp, halved
    lengthwise*

*½ pound crabmeat (preferably lump or backfin), bits of shell and cartilage
    removed, or 1 (6.25-ounce) can crabmeat, well drained*

*2 large egg whites, whisked until frothy*

TOPPING
*2 tablespoons Italian-flavor bread crumbs tossed with 1 tablespoon minced
    scallion*

1. Preheat oven to 350°F. Coat 9-inch pie plate with nonstick cooking spray; set aside.

2. *For crust:* Toss rice with chives and cayenne in large bowl, fold in egg white, then using back of fork, press mixture firmly over bottom and up sides of prepared pie plate. Bake uncovered until set—about 10 minutes. Remove crust from oven but leave oven on.

3. *For filling:* Sauté bacon in medium-size heavy skillet over moderately high heat 2 minutes, stirring often. Add onion, garlic, and flour and cook and stir 1 minute. Slowly whisk in milk, then cook, whisking constantly, until thickened and smooth—about 3 minutes.

4. Mix in lemon zest, salt, black pepper, cayenne, nutmeg, basil, and parsley, transfer to large bowl, and cool 10 minutes. Using large rubber spatula, thoroughly fold in shrimp, crab, and egg whites.

5. Spoon seafood mixture into baked crust and scatter topping evenly over all.

6. Bake uncovered until set like custard and touched with brown—45 to 50 minutes. Cool 5 minutes, then cut into wedges and serve.

RECIPE FROM

*Jessica Gambino; Cañon City, Colorado*

# ANGELA SOMMERS

*Lafayette, Louisiana*

"Tasso cream sauce is standard here in Acadiana," says Angela, a private chef who was born in Connecticut, brought up in Tennessee, and now lives in Louisiana's bayou country. "This recipe is a take-off on a local favorite. I skipped the butter and heavy whipping cream to lighten it up and used it with eggplant rather than the traditional pasta. Then I added wine, basil, and Parmesan for a new twist. This dish is surprisingly quick and easy to prepare and looks as good as it tastes. My boyfriend, who sampled it for me, is not fond of eggplant, so I simply didn't tell him and he never guessed."

# Shrimp in Tasso Cream Sauce with Eggplant Medallions

*Makes 4 servings*

*Tasso, spicily cured Louisiana pork, is not available everywhere. You can substitute a good country ham or, better yet, a spicy smoked turkey sausage as we've done here.*

1 large egg white

½ cup Italian-flavor bread crumbs

1 large eggplant (about 1 pound), peeled and cut into 8 slices ½ inch thick

1 pound shelled and deveined large raw shrimp

¼ teaspoon ground hot red pepper (cayenne)

⅛ teaspoon freshly ground black pepper

1 tablespoon olive oil

¼ cup coarsely chopped spicy, smoked turkey sausage (about ½ medium-size sausage)

1 large clove garlic, minced

¾ cup reduced-sodium, nonfat chicken broth

¼ cup dry white wine

**PER SERVING**

341 calories

....

9 g fat (2 g saturated)

....

182 mg cholesterol

....

922 mg sodium

....

$^1/_2$ cup evaporated skim milk

$^1/_2$ cup thinly sliced scallions (include some green tops) (2 to 3 medium-size scallions)

$^1/_4$ cup freshly grated Parmesan cheese

1. Preheat oven to 400°F. Coat 17 x 11 x 1-inch baking pan with nonstick cooking spray and set aside.

2. Whisk egg white until frothy in pie pan and place bread crumbs in second pie pan. Dip eggplant slices in egg white, turning to coat both sides, then press into crumbs, making sure both sides are nicely breaded.

3. Arrange breaded eggplant slices in prepared pan so they don't touch one another, then bake uncovered for 10 minutes. Turn slices and bake uncovered until golden brown—about 10 minutes more.

4. Meanwhile, season shrimp with cayenne and black pepper. Heat olive oil in large heavy skillet over moderately high heat until ripples appear on skillet bottom—1$^1/_2$ to 2 minutes. Add shrimp, sausage, and garlic and sauté, stirring now and then, for 2 minutes.

5. Add chicken broth, wine, and evaporated milk and bring to a boil, stirring frequently. Using slotted spoon, lift shrimp and sausage to small bowl, cover, and keep warm.

6. Boil skillet liquid uncovered over moderately high heat 5 minutes until reduced by about half. Return shrimp and sausage to skillet, add scallions and Parmesan, then cook and stir just until cheese melts and sauce coats shrimp nicely—1 to 2 minutes.

7. To serve, arrange two eggplant slices on each of four heated dinner plates, then ladle shrimp mixture on top.

RECIPE FROM

*Angela Sommers; Lafayette, Louisiana*

Married to a college professor and mother of two young sons, Laura works as a Historic Preservationist in the Amana Colonies National Historic Landmark. A disappointing meal in a restaurant motivated her to invent this spicy shrimp recipe: "I ordered a dish that I thought I would like from the menu description, but it was *not at all* what I expected! So I came home and started to put together the dish I thought I had ordered. I changed some ingredients, dropped some, added others. After two or three tries I had it! My family loves it—especially seven-year-old Tobin."

# *Chipotle-Beer Shrimp with Pasta*

*Makes 4 servings*

*Beer does wonderful things for shrimp by heightening their sea-sweet flavor. First the shrimp marinate briefly in a light lager, then the beer goes into the tomato sauce and is cooked down, down, down. The shrimp are added for the final five minutes—just long enough for them to cook through.*

NOTE: *These shrimp would be equally good served over fluffy boiled rice.*

*¾ pound medium-size shelled and deveined raw shrimp*

*1 cup lager beer*

*¼ cup coarsely chopped fresh cilantro*

*1 tablespoon olive oil*

*1 cup coarsely chopped yellow onion (about 1 medium-large onion)*

*3 medium-size cloves garlic, minced*

*1 (14.5-ounce) can low-sodium diced tomatoes, drained*

*1 chipotle pepper canned in adobo sauce, drained, seeded, and moderately finely chopped (see headnote for Smoked Sausage Tacos with Mango-Chipotle Sauce, page 102.)*

| PER SERVING |
| :---: |
| 393 calories |
| .... |
| 6 g fat (1 g saturated) |
| .... |
| 129 mg cholesterol |
| .... |
| 497 mg sodium |
| .... |

*1 (8-ounce) package spaghettini, cooked and drained according to package directions*

OPTIONAL TOPPINGS
*¼ cup freshly grated Romano cheese*
*¼ cup coarsely chopped fresh cilantro*

1. Place shrimp, beer, and cilantro in a medium-size bowl, turning shrimp in beer to coat, then let stand at room temperature while you proceed with recipe.

2. Heat olive oil in large heavy skillet over moderately high heat until ripples appear on skillet bottom—1½ to 2 minutes. Add onion and garlic and sauté, stirring now and then, until wilted—about 3 minutes.

3. Set skillet off heat and drain beer from shrimp directly into skillet. Add tomatoes and *chipotle* pepper, return to moderately high heat, and bring to a quick boil. Adjust heat so mixture bubbles gently, and simmer uncovered until the consistency of pasta sauce—about 15 minutes.

4. Add shrimp and cilantro, cover, and cook over low heat just until shrimp turn pink and are cooked through—about 5 minutes.

5. Dump hot spaghettini into large heated bowl, add shrimp mixture, and toss well.

6. To serve, divide pasta among four heated dinner plates and top each portion, if desired, with sprinklings of grated cheese and chopped cilantro.

RECIPE FROM
*Laura Hoover; Swisher, Iowa*

## GAIL S. CHAMMAVANIJAKUL

*Dallas, Texas*

A graduate student in theology and mother of a toddler, Gail was born and brought up in Thailand. "My husband introduced me to this dish—one of his childhood favorites—when we were newlyweds," she told us. "It is the creation of his mother, one of the greatest cooks I know. Not only is it simple to make, it's also very light but filling. I've adapted the recipe to make it lower in fat while the taste and creaminess remain the same. For our family, this is the ultimate comfort food. It fills our tummies (without piling on pounds!) and reminds us of our beloved homeland on the other side of the globe."

# *Creamy Shrimp with Rice*

*Makes 4 to 6 servings*

*A most unusual, most accommodating risottolike recipe of Asian flavor that uses converted or long-grain rice instead of short-grain arborio. First you cook the rice, then you add everything else. Talk about one-dish dinners!*

NOTE: *If you're unable to find fresh shiitake or cremini mushrooms, the good old white supermarket variety will work nicely.*

1 cup uncooked converted or long-grain rice

2 medium-size cloves garlic, finely minced

1 (14.25-ounce) can reduced-sodium, nonfat chicken broth

¾ pound medium-size shelled and deveined raw shrimp

¼ pound fresh shiitake or cremini mushrooms, stemmed and thinly sliced (see Note)

1 large egg, lightly beaten

1 (8-ounce) can sliced water chestnuts, drained

2 medium-size scallions, trimmed and thinly sliced (include some green tops)

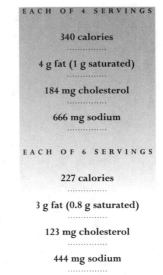

EACH OF 4 SERVINGS

340 calories

4 g fat (1 g saturated)

184 mg cholesterol

666 mg sodium

EACH OF 6 SERVINGS

227 calories

3 g fat (0.8 g saturated)

123 mg cholesterol

444 mg sodium

*2 tablespoons reduced-sodium soy sauce*

*¼ teaspoon freshly ground black pepper*

*2 tablespoons coarsely chopped fresh cilantro*

1. Cook rice according to package directions in large heavy saucepan.

2. Lightly mix in garlic and chicken broth, bring to a boil over moderately high heat, and cook uncovered, stirring occasionally, for 5 minutes.

3. Gently add shrimp, mushrooms, egg, water chestnuts, scallions, soy sauce, and pepper. Reduce heat to moderate, cover, and cook 5 minutes, stirring every now and then. Turn heat off and let stand, still covered, 10 minutes.

4. To serve, mound shrimp and rice mixture in large heated bowl and sprinkle with cilantro.

RECIPE FROM

*Gail S. Chammavanijakul; Dallas, Texas*

"I get ideas from recipes and TV cooking shows, then modify them to meet my husband's and my likes and needs," explains Betty, a retired medical technologist and business computer professor who learned to cook from her mother and grandmother. "I'm a diabetic and need to watch what I cook. To meet my husband's medical needs I also have to use little or no fat. So I revise recipes until my husband says, 'Make so and so again.'" Even though both Fauerbachs like asparagus and shrimp, Betty experimented with four versions of her casserole dish before she considered it perfect.

# *Shrimp and Asparagus Casserole*

*Makes 4 servings*

*Resist the temptation to use frozen or canned asparagus for this recipe. It will cook down to mush. And when cooking the fresh asparagus, take it from the heat when it's still a bit crisp and plunge at once into ice water to stop the cooking and set the bright green color. This is what pros call "shocking" the asparagus.*

*½ pound fresh asparagus, trimmed and cut into 1-inch lengths*

*1 tablespoon unsalted butter*

*½ pound medium-size mushrooms, stemmed and thinly sliced*

*1 cup coarsely chopped yellow onion (about 1 medium-large onion)*

*1 tablespoon cornstarch*

*¼ teaspoon ground nutmeg (or better yet, freshly grated)*

*¼ teaspoon ground white pepper*

*¼ teaspoon salt*

*¾ cup skim milk*

*¼ cup dry sherry*

| PER SERVING |
| --- |
| 184 calories |
| 6 g fat (3 g saturated) |
| 98 mg cholesterol |
| 273 mg sodium |

*½ pound shelled and deveined large raw shrimp, halved lengthwise*

*3 tablespoons freshly grated Parmesan cheese*

1. Preheat oven to 450°F.

2. Bring large pan of water to a boil over high heat. Add asparagus and cook uncovered 4 minutes. Drain asparagus, plunge into ice water, and set aside.

3. Melt butter in large heavy skillet over moderate heat. Add mushrooms and onion and sauté, stirring occasionally, until limp but not brown—about 5 minutes.

4. Blend in cornstarch, nutmeg, pepper, and salt, then mix in milk and sherry and, stirring constantly, bring quickly to a boil. Adjust heat so mixture bubbles, and cook, stirring all the while, until thickened—about 3 minutes.

5. Add shrimp and cook uncovered just until shrimp turn pink—about 2 minutes. Meanwhile, drain asparagus well, then add to shrimp mixture.

6. Turn shrimp mixture into ungreased 1-quart casserole and scatter Parmesan evenly on top.

7. Bake uncovered until bubbly and lightly golden—about 10 minutes. Serve at once.

RECIPE FROM

*Betty Fauerbach; Clyde, North Carolina*

## REBECCA L. BALENT

*Exeter, Pennsylvania*

This thirty-two-year-old businesswoman learned to cook as a child from her mother, sisters, and an Italian baby-sitter who inspired her lifelong love of pasta. Ten years ago, on a strict diet program and unable to stomach even one more piece of broiled fish or grilled chicken breast, she decided to combine some of the foods that *were* permitted on her diet to create a dish she might actually enjoy. The happy result: "I whipped up this linguine with clam sauce; it was a success on the first try and everyone loves it—even my two little dogs think 'Mom' is a very good cook!"

# Rebecca's Linguine with White Clam Sauce

*Makes 4 servings*

*For a dramatic presentation, leave half the clams in their shells, then arrange artfully over the pasta just before serving. The best clams to use for this recipe are tiny littlenecks. But if you live beyond the sound of the surf where fresh clams are unavailable, substitute canned clams.*

NOTE: *In Italy, freshly grated cheese is not usually served with seafood pastas. But Romano works well here.*

1 tablespoon olive oil

3 medium-size cloves garlic, minced

2 dozen littleneck clams in the shell, scrubbed,
    or 1 (10-ounce) can chopped clams, with their liquid

1 (8-ounce) bottle clam juice

2 tablespoons cornstarch blended with ½ cup cold water

2 tablespoons chopped fresh Italian (flat-leaf) parsley

⅛ teaspoon freshly ground black pepper

1 (8-ounce) package linguine, cooked and drained according to package
    directions

4 tablespoons freshly grated Romano cheese

| PER SERVING |
| --- |
| 335 calories |
| .... |
| 7 g fat (2 g saturated) |
| .... |
| 25 mg cholesterol |
| .... |
| 291 mg sodium |
| .... |

1. Heat olive oil in fairly shallow, heavy 2-quart Dutch oven over moderately high heat until ripples appear on pan bottom—1 ½ to 2 minutes. Add garlic and sauté, stirring often, 1 minute.

2. Carefully add unshucked clams, a few at a time so oil doesn't spatter. Pour in clam juice, raise heat to high, and bring to a boil. Cover and boil, jiggling pan from time to time, until all clams open—about 6 minutes.

3. Discard at once any clams that do not open. Either they were dead when they went into the pot or they were filled with mud. In either case, unopened clams should never be eaten. Transfer half the opened clams to large bowl and reserve. Shuck the rest, coarsely chop, and set aside.

4. Whisk cornstarch mixture into hot clam broth and boil over moderate heat, whisking constantly, until thickened and smooth—about 2 minutes. Add reserved chopped clams or canned clams and their liquid if using, parsley, and pepper, and bring just to serving temperature.

5. Pile hot linguine in large heated pasta bowl or deep platter, pour clam sauce over all, and toss well. Top with reserved unshucked clams, sprinkle with cheese, and serve at once.

RECIPE FROM

*Rebecca L. Balent; Exeter, Pennsylvania*

## VERONICA JOHNSON

*Seattle, Washington*

Former flight attendant Veronica is married to an airline captain and has two grown children—a son and a daughter. While still a child in Manitoba, Canada, she learned from her Polish mother how to cook good-tasting, healthy European food, and has never had a weight problem. "We don't even own a scale," she says. She developed this elegant but easy crabmeat dish because she wanted to extend the natural basic combination of seafood and lemons to include pasta. It took a lot of trial and error, Veronica admits, to come up with this particular combo. But it was worth all the time and trouble. "My family and friends just *love* it!"

# Linguine with Crab and a Touch of Lemon

*Makes 4 servings*

*Few main dishes are quicker or easier than this one. So that things move without a hitch, let the linguine cook while you prepare the crab and lemon. Both are done in minutes.*

1 tablespoon olive oil

3 medium-size cloves garlic, minced

1 (14-ounce) can artichoke hearts, drained and halved lengthwise

1½ tablespoons flour

1 (14.25-ounce) can reduced-sodium, nonfat chicken broth

1½ teaspoons chopped, drained capers

½ pound crabmeat (preferably lump or backfin), bits of shell and cartilage removed, or 1 (6.25-ounce) can crabmeat, well drained

2 tablespoons chopped fresh Italian (flat-leaf) parsley

2 tablespoons fresh lemon juice

⅛ teaspoon freshly ground black pepper

1 (8-ounce) package linguine, cooked and drained according to package directions

| PER SERVING |
| --- |
| 314 calories |
| 7 g fat (1 g saturated) |
| 59 mg cholesterol |
| 599 mg sodium |

1. Heat olive oil in large heavy skillet over moderately high heat until ripples appear on skillet bottom—1$\frac{1}{2}$ to 2 minutes. Add garlic and sauté, stirring now and then, 1 minute. Add artichokes, cook and stir 30 seconds, then blend in flour.

2. Slowly whisk in chicken broth, then cook, whisking constantly, 1 minute more. Add capers, reduce heat to low, and simmer uncovered 2 minutes. Add crabmeat, parsley, lemon juice, and pepper and toss well.

3. Dump drained linguine into large heated serving bowl, add crabmeat mixture, toss well, and serve.

RECIPE FROM
*Veronica Johnson; Seattle, Washington*

# SALLY CLARK

## Belding, Michigan

"No more pork chops and gravy for breakfast!" Sally promised herself when she joined *Good Morning America*'s Cut the Calories program. Making better choices and exercising "volume control" at each meal allowed this mother of three to lose twenty pounds while continuing to win prizes at local apple festivals for her pies and cakes. Although she says her own mother influenced her cooking most strongly, she also paid attention to her father's advice: Don't be afraid to experiment! Her crab enchiladas took twenty years of experimenting to perfect but today they top the request list at family get-togethers.

# *Crab Enchiladas*

### *Makes 4 servings*

*If you are cutting down on salt, choose low- or reduced-sodium salsa, vegetable juice, and enchilada sauce when preparing this recipe. Also, use fresh lump crabmeat instead of canned crabmeat, which is heavily freighted with salt. To trim the fat content somewhat, we call for low-fat cheeses—not nonfat, which are unpleasantly rubbery.*

*1 tablespoon olive oil*

*1 cup coarsely chopped yellow onion (about 1 medium-large onion)*

*2 large cloves garlic, minced*

*1 (4.5-ounce) can chopped green chilies, rinsed and drained*

*1 cup bottled mild tomato salsa (preferably low-sodium)*

*1 (10-ounce) can mild enchilada sauce (preferably low-sodium)*

*1 cup canned vegetable juice (preferably low-sodium)*

*1/4 teaspoon ground cumin*

*3/4 pound crabmeat (preferably lump or backfin), bits of shell and cartilage removed, or 2 (6.25-ounce) cans crabmeat, well drained*

*1/4 cup moderately finely shredded low-fat Monterey jack cheese*

| PER SERVING |
| :---: |
| 431 calories |
| .... |
| 13 g fat (4 g saturated) |
| .... |
| 99 mg cholesterol |
| .... |
| 794 mg sodium |
| .... |

*¼ cup moderately finely shredded low-fat extra-sharp Cheddar cheese*

*Eight 6-inch corn tortillas*

1. Heat olive oil in large heavy skillet over moderately high heat until ripples appear on skillet bottom—1½ to 2 minutes. Add onion and garlic and sauté, stirring now and then, until wilted—about 2 minutes.

2. Stir in chilies, salsa, enchilada sauce, vegetable juice, and cumin; adjust heat so mixture bubbles gently, and simmer uncovered until flavors marry—about 30 minutes.

3. Meanwhile, preheat oven to 350°F. Also coat a 13 x 9 x 2-inch baking dish with nonstick cooking spray and set aside.

4. Using wooden spoon, gently mix 1 cup hot skillet sauce with crabmeat, Monterey jack, and Cheddar. Keep remaining sauce warm to ladle over finished enchiladas.

5. To assemble enchiladas, first soften each tortilla by dipping quickly in skillet sauce. Divide crab mixture evenly among tortillas leaving ½-inch margins all round, then roll up and place seam side down in prepared baking dish.

6. Bake enchiladas uncovered until bubbly and cheese melts—about 20 minutes.

7. To serve, place two enchiladas on each of four heated dinner plates and pass remaining sauce.

RECIPE FROM

*Sally Clark; Belding, Michigan*

# MAROLYN B. PATTON

*Yerington, Nevada*

Born in Rio Tinto, once a prosperous copper-mining community and today a ghost town, Marolyn still considers Nevada her home, although she and her husband, both retired, spend most of the year traveling in their motor home. "Usually we spend the summer in Idaho and the winter in Mexico," Marolyn says, "and wherever we are, we fish." The Pattons enjoy eating fish as well as catching them, and Marolyn developed this savory dish at her husband's request—he'd been ordering Cioppino every chance he got in seafood restaurants. This particular Cioppino is an adaptation of one they both liked.

## *Cioppino*

*Makes 6 servings*

*This California classic is believed to have been created in the early 1900s by commercial fishermen off the coast of San Francisco. They simply combined galley staples—olive oil, garlic, onions, canned tomatoes—with whatever their nets fetched up. This isn't an authentic Cioppino, but it is good. Accompany, if you like, with hot red pepper sauce.*

NOTE: *To reduce the sodium content of this recipe, use low- or reduced-sodium canned tomatoes.*

*1 teaspoon olive oil*

*1¹/₂ cups finely chopped yellow onion (about 1 large onion)*

*1 cup finely diced green bell pepper (about 1 medium-size pepper)*

*³/₄ cup finely chopped celery (about 3 small ribs)*

*8 medium-size cloves garlic, minced*

*2 (28-ounce) cans plum tomatoes, with their liquid*

*2 (4.25-ounce) jars chopped green chilies, with their liquid*

*¹/₂ cup beer*

**PER SERVING**

310 calories

....

4 g fat (0.6 g saturated)

....

146 mg cholesterol

....

988 mg sodium

....

*3 tablespoons minced fresh parsley*

*2 tablespoons chopped fresh basil, or 2 teaspoons dried leaf basil, crumbled*

*½ teaspoon dried leaf oregano, crumbled*

*¼ teaspoon dried leaf marjoram, crumbled*

*¼ teaspoon dried leaf thyme, crumbled*

*1 teaspoon chili powder*

*¼ teaspoon freshly ground black pepper*

*⅛ teaspoon ground hot red pepper (cayenne)*

*1 pound boned and skinned halibut, cod, or other lean white fish, cut into
    1-inch chunks*

*½ pound sea scallops, halved if large*

*16 medium-size shelled and deveined raw shrimp (about ¾ pound)*

*½ pound Dungeness or lump crabmeat, bits of shell and cartilage removed, or
    1 (6.25-ounce) can crabmeat, drained well*

1. Heat olive oil, onion, green pepper, and celery in very large heavy saucepan over low heat, stirring often, until onion is wilted but not brown—about 5 minutes.

2. Add all remaining ingredients except halibut, scallops, shrimp, and crab and bring to a boil over high heat. Adjust heat so mixture bubbles gently, cover, and simmer 1 hour, stirring occasionally.

3. Add halibut, scallops, shrimp, and crab, and bring quickly to a boil. Adjust heat so mixture barely trembles, cover, and cook, stirring occasionally, 10 minutes— no longer or you will toughen the fish.

4. Ladle into heated soup plates and serve with crusty chunks of bread.

RECIPE FROM

*Marolyn B. Patton; Yerington, Nevada*

# PATRICIA CASSARO

## *Dallas, Texas*

This mother of three adult daughters works in the construction business as an administrative assistant. Originally from Chicago, she enjoys cooking—especially Italian and Mexican cuisine—and has won two national recipe contests. The idea for this unusual dish came from a childhood memory of her mother or grandmother sautéing peppers, potatoes, and onions together. "I decided to add broth and put it in the blender, then added the other ingredients and topped it off with grilled shrimp. When I tested it on my grandson, he said it was the best!"

# *Red Pepper Soup with Pan-Grilled Shrimp*

*Makes 4 servings*

*To make the best use of your time, shell and devein the shrimp while the soup simmers.*

NOTE 1: *It's important that you purée the hot soup in small batches; otherwise it may spew out of the food processor and scald you.*

NOTE 2: *Sweet white onions include Bermudas, Vidalias, and Walla-Wallas.*

**PER SERVING**

244 calories
....
9 g fat (2 g saturated)
....
46 mg cholesterol
....
367 mg sodium
....

SOUP
2 tablespoons olive oil

3 large red bell peppers, stemmed, halved, and seeded, then each half cut lengthwise into strips ¼ inch wide

1½ cups finely chopped sweet white onion (about 1 medium-large onion) (see Note 2)

6 large cloves garlic, minced

1 large baking potato (about 10 ounces), peeled and cut into medium dice

2 (14½-ounce) cans reduced-sodium chicken broth

2 tablespoons chopped fresh basil, or 2 teaspoons dried leaf basil, crumbled

1 teaspoon dried leaf oregano, crumbled

*1 teaspoon dried leaf thyme, crumbled*

*¼ teaspoon salt*

*¼ teaspoon freshly ground black pepper*

*2 tablespoons fresh lemon juice*

TOPPING
*16 large raw shrimp (about 10 ounces), shelled and deveined*

*1 large clove garlic, finely minced*

*⅛ teaspoon salt*

*5 tablespoons minced fresh parsley*

1. *For soup:* Heat olive oil in large heavy saucepan over moderately high heat until ripples appear on pan bottom—about 1½ minutes. Add bell peppers, onion, and garlic, and cook, stirring now and then, until limp—about 5 minutes.

2. Add potato, chicken broth, basil, oregano, thyme, salt, and black pepper and bring to a boil. Reduce heat so mixture bubbles gently, cover, and cook until potato is tender—about 15 minutes.

3. Purée soup in small batches in food processor, churning until very smooth—about 4 minutes per batch. Return soup to pan and mix in lemon juice. Set over low heat and keep soup warm.

4. *For topping:* Coat large heavy skillet with nonstick cooking spray and heat 1 minute over moderate heat. Add shrimp and cook just until shrimp turn white—about 2 minutes per side. Add garlic, salt, and 1 tablespoon parsley and toss lightly.

5. To serve, ladle hot soup into four heated soup plates, then top each portion with 4 shrimp and 1 tablespoon minced parsley.

RECIPE FROM
*Patricia Cassaro; Dallas, Texas*

# DONNA BOOTH TURRISI

## Pawcatuck, Connecticut

"We always lived on the coast," writes this New Englander. "Quahogs were plentiful and most times we dug them ourselves. We grew up on stuffed clams, clam fritters, and quahog chowder. As the years rolled by and I became more conscious of fat and calories, my original chowder with lots of butter and bacon was out of the question—my husband and I needed to be able to enjoy this regional recipe guilt-free! We were not giving up quahog chowder!" After modifying her chowder to reduce the fat, Donna served it to family and friends. "They raved about it and did not know it was healthy as well as scrumptious!"

# Stonington Clam Chowder

## Makes 6 servings

*You can make a meal of this chowder and need only a crisp green salad to accompany it.*

NOTE: *If you are not keeping an eye on your salt intake, substitute an 8-ounce bottle of clam juice for 1 cup of the water called for in this recipe. The chowder will be even richer.*

1 slice smoky lean bacon, minced

2 teaspoons unsalted butter

1½ cups finely chopped yellow onion
    (about 1 large onion)

⅓ cup finely chopped celery (about 1 small rib)

1 tablespoon flour

3 large all-purpose potatoes (about 10 ounces each),
    peeled and cut into ½-inch dice

2 cups water, or 1 cup water and 1 (8-ounce) bottle clam juice

1½ pints shucked quahogs or cherrystone clams, very coarsely chopped
    (reserve liquid)

2 tablespoons minced fresh parsley

¼ teaspoon freshly ground black pepper

18 fat-free soda crackers, very coarsely crumbled

**PER SERVING**

288 calories

....

5 g fat (2 g saturated)

....

35 mg cholesterol

....

187 mg sodium

....

1. Cook bacon in large heavy saucepan over moderately high heat until golden and almost all drippings have cooked out, 3 to 4 minutes.

2. Reduce heat to low, add butter, onion, and celery, and cook and stir until onion is limp, about 5 minutes. Blend in flour.

3. Add potatoes and water and quickly bring to a boil. Adjust heat so liquid bubbles gently; cover and simmer, stirring occasionally, until potatoes are almost tender, about 15 minutes.

4. Add clams and their liquid, re-cover, and simmer slowly for 5 minutes. Stir in parsley and pepper, turn off heat, and let stand 10 minutes.

5. Divide crackers among six heated soup plates. Ladle in hot chowder and serve.

RECIPE FROM

*Donna Booth Turrisi; Pawcatuck, Connecticut*

# POULTRY

Oven-Fried Chicken with Andouille Sausage *(Grand Prize Winner, Entrées)*     50

Chicken Cutlets with Roasted Red Peppers, Clelia Style *(Finalist, Entrées)*     52

Chicken Breasts and Fresh Tomatoes with Capers     54

Tasty Tangerine-Grilled Chicken     56

Low-Fat Tequila-Lime Chicken     58

Feta-Stuffed Chicken with Cucumber-Dill Sauce     60

Oriental Chicken in a Garden     62

Cajun Chicken Pasta     64

Lean Caribbean Chicken with Rice     66

Dijon Rosemary Chicken     68

Chicken Parmesan     70

Roasted Chicken with Black Bean Sauce     72

Coq au Vin     74

Curried Chicken     76

Slickrock Mesa Chicken Stew     78

Chicken and Vegetable Enchiladas with Sour Cream and Scallions     80

Black Bean and Chicken Enchiladas with Green Chili Sauce     83

Pecos Chicken-Cornbread Salad     85

Stuffed Turkey Cutlets     87

Oven-Fried Turkey Feathers with Jalapeño Pepper Mayonnaise     89

Curried Turkey Roulade with Ruby Sauce     91

Turkey Salsa Meat Loaf *(Finalist, Entrées)*     94

Spaghetti Squash with Parmesan-Turkey Balls     96

Labladie's Lite Chili     98

Tortilla Quiche     100

Smoked Sausage Tacos with Mango-Chipotle Sauce     102

Cabbage Soup with Turkey Sausage     104

## SANDY GREENE

*Wayne, Pennsylvania*

Sandy works from her home as a QVC representative. One wintry Pennsylvania day when she was feeling housebound, she invented this unique entrée and on a whim, entered it in the *Good Morning America* Cut the Calories Cook-Off and took top honors in the Entrée Category. "For years I've made oven-fried chicken with a rice cereal coating," she says, "so I simply experimented with different seasonings. Watching Emeril Lagasse inspired me to add the andouille sausage." Sandy, who makes creative cooking sound easy, adds that she has been influenced about equally by her mother and television's Food Network.

GRAND PRIZE WINNER, ENTRÉES

# Oven-Fried Chicken with Andouille Sausage

*Makes 4 servings*

*If you can find low-fat andouille sausage, you can up the amount in this recipe to 4 ounces without sabotaging the fat and calorie counts. Otherwise, stick with the 2 ounces called for here.*

**CHICKEN**

*2 ounces andouille sausage, finely chopped*

*1 cup crisp rice cereal (not flakes)*

*¼ cup freshly grated Parmesan cheese*

*2 teaspoons sweet paprika*

*½ teaspoon ground cumin*

*¼ teaspoon salt*

*⅛ teaspoon freshly ground black pepper*

*3 large cloves garlic, finely minced*

*1 large egg*

*4 (5-ounce) boneless, skinless chicken breast halves*

**PER SERVING**

289 calories
....

7 g fat (2 g saturated)
....

151 mg cholesterol
....

556 mg sodium
....

½ *cup nonfat plain yogurt*

1 *tablespoon minced fresh parsley*

2 *teaspoons fresh lemon juice*

½ *teaspoon ground cumin*

⅛ *teaspoon salt*

1. Preheat oven to 350°F. Coat baking sheet with nonstick cooking spray and set aside.

2. *For chicken:* Cook sausage in medium-size skillet over moderate heat until lightly browned and almost all fat cooks out—about 3 minutes. With slotted spoon, lift sausage to paper toweling to drain. Discard skillet drippings.

3. Place cereal in plastic bag and roughly crush with rolling pin. Transfer cereal to large bowl and mix in cheese, paprika, cumin, salt, and pepper. Add drained sausage and garlic and toss well to mix.

4. Beat egg until frothy in medium-size bowl. Dip each piece of chicken into egg, then into cereal mixture, pressing to coat.

5. Arrange chicken pieces, not touching, on prepared baking sheet and bake uncovered until well done in center—about 30 minutes.

6. *For sauce:* Whisk together all ingredients in a small bowl.

7. As soon as chicken tests done, serve. Pass sauce separately.

RECIPE FROM

*Sandy Greene; Wayne, Pennsylvania*

## CLELIA GRACEFFA EGAN

*Needham, Massachusetts*

Born in Naples, Clelia had already learned from her mother and grandmother how to cook Italian when, as a teenager, she moved with her family to America. Today, married to a financial consultant and working full time herself as administrative assistant to an attorney and CPA, she finds time to try old favorites in new ways—like the evening she came home from work with chicken cutlets and just half an hour till dinnertime. "I decided to make the cutlets different with whatever low-calorie ingredients I had on hand," she recalls. "This recipe took me twenty to twenty-five minutes to put together and my family loved it instantly!"

### FINALIST, ENTRÉES

# Chicken Cutlets with Roasted Red Peppers, Clelia Style

*Makes 4 servings*

*Here's the easiest way to toast pignoli (pine nuts): Place nuts in a dry 10-inch nonstick skillet, set over moderate heat, and toss constantly until golden brown. This will take about 5 minutes.*

*3 large red bell peppers, stemmed, quartered, and seeded*

*4 (5-ounce) boneless, skinless chicken breast halves*

*2 tablespoons flour mixed with ¼ teaspoon salt and ⅛ teaspoon freshly ground black pepper (seasoned flour)*

*2 tablespoons olive oil*

*2 large cloves garlic, finely minced*

*1 cup dry white wine*

*3 tablespoons well-drained small capers*

*3 tablespoons toasted pignoli (pine nuts) (see headnote above)*

| PER SERVING |
|---|
| 342 calories |
| .... |
| 12 g fat (2 g saturated) |
| .... |
| 82 mg cholesterol |
| .... |
| 435 mg sodium |
| .... |

1. Set broiler rack 3 inches from heating element and preheat broiler.

2. Arrange bell peppers skin-side up on broiler pan and broil 3 inches from heat until lightly charred and skin begins to pull away—about 5 minutes. Slip peppers into plastic bag, seal, and let stand 15 minutes. When cool enough to handle, peel peppers and cut lengthwise into strips $1/2$ inch wide.

3. Dredge chicken in seasoned flour, shaking off excess.

4. Heat olive oil in large heavy skillet over moderately high heat until ripples appear on skillet bottom—about $1\frac{1}{2}$ minutes. Add chicken and brown 5 minutes on each side. Lift chicken to plate and keep warm.

5. Reduce heat to low, add garlic to skillet, and cook just until limp—about 30 seconds. Add wine, roasted peppers, and capers and cook, stirring, for 1 minute.

6. Return chicken to skillet, spoon peppers and pan juices on top, cover, and simmer just until chicken is well done in center—8 to 10 minutes.

7. To serve, arrange chicken on heated platter, spoon peppers and pan juices on top, then sprinkle with toasted pignoli.

RECIPE FROM

*Clelia Graceffa Egan; Needham, Massachusetts*

## SUSAN E. HULBURT

*Sugar Land, Texas*

Susan, a fourth-grade schoolteacher, likes to cook Southern (U.S.) and Mediterranean dishes and controls her weight by following a "sensible, low-fat, well-rounded diet filled with fruits, vegetables, and herbs in season." She also enjoys gardening and finds that her small kitchen garden inspires her to create special recipes that will allow her to use her vegetables and fresh herbs to full advantage. "I have been making and serving this chicken dish for several years," she told us, "because friends and family love it."

# *Chicken Breasts and Fresh Tomatoes with Capers*

*Makes 4 servings*

*To flatten chicken breasts to uniform thickness without tearing them, pound between sheets of plastic wrap. The best implement to use is a cutlet bat, but a rolling pin works well, too.*

4 (5-ounce) boneless, skinless chicken breast halves,
    pounded until $^1/_2$ inch thick (see headnote above)

2 tablespoons flour

2 tablespoons olive oil

$^1/_2$ cup coarsely chopped yellow onion
    (about 1 small onion)

3 large cloves garlic, finely minced

4 cups coarsely diced, cored but not peeled firm-ripe
    tomatoes (about 2 large tomatoes or $1^3/_4$ pounds)

1 cup nonfat, low-sodium chicken broth

$^1/_4$ cup Burgundy or other dry red wine (optional)

2 tablespoons tomato paste

2 tablespoons chopped fresh basil, or 2 teaspoons dried leaf basil, crumbled

2 tablespoons chopped fresh oregano, or 1 teaspoon dried leaf oregano,
    crumbled

| PER SERVING |
| :---: |
| 307 calories |
| .... |
| 9 g fat (1 g saturated) |
| .... |
| 82 mg cholesterol |
| .... |
| 417 mg sodium |
| .... |

*¼ teaspoon salt*

*¼ teaspoon freshly ground black pepper*

*2 tablespoons well-drained small capers*

1. Dredge chicken evenly on both sides with flour, shaking off excess.

2. Heat olive oil in large heavy skillet over moderately high heat until ripples appear on skillet bottom—about 1½ minutes. Add chicken and sauté until golden brown—3 to 5 minutes on each side. Lift chicken to paper toweling to drain.

3. Reduce heat to moderate, add onion and garlic to skillet, and cook, stirring, until nicely wilted—about 3 minutes. Add tomatoes and cook uncovered 3 minutes. Mix in chicken broth, wine, if you like, tomato paste, basil, oregano, salt, and black pepper and bring to a simmer.

4. Reduce heat to low, then return chicken to pan, pushing into sauce. Add capers, cover, and simmer until chicken shows no signs of pink in center—8 to 10 minutes.

5. Lift chicken to heated platter, cover loosely to keep warm. Raise heat under skillet to moderately high and boil tomato mixture uncovered until consistency of pasta sauce—8 to 10 minutes.

6. Spoon sauce over chicken and serve at once. Accompany, if you like, with boiled white or brown rice.

RECIPE FROM

*Susan E. Hulburt; Sugar Land, Texas*

# KIM DAYNA SHAFER

*Barstow, California*

"For this recipe, I used tangerines because they were in season in the markets," Kim wrote in describing her piquant chicken recipe. "It's their freshness that creates the wonderful flavor in the meat. I worked on this dish until my husband said he never wanted to taste another grilled chicken breast (for at least a month!). My family and and friends all love it and request it often." Applying the same quality of dedication to a diet program as she uses in perfecting recipes, Kim lost ninety-five pounds and has maintained the loss for more than ten years.

# Tasty Tangerine-Grilled Chicken

*Makes 4 servings*

*Far and away the easiest way to marinate chicken (or anything else) is to mix the marinade in a sturdy plastic zipper bag, add the chicken, and set in the refrigerator, turning the bag over every hour or so. No muss, no fuss.*

NOTE 1: *To pound chicken thin without tearing it, place between sheets of plastic wrap and use a smooth cutlet bat or a rolling pin.*

NOTE 2: *If you have no grill pan, simply use a large heavy skillet coated with nonstick cooking spray. Sauté the chicken breast halves, two at a time, over moderately high heat and allow about 4 minutes on each side.*

*½ cup fresh tangerine juice*

*2 tablespoons reduced-sodium soy sauce*

*3 medium-size cloves garlic, minced*

*1 tablespoon peeled and minced fresh ginger*

*1 tablespoon honey*

*2 teaspoons finely grated tangerine zest*

*4 (5-ounce) boneless, skinless chicken breast halves,
    pounded to a thickness of about ⅜ inch*

**PER SERVING**

195 calories

....

2 g fat (0.5 g saturated)

....

82 mg cholesterol

....

393 mg sodium

....

1. Place all ingredients except chicken breasts in sturdy jumbo-size plastic zipper bag; seal and shake to combine.

2. Add chicken, press out air, reseal, and turn this way and that to coat. Set in refrigerator for 4 hours, turning bag every hour or so.

3. When chicken has only 20 minutes more to marinate, preheat oven to 350°F.

4. When ready to grill chicken, set 10-inch cast-iron grill pan over moderate heat for 2 minutes. Remove from heat and coat well with nonstick cooking spray. Place two breast halves on pan and grill 2 minutes over moderately high heat. Give an eighth or quarter turn, still same side up, so you get crisscross grill marks. Turn breasts over and grill flip sides the same way, again creating cross-hatch grill marks.

5. Transfer grilled chicken to ungreased 13 x 9 x 2-inch baking pan and set aside. Grill remaining two breast halves exactly the same way, then add to baking pan.

6. Pour marinade into small saucepan and bring quickly to a boil over moderately high heat. Strain marinade evenly over chicken.

7. Bake uncovered until chicken shows no signs of pink in center, about 8 minutes. Serve at once, topping each portion with tangerine pan drippings.

RECIPE FROM

*Kim Dayna Shafer; Barstow, California*

# SANDY FULLER

*Odessa, Florida*

Sandy was born in England, moved to Tampa when she was seven, and today she and her husband, a financial planner, have six children ranging in age from just under two to twenty-two. Not surprisingly, Sandy likes recipes that don't require much preparation time. She got the idea for this zesty tequila-lime chicken while trying to re-create a dish she'd sampled in a restaurant. "I wanted to replicate the taste without using much fat," she says, "so I experimented with basic cream sauce recipes, replacing fat with other ingredients. My family always enjoys this recipe."

# *Low-Fat Tequila-Lime Chicken*

*Makes 4 servings*

*Resist the temptation to use bottled lime juice in this recipe. It has an unpleasant metallic taste.*

NOTE 1: *Low-fat tortillas (about 98 percent fat-free) are becoming more widely available—several brands are now in national distribution.*

NOTE 2: *For this recipe, you'll need a large heavy skillet with a heatproof handle—preferably a 10-inch cast-iron one—that can go from stovetop to oven.*

SAFETY TIP: *When adding tequila—or, for that matter, any wine or spirits—to a hot mixture, always remove the pan from the heat. If you don't, the pan contents may catch fire.*

4 (7-inch) low-fat flour tortillas, cut into strips about 1½ inches wide

4 (5-ounce) boneless, skinless chicken breast halves

¼ teaspoon salt

⅛ teaspoon freshly ground black pepper

1 tablespoon olive oil

**PER SERVING**

401 calories

....

12 g fat (5 g saturated)

....

102 mg cholesterol

....

614 mg sodium

....

*1 (14.25-ounce) can reduced-sodium, nonfat chicken
    broth whisked until smooth with 2 tablespoons cornstarch*

*3 tablespoons tequila*

*½ cup finely shredded low-fat Swiss cheese*

*¼ cup fresh lime juice*

*2 tablespoons low-fat sour cream*

*2 tablespoons freshly grated Parmesan cheese*

1. Preheat oven to 350°F.

2. Spray tortilla strips with nonstick cooking spray, tossing to coat evenly, then spread on jelly-roll pan or large baking sheet and bake uncovered until crisp, about 7 minutes, turning after 3 minutes. Remove from oven and reserve. Leave oven on.

3. Sprinkle chicken evenly with salt and pepper. Heat olive oil in large heavy skillet (see Note 2) over moderately high heat until ripples appear on pan bottom—1½ to 2 minutes. Add chicken and brown 5 minutes on each side. Transfer chicken to oven and bake uncovered until chicken shows no signs of pink in center—8 to 10 minutes. Turn chicken once as it bakes.

4. When chicken tests done, transfer to heated platter, cover loosely with foil, and keep warm. Add broth mixture to skillet, set over low heat, and cook, stirring and scraping up brown bits, until mixture bubbles and thickens—2 to 3 minutes.

5. Remove skillet from heat, add tequila and all remaining ingredients, stirring well to mix. Return to low heat and cook and stir just until mixture steams—about 1 minute longer.

6. To serve, divide tortilla strips among four heated dinner plates, place chicken on top, then ladle sauce evenly over all.

RECIPE FROM
*Sandy Fuller; Odessa, Florida*

## LISA STIFT

### *Salem, New Hampshire*

"I was trying to come up with a lunch meal for two dieting friends," explained Lisa, who learned to cook from her mother, a home economics teacher. "I knew they liked feta cheese and spinach and could have chicken on their diet, so I figured I could make a Greek-style dish with lemon and cucumber. My husband's Aunt Pat has a recipe where you make a pocket in the meat and fill it with stuffing. That way I could place the spinach and feta in the meat without the cheese melting off. Watching *GMA* and Emeril Lagasse taught me to wrap the chicken in foil to keep it moist while cooking. The cucumber sauce was similar to the sauce in a gyro. My friends were impressed!"

# *Feta-Stuffed Chicken with Cucumber-Dill Sauce*

### *Makes 4 servings*

*"Sealed in silver" describes these stuffed chicken breasts because they bake in packets of foil—to shape them, you'll need four 12-inch lengths of aluminum foil, not heavy-duty. The time to make the sauce is while the chicken is in the oven.*

TIP: *To make yogurt drain more quickly and completely, cut through it with knife in a crisscross pattern, then dump into a very fine sieve or a larger-mesh sieve lined with a coffee filter. Draining yogurt rids it of much of its sourness.*

CHICKEN
*4 (5-ounce) boneless, skinless chicken breast halves*

*12 large fresh spinach leaves, stemmed*

*4 (1-inch) cubes reduced-fat feta cheese, each cut into 4 slices*

*4 teaspoons fresh lemon juice*

*2 teaspoons finely grated lemon zest*

| PER SERVING |
| :---: |
| 248 calories |
| .... |
| 6 g fat (3 g saturated) |
| .... |
| 93 mg cholesterol |
| .... |
| 647 mg sodium |
| .... |

*¼ teaspoon salt*

*⅛ teaspoon freshly ground black pepper*

SAUCE

*1 medium-size cucumber, trimmed, peeled, and sliced 1 inch thick*

*1 (8-ounce) carton nonfat plain yogurt, well drained (see Tip)*

*2 tablespoons freshly snipped dill (no substitute)*

*2 teaspoons fresh lemon juice*

1. Preheat oven to 350°F.

2. *For chicken:* Working from the thick edge of each chicken breast and cutting toward the thin edge, make pita-like pocket in each breast, then place on 12-inch length of foil (see headnote).

3. Lay 3 spinach leaves flat inside each pocket; then add 4 slices feta, lying side by side. Drizzle ½ teaspoon lemon juice inside each pocket and sprinkle in ½ teaspoon lemon zest. Finally, drizzle another ½ teaspoon lemon juice over each chicken breast and sprinkle with salt and pepper.

4. Working with one packet at a time, lift two longer sides of foil so edges meet, then roll down toward chicken, creating a little tent. Next, fold sides of tent in toward chicken to seal.

5. Place foil packets on large baking sheet and bake until chicken shows no signs of pink in center—25 to 30 minutes.

6. *Meanwhile, prepare sauce:* Drain cucumber slices in coffee filter–lined sieve 5 minutes, then pulse with all remaining ingredients in food processor or electric blender until nearly smooth but with a few small pieces of cucumber still showing, about 45 seconds.

7. To serve, open foil packets and place on heated dinner plates. Spoon cucumber sauce onto plate or into packets beside chicken or, if you prefer, pass separately.

RECIPE FROM

*Lisa Stift; Salem, New Hampshire*

# VIRGINIA C. ANTHONY

*Jacksonville, Florida*

Born in New Jersey but brought up in Florida, Virginia has a retired husband, two children, and three grandchildren, all of whom enjoy her cooking. She has won or placed in numerous recipe contests, and likes to cook "anything"—especially dishes she dreams up herself, like this stir-fry, which she's been perfecting ever since she first tried it in 1971. "When I created it, fresh ginger, snow peas, and yellow peppers weren't readily available," she recalls. Now she can easily find the colorful, crisp-fresh vegetables she insists upon.

# Oriental Chicken in a Garden

*Makes 4 to 6 servings*

*Few recipes are more colorful or nutritious than this one, which brims with tomatoes and red, yellow, and green bell peppers.*

TIP 1: *The fastest way to core and seed bell peppers is to halve them lengthwise; then, with a sharp paring knife, cut out the core and pithy innards to which most of the seeds cling. A quick tap of the knife will free any remaining seeds. Once this is done, all that's needed is to cut the peppers into the 1-inch squares this recipe calls for.*

TIP 2: *The rice will take about 20 minutes to cook, so put it on at the outset.*

>*3 tablespoons reduced-sodium soy sauce*
>
>*2 tablespoons plus 1 teaspoon cornstarch*
>
>*2 teaspoons Chinese rice wine or dry sherry*
>
>*1 teaspoon Oriental roasted sesame oil*
>
>*2 large cloves garlic, finely minced*
>
>*¼ teaspoon freshly ground black pepper*
>
>*4 (5-ounce) boneless, skinless chicken breast halves, cut into 1-inch cubes*
>
>*1 tablespoon peanut oil*
>
>*3 medium-size ribs celery, trimmed and thinly sliced on the bias*
>
>*6 ounces fresh snow peas, strings removed*
>
>*1 medium-size red bell pepper, cored, seeded, and cut into 1-inch squares (see Tip 1)*

1 medium-size green bell pepper, cored, seeded,
and cut into 1-inch squares

1 medium-size yellow bell pepper, cored, seeded,
and cut into 1-inch squares

8 medium-size scallions, trimmed and thinly sliced
(include some green tops)

1 (1-inch) cube fresh ginger, peeled and finely minced

1 (14.25-ounce) can reduced-sodium, nonfat chicken broth

½ teaspoon sugar

2 medium-size firm-ripe tomatoes, each cored and
cut into 8 wedges but not peeled

1 cup converted rice, cooked according to package
directions

| EACH OF 4 SERVINGS |
| --- |
| 488 calories |
| ..... |
| 8 g fat (2 g saturated) |
| ..... |
| 84 mg cholesterol |
| ..... |
| 647 mg sodium |
| ..... |
| EACH OF 6 SERVINGS |
| 326 calories |
| ..... |
| 5 g fat (1 g saturated) |
| ..... |
| 56 mg cholesterol |
| ..... |
| 431 mg sodium |
| ..... |

1. Combine 1 tablespoon soy sauce, 1 teaspoon cornstarch, the rice wine and sesame oil, half the garlic, and all the black pepper in medium-size bowl. Add chicken, turning to coat, and set aside.

2. Heat peanut oil in very large heavy skillet or wok over moderately high heat until ripples appear on skillet bottom—1½ to 2 minutes. Add celery and snow peas and stir-fry 2 minutes.

3. Add remaining garlic; red, green, and yellow bell peppers; scallions and ginger; and stir-fry 2 minutes. Scoop into large bowl and reserve.

4. Blend remaining 2 tablespoons cornstarch into skillet drippings, then whisk in chicken broth, sugar, and remaining 2 tablespoons soy sauce. Cook, stirring constantly, until lightly thickened, about 2 minutes.

5. Add chicken and any marinade to skillet, adjust heat so mixture bubbles gently, cover, and cook until chicken shows no tinges of pink in center, about 5 minutes.

6. Return reserved vegetables to skillet, add tomatoes, toss quickly to mix, then cover and cook 2 minutes more.

7. To serve, bed rice on large, deep, heated platter and top with chicken mixture.

RECIPE FROM

*Virginia C. Anthony; Jacksonville, Florida*

Kathy, a judicial assistant to a U.S. district judge, is married to an electronics technician. Originally from Michigan, she likes living in the Black Hills "banana belt" where the mild climate permits virtual year-round golf—she and her husband play several times a week. It was at a local country club that Kathy tasted a chicken dish she and a friend later tried to re-create. "I don't know that our attempt was all that similar to the original," she confessed, "but my husband and I both like it and serve it often to guests. It's convenient (all in one pan) and tastes just as good the next day."

# Cajun Chicken Pasta

*Makes 6 servings*

*The sauce in this recipe has all the creaminess of Alfredo—without the heavy cream. Evaporated skim milk blended with flour does the trick!*

**4 (5-ounce) boneless, skinless chicken breast halves, cut crosswise into strips ¼ inch wide**

**1 tablespoon plus ½ teaspoon Cajun seasoning**

**1 tablespoon olive oil**

**1 medium-size red bell pepper, cored, seeded, and cut lengthwise into strips ¼ inch wide**

**6 ounces mushrooms, stemmed and thinly sliced**

**½ cup coarsely chopped yellow onion (about 1 small onion)**

**2 tablespoons flour**

**2 medium-size cloves garlic, finely minced**

**1 teaspoon finely grated lemon zest**

**½ teaspoon dried leaf basil, crumbled**

**⅛ teaspoon freshly ground black pepper**

**1 (12-ounce) can evaporated skim milk**

**PER SERVING**

330 calories

····

6 g fat (2 g saturated)

····

60 mg cholesterol

····

559 mg sodium

····

1 (8-ounce) package fettuccine, cooked and drained according to package
    directions
¼ cup freshly grated Parmesan cheese
2 tablespoons coarsely chopped fresh Italian (flat-leaf) parsley

1. Place chicken in large bowl, add 1 tablespoon Cajun seasoning, toss well, and set aside.

2. Heat olive oil in medium-size Dutch oven over moderately high heat until ripples appear on pan bottom—1½ to 2 minutes. Add chicken, cover, and cook, stirring occasionally, until nearly done—about 5 minutes. Add red bell pepper, mushrooms, and onion, cover and cook, stirring occasionally, 5 minutes more.

3. Meanwhile, whisk together flour, remaining ½ teaspoon Cajun seasoning, garlic, lemon zest, basil, black pepper, and evaporated skim milk.

4. Add flour mixture to chicken, bring to quick boil over high heat, then adjust heat so mixture bubbles gently, and simmer uncovered, stirring occasionally, until sauce thickens and no raw taste of starch remains—about 3 minutes. If sauce seems thick, stir in 3 to 4 tablespoons water.

5. Dump hot drained fettuccine into Dutch oven, toss all well, then transfer to large heated serving bowl.

6. Scatter cheese and parsley on top and serve at once.

RECIPE FROM
*Kathy Cline; Rapid City, South Dakota*

# MELISSA JUARBE

## Parsons, Kansas

Born in Nebraska and brought up in Missouri, Melissa is married to a computer analyst and has one daughter just graduating from college. As the manager of a delicatessen, she has a professional as well as a personal interest in food and often makes use of cooking ideas learned from her Italian mother and Puerto Rican mother-in-law. This chicken recipe, her "signature dish," is an adaptation of her mother-in-law's standard *arroz con pollo,* updated through the use of lean chicken breasts, less fat, more vegetables, raisins to counteract the saltiness of the olives, and some substitutions for seasonings not available stateside.

# Lean Caribbean Chicken with Rice

### Makes 4 servings

*Such a quick and easy skillet dinner. So that everything will be ready to serve at the same time, cook the rice while you cook the chicken. For 2 cups cooked rice, you'll need about 3/4 cup converted rice.*

TIP: *If you should have 2 cups leftover cooked rice, so much the better. Dump into a large fine sieve, set over a pan containing about one inch simmering water, tent with foil, and heat about 5 minutes. Fluff with a fork and serve.*

4 (5-ounce) boneless, skinless chicken breast
   halves

1/2 teaspoon salt

1/4 teaspoon freshly ground black pepper

2 tablespoons olive oil

1 cup coarsely chopped yellow onion
   (about 1 medium-large onion)

2 medium-size cloves garlic, minced

1/2 cup thinly sliced peeled carrot (1 small carrot)

1/2 large green bell pepper, cored, seeded, and cut lengthwise into strips
   1/2 inch wide

**PER SERVING**

396 calories
....
10 g fat (1 g saturated)
....
82 mg cholesterol
....
494 mg sodium
....

$^{1}/_{2}$ *large red bell pepper, cored, seeded, and cut lengthwise into strips* $^{1}/_{2}$ *inch wide*

$^{1}/_{2}$ *large yellow bell pepper, cored, seeded, and cut lengthwise into strips* $^{1}/_{2}$ *inch wide*

*2 tablespoons golden seedless raisins*

*2 tablespoons coarsely chopped pimiento-stuffed green olives or olive salad*

*1 cup low-fat, low-sodium tomato sauce*

*1 cup water*

$^{1}/_{4}$ *cup coarsely chopped fresh cilantro*

$^{1}/_{2}$ *teaspoon dried leaf oregano, crumbled*

$^{1}/_{2}$ *teaspoon ground cumin*

$^{1}/_{2}$ *teaspoon hot red pepper sauce*

*2 cups cooked white rice*

1. Sprinkle chicken on both sides with salt and pepper.

2. Heat 1 tablespoon olive oil in very large heavy skillet over moderately high heat until ripples appear on skillet bottom—about $1^{1}/_{2}$ minutes. Add chicken and sauté until golden brown—3 to 5 minutes on each side. Lift chicken to paper toweling to drain.

3. Add remaining 1 tablespoon olive oil to skillet, again heat till ripples appear on pan bottom, then add onion, garlic, carrot, green, red, and yellow peppers, and cook, stirring often, until nicely wilted—about 5 minutes.

4. Return chicken to skillet, add all remaining ingredients except rice, and bring to a boil. Adjust heat so mixture bubbles gently, cover, and cook just until chicken shows no pink in center—about 15 minutes.

5. Raise heat to moderately high and boil uncovered until carrots are tender and sauce is consistency of pasta sauce—about 5 minutes.

6. Divide rice among four heated dinner plates, spoon chicken mixture on top, and serve.

RECIPE FROM

*Melissa Juarbe; Parsons, Kansas*

Nadine and her husband Douglass, both accountants by profession, frequently dine alone now that their son and daughter are in their twenties. "I often create recipes using ingredients that my husband and I especially like," says Nadine. But having lost ten pounds and kept them off, she keeps an eye on the fat and calories, too. "We both love using white wine in sauces," she continues. And because she grows her own rosemary, it's always available fresh. With these two ingredients in mind, Nadine worked with this low-fat, low-cal chicken recipe for a couple of months until it met with approval. Now she and Douglass enjoy the dish often on cold winter evenings.

# *Dijon Rosemary Chicken*

*Makes 4 servings*

*Nadine Clapp, who submitted this recipe, suggests serving it with fluffy boiled rice and a well-chilled chardonnay. She bakes her chicken instead of finishing it on the stovetop, a method we favor because it's quicker. If you have an ovenproof skillet, you can transfer the chicken to a preheated 350°F oven in step 4 as soon as the sauce bubbles. Cover and bake until the chicken shows no tinge of pink in the center—25 to 30 minutes. Or you can do as Nadine does and transfer everything to a lidded casserole (but you'll have an extra dish to wash).*

NOTE: *You should use fresh rosemary for this recipe—the dried lacks the requisite resiny-lemony flavor.*

**4 (5-ounce) boneless, skinless chicken breast halves**

**¼ teaspoon salt**

**⅛ teaspoon freshly ground black pepper**

**1 tablespoon olive oil**

**3 medium-size cloves garlic, finely minced**

PER SERVING

255 calories
....
4 g fat (0.7 g saturated)
....
85 mg cholesterol
....
455 mg sodium
....

*1 tablespoon finely chopped fresh rosemary plus 4 small sprigs for garnishing*

*1 tablespoon flour*

*$^1/_2$ cup dry white wine*

*1 cup evaporated skim milk*

*$1^1/_2$ tablespoons Dijon mustard*

1. Sprinkle chicken on all sides with salt and pepper.

2. Heat olive oil in very large nonstick skillet over moderately high heat until ripples appear on skillet bottom—$1^1/_2$ to 2 minutes. Add chicken and brown 5 minutes on each side. Lift chicken to large plate and reserve.

3. Add garlic, chopped rosemary, and flour to skillet and cook and stir over moderately high heat for 1 minute. Off heat, whisk in wine and milk. Return skillet to heat and bring to a boil, whisking constantly so sauce doesn't lump.

4. Return chicken to skillet, adjust heat so sauce bubbles gently, cover, and cook, turning chicken and stirring sauce twice, until chicken shows no signs of pink in center—about 10 minutes.

5. Lift chicken to heated serving platter. Quickly whisk mustard into skillet sauce, then pour over chicken. Garnish with rosemary sprigs and serve.

RECIPE FROM

*Nadine Clapp; Kansas City, Missouri*

"I like to try everything," says Leanne of her cooking style. Creating a low-fat version of her mother's Chicken Parmesan was one of her outstanding successes. "I never saw Mom use a recipe for this dish," she recalls. "Her original way of browning the chicken was to use lots of butter, and she wouldn't use anything but a thick slab of whole-milk mozzarella for the topping. I made some adjustments, measured the low-fat mozzarella ever so carefully, and served the fat-reduced dish to my unsuspecting family" (husband Jerry, an executive in the entertainment business, and twelve-year-old stepson Richard). "They never knew the difference!" It's unlikely baby Carly got a taste, but she no doubt will before long.

# Chicken Parmesan

*Makes 4 servings*

*To trim fat, calories, and sodium, choose a marinara (or other tomato-based pasta sauce) that's either low or reduced in fat and sodium. It goes without saying that you should also remove all visible fat from the chicken breasts.*

TIP: *Being soft, mozzarella is often difficult to shred. You'll find the going easier if you chill it well first—20 to 30 minutes in the freezer should do the trick.*

2 tablespoons flour

1 tablespoon freshly grated Parmesan cheese

2 large egg whites

6 tablespoons Italian-flavor bread crumbs

2 medium-size cloves garlic, minced

$1/4$ teaspoon freshly ground black pepper

4 (5-ounce) boneless, skinless chicken breast halves

1 tablespoon olive oil

$1^{1}/2$ cups low-fat, low-sodium marinara sauce

$1/2$ cup shredded part-skim mozzarella cheese

| PER SERVING |
| :---: |
| 363 calories |
| .... |
| 12 g fat (3 g saturated) |
| .... |
| 91 mg cholesterol |
| .... |
| 413 mg sodium |
| .... |

1. Preheat oven to 350°F.

2. Combine flour and Parmesan in shallow bowl. Whisk egg whites until frothy in second shallow bowl, and in third shallow bowl, toss crumbs with garlic and pepper until well mixed.

3. Dredge chicken in flour mixture, shaking off excess. Dip into egg whites, then into crumb mixture, pressing firmly to coat all sides well.

4. Heat olive oil in large heavy skillet over moderate heat for 1½ minutes. Add chicken and brown well—3 to 4 minutes on each side.

5. Pour marinara sauce into ungreased 13 x 9 x 2-inch baking dish, add chicken, and sprinkle with mozzarella.

6. Bake uncovered until bubbling and tipped with brown—about 20 minutes. Serve at once.

RECIPE FROM

*Leanne Guido; Silver Spring, Maryland*

# DONNAMARIE ZOTTER

*Mechanicsburg, Pennsylvania*

DonnaMarie, an attorney who learned to cook by watching her mom and grand-mother "and by reading beautiful, interesting cookbooks," prefers to use only the freshest in-season ingredients. Tasting a very spicy fried chicken appetizer at a restaurant inspired her to create this recipe, which combines black beans and the chili flavorings she and her husband like in a memorable sauce. In her words, "It takes plain ordinary chicken to a new, exciting eating experience." This particular recipe also trims fat and calories, necessary (along with "regular exercise") to keep DonnaMarie from regaining any of the twenty pounds she lost. She adds that the Black Bean Sauce is also great on baked potatoes and as a condiment for pita or roll-up sandwiches.

# *Roasted Chicken with Black Bean Sauce*

*Makes 4 servings*

*You can, if you like, substitute yellow squash for zucchini in this recipe, even sliced mush-rooms, asparagus tips, or whatever seasonal vegetable you fancy.*

NOTE: *Using olive oil–flavored nonstick cooking spray in this recipe means you can reduce the amount of olive oil to 1 tablespoon and significantly pare fat and calories.*

*Olive oil–flavored nonstick cooking spray*

*4 (5-ounce) boneless, skinless chicken breast halves*

*2 medium-size zucchini (about ¾ pound), trimmed, halved lengthwise, then each half cut into 1-inch chunks*

*1½ teaspoons ground cumin*

*1½ teaspoons chili powder*

*¼ teaspoon salt*

*⅛ teaspoon freshly ground black pepper*

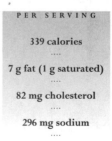

PER SERVING

339 calories
....
7 g fat (1 g saturated)
....
82 mg cholesterol
....
296 mg sodium
....

*1 tablespoon olive oil*

*1 cup coarsely chopped yellow onion (about 1 medium-large onion)*

*2 medium-size cloves garlic, finely minced*

*½ cup dry red wine*

*1 (14.5-ounce) can low-sodium diced tomatoes, drained*

*2 tablespoons finely diced sun-dried tomatoes (not oil-pack)*

*1 (15-ounce) can black beans, rinsed and drained*

1. Preheat oven to 350°F. Coat 13 x 9 x 2-inch baking dish well with olive oil–flavored nonstick cooking spray.

2. Arrange chicken and zucchini in baking dish, sprinkle with 1 teaspoon each ground cumin and chili powder, then all the salt and pepper. Set uncovered in oven and roast until chicken shows no signs of pink in center and zucchini is tender, about 30 minutes.

3. Meanwhile, heat olive oil in medium-size heavy skillet over moderately high heat until ripples appear on pan bottom—1½ to 2 minutes. Add onion and garlic and cook, stirring occasionally, until tender, about 3 minutes. Sprinkle in remaining ½ teaspoon each ground cumin and chili powder, tossing lightly to mix.

4. Add red wine and boil uncovered until reduced by half—2 to 3 minutes. Add canned tomatoes and sun-dried tomatoes, reduce heat to low, and simmer uncovered until flavors merge—2 to 3 minutes. Mix in black beans, cover, and simmer sauce over low heat 5 minutes. Keep warm until ready to serve.

5. To serve, divide black bean sauce among four heated dinner plates, then arrange chicken and zucchini artfully on top.

RECIPE FROM

*DonnaMarie Zotter; Mechanicsburg, Pennsylvania*

Sharon, today a technologist in the highly sophisticated field of magnetic resonance imaging, was born and brought up in Missouri, where she learned to cook from her mother, grandmother, and a great aunt. She had been serving a family favorite, Coq au Vin, for some thirty years before "a thickening waistline" prompted her to start on a Weight Watchers diet program and rethink her cooking practices. "I decided to change all family favorites to lower the fats and calories," she explained. The result? Sharon lost thirty pounds and her family still likes her cooking.

## *Coq au Vin*

### *Makes 6 servings*

*True French Coq au Vin, traditionally made with a plump chicken and about a quarter of a pound of bacon, is hardly slimming fare. This version substitutes a skinned broiler-fryer and trims the fat to a bare-bones level. The best wine to use for this recipe is a French Burgundy, but any well-balanced dry red wine will do. Never use "cooking wine," which dates, it's said, back to Prohibition, and has had salt added to keep chefs from tippling. It's both expensive and inferior.*

*1 large whole head garlic (about 4 ounces)*

*3 tablespoons flour*

*¼ teaspoon salt*

*⅛ teaspoon freshly ground black pepper*

*1 (3¾-pound) broiler-fryer, cut up for frying and all skin and fat removed*

*1 slice extra-lean bacon, coarsely chopped*

*1 tablespoon olive oil*

*1 cup frozen pearl onions, separated but not thawed*

*½ pound medium-size white mushrooms, trimmed and quartered*

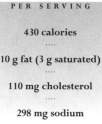

PER SERVING

430 calories
....
10 g fat (3 g saturated)
....
110 mg cholesterol
....
298 mg sodium
....

*1 teaspoon dried leaf thyme, crumbled*

*1 (14.25-ounce) can reduced-sodium, nonfat chicken broth*

*2 cups red Burgundy wine (see headnote)*

*1 pound walnut-size red-skin potatoes, scrubbed and strip of skin removed
around middle*

1. Preheat oven to 350°F. Lay garlic on side, slice ¼ inch off top and discard, then wrap garlic in aluminum foil. Set on middle oven rack and roast until soft—about 40 minutes.

2. Meanwhile, combine flour, salt, and pepper in large pie tin, then dredge chicken in seasoned flour in two batches, each time shaking off excess; set chicken aside.

3. Heat bacon and olive oil in medium-size Dutch oven over moderately high heat until bacon browns lightly and almost all fat cooks out—2 to 3 minutes. Scoop browned bacon bits to paper toweling to drain.

4. Brown chicken well in two batches in drippings over moderately high heat, allowing 10 minutes for each batch and turning chicken after 5 minutes. Lift chicken to platter and reserve. Remove garlic from oven and let stand, still wrapped, until easy to handle—about 10 minutes.

5. Add pearl onions, mushrooms, and thyme to Dutch oven, reduce heat to moderate, and cook, stirring often, until lightly browned—about 5 minutes. Squeeze roasted garlic over vegetables.

6. Return reserved bacon and chicken to pot, add chicken broth, wine, and potatoes, and bring to a boil. Cover Dutch oven, transfer to oven, and bake until potatoes are fork-tender and chicken shows no signs of pink in center—about 1 hour.

7. Arrange chicken on large heated platter, spoon vegetables and gravy on top, and serve.

RECIPE FROM

*Sharon A. Curry; Independence, Missouri*

## DARLA J. DALHOVER

*Cincinnati, Ohio*

Born and brought up in the city where she now lives and works as bookkeeper to a jewelry manufacturer, Darla says she learned both how to cook and how *not* to cook from her mother. Her interest in experimenting with unusual combinations of foods and flavors she attributes to a former co-worker from Sri Lanka who customarily packed in her lunch box foods that Darla considered "really strange," but also irresistible. In the course of becoming a more adventurous cook, Darla found the pounds piling on. She managed to lose seventy of those pounds and has kept them off, thanks to trimming fat and calories from her recipes. This curried chicken, one of her "leaner" creations, is a dish her husband and children especially enjoy.

# Curried Chicken

*Makes 4 servings*

*What's unusual about this recipe is that the chicken is dusted with curry powder, which gives it a lovely golden finish. The sauce contains both curry and chili powder plus green chilies for additional heat. Reduce the amount of chilies if you like things more tepid.*

*4 (5-ounce) boneless, skinless chicken breast halves*

*2 teaspoons curry powder*

*1/2 teaspoon salt*

*1/8 teaspoon freshly ground black pepper*

*1 tablespoon plus 2 teaspoons vegetable oil*

*2 cups coarsely chopped Spanish, Bermuda, or other sweet onion (about 1 large onion)*

*1 (14.5-ounce) can diced tomatoes, with their liquid*

*1 (4.5-ounce) can diced green chilies, rinsed and drained*

*1 1/2 teaspoons chili powder*

*1/2 teaspoon ground cumin*

*1/4 cup water*

*2 cups cooked white rice*

| PER SERVING |
| :---: |
| 391 calories |
| .... |
| 8 g fat (1 g saturated) |
| .... |
| 82 mg cholesterol |
| .... |
| 688 mg sodium |
| .... |

1. Sprinkle chicken with $^1/_2$ teaspoon curry powder, $^1/_4$ teaspoon salt, and the black pepper, rubbing seasonings in well.

2. Heat 1 tablespoon oil in large heavy skillet over moderately high heat until ripples appear on skillet bottom—about $1^1/_2$ minutes. Add chicken and sauté until golden brown—3 to 5 minutes on each side. Lift chicken to paper toweling to drain.

3. Add remaining 2 teaspoons oil to skillet, again heat till ripples appear on pan bottom, then add onion and sauté, stirring often, until wilted—about 5 minutes.

4. Return chicken to pan, add remaining curry powder and salt, tomatoes with their liquid, green chilies, chili powder, cumin, and water. Adjust heat so mixture bubbles gently, cover, and simmer until chicken is tender and shows no signs of pink in center—about 20 minutes.

5. Remove chicken to heated plate, cover loosely to keep warm. If skillet mixture seems thin, boil uncovered until consistency of gravy—about 5 minutes.

6. To serve, divide rice among four heated dinner plates, top with chicken, then spoon curry mixture over all.

RECIPE FROM

*Darla J. Dalhover; Cincinnati, Ohio*

# MARIE VALENZUELA

*Westminster, Colorado*

Marie grew up in Michigan and central Indiana, where watching her grandmother make bread every Saturday inspired her to learn how to cook. Now a policy analyst for the Colorado Department of Labor and Employment (and writer of fiction in her downtime), she still enjoys cooking and adapted this savory dish from a recipe for chicken stew that didn't suit her: "I converted it to a crockpot recipe, reduced the oil [Marie lost fifteen pounds and intends to keep them off], substituted whole spices for ground, added chilis and cilantro." Reactions from friends? "Everyone wants the recipe and there are never any leftovers."

# Slickrock Mesa Chicken Stew

*Makes 6 servings*

*Marie Valenzuela developed this recipe for her slow cooker in which the chicken simmers slowly, ever so slowly to succulence. In all, it takes more than 4 hours. We've worked out a 47-minute stovetop version. If you prefer the slow cooker method, follow our recipe through step 3, then add the chicken mixture in the skillet to the slow cooker along with the tomatoes, picante sauce, cumin, cinnamon, cloves, and corn. Cover and cook on low for 4 hours. Afterward, finish the recipe as directed below in step 5.*

NOTE: *If you opt for the low-fat sour cream topping, add 20 calories, 1 gram fat (1 gram saturated), 5 milligrams cholesterol, and 10 milligrams sodium to each of the per-serving counts below.*

*4 (5-ounce) boneless, skinless chicken breast halves*

*1/4 teaspoon salt*

*1/8 teaspoon freshly ground black pepper*

*1 tablespoon olive oil*

*1 1/2 cups coarsely chopped yellow onion
(about 1 large onion)*

*3 medium-size cloves garlic, finely minced*

**PER SERVING**

211 calories
....
3 g fat (0.5 g saturated)
....
55 mg cholesterol
....
406 mg sodium
....

*1¼ cups coarsely chopped green bell pepper (about 1 large pepper)*

*1 tablespoon minced jalapeño pepper (about 1 small pepper)*

*1 (4.5-ounce) can chopped green chilies, rinsed and drained*

*1 (14.5-ounce) can low-sodium diced tomatoes, with their liquid*

*1 cup bottled mild or medium picante sauce (preferably low-sodium)*

*1 teaspoon ground cumin*

*½ teaspoon ground cinnamon*

*Pinch ground cloves*

*1 (11-ounce) can whole-kernel corn (preferably low-sodium), drained*

*½ cup coarsely chopped fresh cilantro*

*6 tablespoons low-fat sour cream (optional topping)*

1. Cut chicken into 1-inch cubes and toss with salt and pepper; set aside.

2. Heat olive oil in medium-size Dutch oven over moderately high heat until ripples appear on pan bottom—1½ to 2 minutes. Add chicken and brown 5 minutes on each side.

3. Add onion, garlic, bell pepper, jalapeño, and canned green chilies and sauté, stirring occasionally, until vegetables wilt—about 5 minutes.

4. Add tomatoes, picante sauce, cumin, cinnamon, and cloves. Bring to a boil, adjust heat so mixture bubbles gently, cover, and simmer 25 minutes. Stir in corn, cover, and simmer 5 minutes more.

5. Stir in cilantro, ladle into heated soup bowls, and top each portion, if you like, with 1 tablespoon low-fat sour cream. A good accompaniment: low-fat flour tortillas.

RECIPE FROM

*Marie Valenzuela; Westminster, Colorado*

"I used to make traditional high-fat enchiladas with lots and lots of cheese," says Timothy, a claims adjuster who likes to cook almost anything hot and spicy. "But when Cheryl and I started dieting after our son Jonah was born, I had to find ways to change the recipe. I added beans to boost the fiber, cut down on the cheese, and switched to low-fat sour cream. It took a few times to get it right, but I make these low-fat enchiladas often and we like them." Best of all, this slimmed-down version has helped Timothy and his wife lose thirty pounds—and keep those pounds from creeping back on!

# Chicken and Vegetable Enchiladas with Sour Cream and Scallions

*Makes 4 servings*

*More nutritious than most enchiladas, these contain diced red bell pepper and shredded carrot, both high in vitamins A and C. And in keeping with the government's current guidelines for healthful eating, meat (in this case chicken) isn't the heavyweight. In fact, with 5 ounces spread over 4 servings, it's more for texture than anything else.*

NOTE: *This recipe calls for a grilled, boneless chicken breast. You could settle for deli chicken, but if you want to grill the chicken yourself, here's how: Heat a small cast-iron grill pan over moderate heat for 2 minutes. Remove from heat and coat well with nonstick cooking spray. Place chicken breast on pan and grill 2 minutes over moderately high heat. Without turning the breast over, give it an eighth or quarter turn so you get crisscross grill marks. Turn breast over and grill the flip side the same way, but cook it 4 minutes instead of 2. Transfer grill pan to preheated 350°F. oven and bake chicken uncovered until no tinges of pink show in center—8 to 10 minutes.*

ENCHILADAS

*½ cup low-fat sour cream*

*2 tablespoons coarsely chopped fresh cilantro*

*1½ teaspoons ground cumin*

*1 teaspoon chili powder*

*1 tablespoon olive oil*

*1 cup coarsely chopped red onion (about 1 medium-size onion)*

*1 cup coarsely chopped red bell pepper (about 1 medium-size pepper)*

*½ cup coarsely shredded carrot (about 1 medium-small carrot)*

*1 (15-ounce) can black beans, rinsed and drained*

*1 (4.5-ounce) can chopped green chilies, rinsed and drained*

*1 (5-ounce) boneless, skinless chicken breast half, grilled and finely diced (see Note)*

*¼ teaspoon freshly ground black pepper*

*8 (7-inch) low-fat flour tortillas*

TOPPING

*¼ cup thinly sliced scallions (include some green tops) (about 2 medium-size scallions)*

*¼ cup moderately coarsely shredded low-fat Cheddar cheese*

PER SERVING

383 calories
....
8 g fat (3 g saturated)
....
32 mg cholesterol
....
819 mg sodium
....

1. Preheat oven to 350°F. Coat 13 x 9 x 2-inch baking dish well with nonstick cooking spray and set aside.

2. *For enchiladas:* Combine sour cream with cilantro, cumin, and chili powder in small bowl and set aside.

3. Heat olive oil in large heavy skillet over moderately high heat until ripples appear on skillet bottom—1½ to 2 minutes. Add onion, bell pepper, and carrot and sauté, stirring now and then, until limp—about 5 minutes.

4. Remove skillet from heat and mix in black beans, chilies, 2 tablespoons reserved sour cream mixture, chicken, and black pepper.

5. To assemble enchiladas, spoon ½ cup black bean mixture onto center of each tortilla, shaping into log, and roll up.

6. Arrange enchiladas, seam sides down, in prepared baking dish and spread with remaining sour cream mixture.

7. Cover with aluminum foil, dull side up, and bake 25 minutes.

8. Scatter scallions and Cheddar over enchiladas, dividing amounts evenly, and serve.

RECIPE FROM

*Timothy G. Ball; West Seneca, New York*

## SHELLY PLATTEN

*Amherst, Wisconsin*

Raised on a Wisconsin farm, Shelly inherited a love of cooking from her mother and grandmother. Today a freelance artist, mother of two young children, and wife of an elementary schoolteacher, she cooks specialty dishes for family reunions and potluck dinners and has won many recipe contests. Of her layered chicken salad she writes: "I've always enjoyed eating layered trifle desserts served in a pretty bowl, so I decided to try a savory salad version. Since our family likes Mexican food, the idea of layering Mexican chicken with cornbread intrigued me. It's a colorful and different dish to bring to a potluck and knowing that it's low in fat makes it a guilt-free pleasure!" That's important to Shelly because she's lost forty pounds and never gained them back.

# Pecos Chicken-Cornbread Salad

*Makes 6 to 8 servings*

*You can make the cornbread a day ahead of time, then assemble this layered salad shortly before serving. It's a showy affair, perfect for a party.*

CORNBREAD
*1 cup sifted all-purpose flour*

*1 cup yellow cornmeal*

*1 teaspoon baking powder*

*1 teaspoon baking soda*

*½ teaspoon chili powder*

*2 large egg whites, lightly beaten*

*1 cup low-fat (1.5 percent) buttermilk*

*1 (4.5-ounce) can chopped green chilies, rinsed
    and drained*

SALAD
*4 (5-ounce) boneless, skinless chicken breast halves,
    cut into ½-inch cubes*

EACH OF 6 SERVINGS

422 calories

5 g fat (3 g saturated)

65 mg cholesterol

1,163 mg sodium

EACH OF 8 SERVINGS

316 calories

4 g fat (2 g saturated)

49 mg cholesterol

882 mg sodium

*1 (10-ounce) can diced tomatoes with green chilies, drained*

*¼ cup coarsely chopped fresh cilantro*

*1 teaspoon ground cumin*

*½ teaspoon chili powder*

*3 cups thinly sliced romaine (about ½ medium-size head)*

*1 (11-ounce) can corn with diced red and green bell pepper, drained*

*1 (15-ounce) can black beans, rinsed and drained*

*1 cup moderately finely diced green bell pepper (about 1 medium-size pepper)*

*½ cup low-fat sour cream*

*½ cup finely shredded reduced-fat Cheddar cheese*

1. Preheat oven to 400°F. Coat 9 x 9 x 2-inch baking dish with nonstick cooking spray and set aside.

2. *For cornbread:* Combine flour, cornmeal, baking powder, soda, and chili powder in large bowl and make well in center. Quickly whisk together egg whites and buttermilk, dump into well in dry ingredients, and stir only enough to mix. Add green chilies and again stir only enough to mix.

3. Spoon batter into prepared baking dish, spreading to corners, and bake uncovered until a toothpick inserted in center comes out clean—20 to 25 minutes. Cool cornbread to room temperature in upright pan on wire rack, then cut into 1-inch cubes.

4. *For salad:* Heat large heavy skillet over moderately high heat 1½ to 2 minutes. Add chicken and tomatoes with green chilies and bring to a quick boil. Mix in 2 tablespoons cilantro, the cumin, and chili powder. Adjust heat so mixture bubbles gently, cover, and cook 5 minutes, stirring at half-time. Remove from heat and cool to room temperature.

5. To assemble salad, layer ingredients into straight-sided glass bowl this way: half *each* of the cornbread cubes, chicken mixture, romaine, corn, black beans, green bell pepper, sour cream, and cheese. Repeat layers, sprinkle with remaining 2 tablespoons chopped cilantro, and serve.

RECIPE FROM

*Shelly Platten; Amherst, Wisconsin*

## EDWARD CLUKEY

*Terryville, Connecticut*

"I was having a small dinner party for some friends," this cardiovascular specialist and father of two grown-up children wrote, explaining how he happened to originate his unusual and effective dish. "One of our friends preferred low-fat, low-cholesterol foods. I have about fifty cookbooks but could not find anything in them that interested me, and neither could my wife Patsy. I watch as many cooking shows as I can, so I think the recipe I finally put together came from years of watching all those different shows!"

# Stuffed Turkey Cutlets

*Makes 4 servings*

*Boneless, skinless turkey cutlets are now routinely carried by all good supermarkets. Packaged in plastic and ready to go, they are every bit as versatile as veal cutlets but far less expensive. This imaginative recipe uses them to best advantage.*

1 tablespoon olive oil

1 large shallot, minced

1/4 pound lean ground pork

1 large egg white

2 tablespoons soft white bread crumbs

1 tablespoon Cognac

1/2 teaspoon rubbed sage

1/4 teaspoon dried leaf thyme, crumbled

1/2 teaspoon salt

1/2 teaspoon freshly ground black pepper

2 cups small whole spinach leaves

4 (3-ounce) turkey cutlets, flattened slightly if uneven

1 tablespoon freshly grated Parmesan cheese

**PER SERVING**

208 calories

....

7 g fat (2 g saturated)

....

72 mg cholesterol

....

423 mg sodium

....

1. Preheat oven to 375°F. Coat 9 x 9 x 2-inch baking pan with nonstick cooking spray and set aside.

2. Heat olive oil in small heavy skillet over moderately high heat until ripples appear on skillet bottom—$1\frac{1}{2}$ to 2 minutes. Add shallot and sauté, stirring often, until soft—about 3 minutes. Remove from heat and mix in pork, egg white, bread crumbs, Cognac, sage, thyme, and $\frac{1}{4}$ teaspoon each salt and pepper; set aside.

3. Blanch spinach in boiling water 1 minute, drain, and plunge into ice water for 2 to 3 minutes. Drain spinach again and squeeze dry in paper toweling. Set aside.

4. Spread each turkey cutlet with one-fourth of pork mixture, leaving $\frac{1}{4}$-inch margins all around, then lay one-fourth of spinach leaves on top of each. Beginning at short end, roll each cutlet up jelly-roll style as tight as possible.

5. Quickly mix Parmesan cheese with remaining $\frac{1}{4}$ teaspoon salt and pepper on sheet of wax paper and dredge each turkey roll in mixture.

6. Place turkey rolls seam sides down in prepared baking pan and bake uncovered until instant-read meat thermometer inserted in center of roll reaches 170°F. Remove turkey rolls from oven and let stand 5 minutes.

7. To serve, cut each turkey roll on the diagonal into slices $\frac{1}{2}$ inch thick and arrange on heated dinner plates.

RECIPE FROM

*Edward Clukey; Terryville, Connecticut*

# RICHARD RIZZIO JR.

*Troy, Michigan*

A technical systems coordinator for electronic security in a large Detroit hospital, forty-seven-year-old Richard has loved to cook ever since his mother and grandmother taught him how back when he was growing up in Michigan's "U.P." (Upper Peninsula). Like many good cooks, he found the weight creeping on, but thanks to a diet his doctor put him on, he's lost thirty pounds and managed to keep most of them off. "Looking for a fast and easy recipe that was also good for you," he created Turkey Feathers with Jalapeño Pepper Mayonnaise—a big hit with his wife Joanie. Richard clearly has a feel for food. He's won five cooking contests including the National Oyster Cook-Off in Maryland.

# Oven-Fried Turkey Feathers with Jalapeño Pepper Mayonnaise

*Makes 4 servings*

*Richard Rizzio Jr., who created this recipe, says the breading used here for turkey cutlets is a family favorite, something he uses to coat everything from artichokes to oysters. Our recipe tester says his turkey feathers would be great in a sandwich spread with the jalapeño mayo.*

TIP: *So that the mayonnaise has time to mellow, make it as soon as the turkey goes into the oven.*

NOTE: *If you're on a low-sodium diet, you may be interested to know that you can reduce the amount of sodium to a mere 172 mg per serving by using plain bread crumbs instead of the Italian-flavor ones called for here.*

**TURKEY**
*½ cup Italian-flavor bread crumbs*
*2 tablespoons freshly grated Parmesan cheese*
*1 tablespoon finely chopped fresh Italian (flat-leaf) parsley*

*1 large clove garlic, minced*

*⅛ teaspoon freshly ground black pepper*

*4 (3-ounce) turkey cutlets, pounded to a thickness of ⅛ inch*

*1 tablespoon olive oil*

MAYONNAISE

*3 tablespoons low-fat sour cream*

*2 tablespoons low-fat mayonnaise*

*1 to 2 teaspoons finely chopped, seeded green jalapeño pepper (preferably fresh), depending on how hot you like things*

*1 to 2 teaspoons finely chopped, seeded red jalapeño pepper (preferably fresh), again depending on how hot you like things*

*1 tablespoon fresh lemon juice*

*1 teaspoon finely grated lemon zest*

*⅛ teaspoon freshly ground black pepper*

PER SERVING

299 calories
....
15 g fat (4 g saturated)
....
61 mg cholesterol
....
672 mg sodium
....

1. Preheat oven to 350°F. Coat a 17 x 11 x 1-inch baking pan with nonstick cooking spray and set aside.

2. *For turkey:* Combine bread crumbs, Parmesan, parsley, garlic, and black pepper in pie pan. Dip turkey cutlets in olive oil, turning to coat both sides, then press into crumb mixture, making sure both sides are nicely breaded.

3. Arrange breaded cutlets in prepared pan so they don't touch one another, then bake uncovered for 10 minutes. Turn cutlets and bake uncovered until golden brown, firm to the touch, and no tinges of pink show in center—10 to 15 minutes more.

4. *For mayonnaise:* Mix all ingredients together in small glass or porcelain bowl, cover with plastic wrap, and let stand at room temperature until turkey is done.

5. To serve, arrange turkey cutlets on four heated dinner plates and spoon a heaping tablespoon mayonnaise alongside each.

RECIPE FROM

*Richard Rizzio Jr.; Troy, Michigan*

## ROBIN WILSON

*San Jose, California*

Brought up in the Pacific Northwest, Robin learned to cook from his mother when he was seven, and by the age of eleven was watching cooking shows on television and declaring his firm intention to become a chef. Today, at eighteen, he is an assistant cook for a caterer and hopes to study at Johnson & Wales University, a well-known culinary school in Providence, Rhode Island, before opening his own restaurant or catering service. Robin, who likes to experiment, created this dish using Indian spices and cranberries he found in his mom's cupboard. "I started with something popular—turkey," he says in describing his recipe. "I had recently been introduced to Indian cuisine, so I took some spices and combined them with the turkey, rolled it to make it look nice, and added a complementary sauce."

# Curried Turkey Roulade with Ruby Sauce

*Makes 6 servings*

*Butterflying and pounding a turkey breast isn't as neat as peeling a potato so our best advice is to coax your butcher into doing these jobs for you. Then you're ready to roll—no pun intended.*

NOTE 1: *If you must do these jobs yourself, here's how: First butterfly the turkey breast by starting on one long side and cutting almost—but not quite—through to the opposite side so you can open the two halves like a book. Next, cover the opened turkey breast with plastic wrap and, using a cutlet bat or rolling pin, pound to a uniform thickness of ¾ inch. The plastic wrap makes it easier to pound the meat without tearing or punching holes in it.*

NOTE 2: *Basmati rice, which this recipe calls for, is a slender-grained Indian rice of delicate nutty flavor. Most better supermarkets now stock it in their international food sections. And all Middle Eastern and Asian groceries carry it. If you can't find it, substitute long-grain or converted white rice.*

**TURKEY**

$1\frac{1}{2}$ teaspoons ground cumin

$1\frac{1}{2}$ teaspoons curry powder

$\frac{1}{8}$ teaspoon salt

$\frac{1}{8}$ teaspoon freshly ground black pepper

1 ($2\frac{1}{2}$-pound) boneless, skinless turkey breast half, butterflied and pounded to a thickness of $\frac{3}{4}$ inch (see headnote)

**FILLING**

$1\frac{1}{4}$ cups reduced-sodium, nonfat chicken broth

$\frac{1}{4}$ cup dried cranberries

2 teaspoons olive oil

$\frac{1}{4}$ cup coarsely chopped yellow onion (about 1 very small onion)

$\frac{1}{4}$ cup finely diced carrot (about $\frac{1}{2}$ medium-small carrot)

$\frac{1}{4}$ cup finely diced celery (about $\frac{1}{2}$ medium-small celery rib)

$\frac{1}{2}$ cup basmati rice (see headnote)

$\frac{1}{8}$ teaspoon salt

$\frac{1}{8}$ teaspoon freshly ground black pepper

$\frac{1}{4}$ cup slivered almonds

**SAUCE**

$\frac{3}{4}$ cup jellied cranberry sauce

$\frac{3}{4}$ cup reduced-sodium, nonfat chicken broth

$1\frac{1}{2}$ tablespoons balsamic vinegar

**PER SERVING**

405 calories

....

6 g fat (1 g saturated)

....

118 mg cholesterol

....

232 mg sodium

....

1. Preheat oven to 350°F.

2. *For turkey:* Combine cumin, curry powder, salt, and pepper and rub evenly over turkey. Cover and refrigerate while you prepare filling.

3. *For filling:* Bring $\frac{1}{4}$ cup chicken broth to boiling in very small nonreactive saucepan over high heat. Remove from heat, add dried cranberries, and set aside to plump.

4. Heat olive oil in small heavy saucepan over moderately high heat until ripples

appear on pan bottom—$1\frac{1}{2}$ to 2 minutes. Add onion, carrot, and celery and sauté, stirring often, until vegetables soften—about 3 minutes.

5. Add remaining 1 cup broth and bring quickly to a boil. Add rice, salt, and pepper, reduce heat to low, cover, and simmer until tender—about 15 minutes. Remove rice from heat, add plumped dried cranberries and slivered almonds, toss lightly with fork, then cool 10 minutes.

6. *To make turkey roulade:* Lay butterflied turkey breast flat on counter, spread with rice mixture, leaving 1-inch margins all around, then starting at a short end, roll up jelly-roll style as tight as possible. Tie roll with cotton butcher's twine in four places, spacing about $1\frac{1}{2}$ inches apart.

7. Place roulade in ungreased 9 x 9 x 2-inch baking pan and roast uncovered until instant-read meat thermometer, inserted in center of roll, reaches 170°F—$1\frac{3}{4}$ to 2 hours. Remove roulade from oven, cover loosely with foil, and let stand 20 minutes.

8. *Meanwhile, prepare sauce:* Place cranberry sauce in small nonreactive skillet and break up with fork. Whisk in chicken broth and bring to a boil over moderate heat. Adjust heat so mixture bubbles gently and simmer uncovered 2 minutes. Mix in vinegar and simmer uncovered 30 seconds more—sauce should be syrupy.

9. To serve, remove strings from turkey roulade, then slice about $\frac{3}{8}$ inch thick. Divide slices among six heated dinner plates and spoon sauce alongside.

RECIPE FROM
*Robin Wilson; San Jose, California*

Sarah has two children and two grandchildren, and in thirty-two years of marriage has cooked a lot of family meals. "At my age," she says, "my goal has shifted from losing weight—I'm hypothyroid and it's almost impossible to lose—to living a healthier lifestyle and trying to stay fit. With traditional meat loaf so high in fat content it was a challenge to turn it into a low-fat entrée. Everyone loves my homemade salsa, so I used it in the recipe combined with additional chopped vegetables and oats for fiber. It tastes surprisingly great!"

FINALIST, ENTRÉES

# Turkey Salsa Meat Loaf

*Makes 6 servings*

*The trouble with ground turkey—especially ground lean white meat—is that it can be as dry as wood chips. Not so in this recipe because the oatmeal holds and absorbs juices. Helping to lower the fat content while adding plenty of punchy flavor is a spicy nonfat salsa.*

1 tablespoon olive oil

1 cup finely chopped yellow onion (about 1 medium-large onion)

1/2 cup finely chopped carrot (about 1 medium-small carrot)

1/4 cup finely chopped celery (about 1 small rib)

1 pound extra-lean ground turkey breast

1 cup old-fashioned rolled oats (not quick-cooking)

1/2 cup plus 3 tablespoons nonfat tomato salsa (as hot as you like)

1 large egg

2 tablespoons minced fresh Italian (flat-leaf) parsley

3/4 teaspoon salt

1 teaspoon freshly ground black pepper

**PER SERVING**

227 calories

....

10 g fat (2 g saturated)

....

95 mg cholesterol

....

621 mg sodium

....

1. Preheat oven to 375°F. Coat 8½ x 4½ x 2¾-inch loaf pan with nonstick cooking spray and set aside.

2. Heat olive oil in medium-size heavy skillet over moderately high heat for 1 minute. Add onion, carrot, and celery and stir-fry until limp—about 5 minutes.

3. Transfer skillet mixture to large bowl. Add turkey, rolled oats, ½ cup salsa, and all remaining ingredients. Mix well.

4. Pat mixture into prepared pan and bake uncovered 30 minutes. Spread remaining 3 tablespoons salsa on top and bake until meat loaf is set and juices run clear—about 15 minutes longer. A meat thermometer inserted in middle of loaf should read 180°F.

5. Remove meat loaf from oven and let stand in upright pan 15 minutes; this firms up the loaf and allows the juices to settle.

6. Cut into six thick slices and serve.

RECIPE FROM

*Sarah Tackett; Springfield, Ohio*

*Richmond, Virginia*

Ellen and her husband James, who married recently, are both bankers and both from large Virginia families. Both enjoy biking, hiking, music, and many other activities, but they don't always share the same food preferences. "I'm learning to make some adjustments," Ellen says. One of her recent creations is this company dish in which she substitutes ground turkey for hamburger (Ellen doesn't eat red meat) and uses zucchini, squash, peppers, and basil fresh from her own vegetable garden.

# Spaghetti Squash with Parmesan-Turkey Balls

*Makes 4 servings*

*These unusual turkey balls are moistened by finely chopped pimiento-stuffed green olives. Freshly grated Parmesan adds a certain nutty flavor and also helps bind the meatball mixture.*

NOTE: *The spaghetti squash and turkey balls are especially good with freshly grated Parmesan sprinkled over all just before serving. But for serious calorie-, fat-, and sodium-counters, we've made the additional Parmesan optional. Topping each portion with 1 tablespoon grated Parmesan will add 29 calories, 2 grams fat (1 gram unsaturated), 5 milligrams cholesterol, and 116 milligrams sodium to the nutritive counts given below.*

*1 small to medium-size spaghetti squash*
*(1¾ pounds), halved lengthwise and seeded*

*1 cup water*

*1 pound lean ground turkey*

*¼ cup finely chopped pimiento-stuffed green olives*

*3 tablespoons freshly grated Parmesan cheese*

*1 tablespoon olive oil*

*1 cup coarsely chopped green bell pepper (about 1 medium-size pepper)*

PER SERVING

329 calories

....

16 g fat (4 g saturated)

....

93 mg cholesterol

....

443 mg sodium

....

*¼ cup coarsely chopped red onion (about 1 very small onion)*

*1 cup thinly sliced, stemmed mushrooms (about 4 medium-size mushrooms)*

*½ cup thinly sliced zucchini (about ½ small zucchini)*

*½ cup thinly sliced yellow squash (about ½ small yellow squash)*

*2 (8-ounce) cans low-fat, low-sodium tomato sauce*

*2 tablespoons coarsely chopped fresh basil*

OPTIONAL TOPPING
*4 tablespoons freshly grated Parmesan cheese*

1. Preheat oven to 350°F. Place spaghetti squash halves, cut sides down, in ungreased 13 x 9 x 2-inch baking pan, pour water around squash, and bake uncovered until squash feels tender—about 45 minutes.

2. Meanwhile, combine turkey, olives, and Parmesan in small bowl, then shape into 16 walnut-size balls.

3. Heat olive oil in large heavy nonstick skillet over moderately high heat until ripples appear on skillet bottom—1½ to 2 minutes. Add turkey balls and brown lightly on all sides—about 6 minutes in all; drain on paper toweling.

4. Transfer turkey balls to second ungreased 13 x 9 x 2-inch baking pan; add bell pepper, onion, mushrooms, zucchini, and yellow squash, arranging so turkey balls are covered. Pour tomato sauce evenly over all.

5. Bake uncovered in same oven with spaghetti squash until vegetables are tender and turkey balls show no tinges of pink in center—about 30 minutes.

6. To serve, fork spaghetti squash into pastalike strands and divide among four heated dinner plates.

7. Quickly toss turkey balls with vegetables and tomato sauce, right in pan. Then ladle over spaghetti squash, dividing total amount equally. Sprinkle with chopped basil and, if you like, top each portion with 1 tablespoon freshly grated Parmesan.

RECIPE FROM
*Ellen Featherstone; Richmond, Virginia*

## JO ANNE C. WHITE

*Winnsboro, Texas*

Jo Anne, known locally as "Labladie" because of her willingness to take in home-less Labradors, owns six dogs, including three black Labs. An antique dealer today, she was working away from home every day in interior design back in 1972 when her husband's high cholesterol level prompted her to cut fats from the family diet. This posed a challenge: "Back then there were few low-fat recipes or substitutes and I *had* to be inventive in my cooking!" She had a daughter and six sons to feed, too—from teenagers down to a two-year-old toddler. "One of my best quick fixes," Jo Anne says, "is this satisfying chili made with ground turkey instead of beef."

## *Labladie's Lite Chili*

*Makes 6 Servings*

*Classic chilis brim with fat, calories, and cholesterol. This one, made with lean ground turkey, removes the lion's share of all three and yet its flavor is surprisingly rich.*

1 tablespoon olive oil

1½ cups coarsely chopped yellow onion (about 1 large onion)

1½ cups coarsely chopped green bell pepper (about 1 large pepper)

2 medium-size cloves garlic, minced

1 pound ground turkey (a 50-50 mix of light meat and dark)

1 tablespoon chili powder

1 tablespoon ground cumin

1 teaspoon dried leaf oregano, crumbled

1 teaspoon dried leaf basil, crumbled

1 teaspoon ground coriander

½ teaspoon red pepper flakes

**PER SERVING**

284 calories

....

13 g fat (4 g saturated)

....

71 mg cholesterol

....

466 mg sodium

....

*1 (15-ounce) can low- or reduced-sodium diced tomatoes, with their liquid*

*1 cup chicken broth*

*1 tablespoon tomato paste*

*1 (15-ounce) can pinto beans, rinsed and drained*

*6 tablespoons low-fat sour cream*

1. Heat olive oil in very large heavy saucepan over moderately high heat for 1 minute. Add onion, bell pepper, and garlic and stir-fry until limp—about 5 minutes. Scoop onto plate and reserve.

2. Coat bottom and sides of saucepan with nonstick cooking spray and set over moderately high heat. Add turkey and sauté, stirring constantly and breaking up large clumps, until no longer pink and beginning to brown—5 to 6 minutes. Mix in chili powder, cumin, oregano, basil, coriander, and red pepper flakes.

3. Return reserved cooked onion–bell pepper mixture to saucepan, add tomatoes, chicken broth, and tomato paste, and bring quickly to a boil. Adjust heat so mixture bubbles gently, cover, and simmer 30 minutes.

4. Add pinto beans, cover, and simmer 10 minutes more.

5. Ladle into heated soup plates, top each portion with 1 tablespoon sour cream, and serve.

RECIPE FROM
*Jo Anne C. White; Winnsboro, Texas*

## GAYLA J. McALARY

*Jenks, Oklahoma*

In her career as chef on private yachts, Gayla has had both the budget and opportunity to create "fabulous recipes," and has found that the owners and their "rich and famous" guests are always interested in light, healthful, gourmet cuisine—"They pay me to watch their diets!" she comments. "But working in a galley at sea can be trying," she continues. "Making easy, time-efficient recipes allows me more time out of the galley to see the world—which also gives me insight into the cuisines of different countries and lots of ideas to incorporate into my own cooking."

# *Tortilla Quiche*

*Makes 8 servings*

*A single large tortilla serves as the crust for this quiche strewn with chopped crisp turkey bacon, broccoli, mushrooms, onion, and bell pepper. You can, if you like, substitute frozen egg product for the eggs and egg whites called for below—Gayla McAlary, who sent us this recipe, usually does. One (8-ounce) carton, thawed, the equivalent of four whole eggs, will be sufficient.*

2 slices smoked turkey bacon

1 (10-inch) flour tortilla

1 tablespoon olive oil

$\frac{1}{2}$ cup thinly sliced, stemmed mushrooms
   (about 2 medium-size mushrooms)

$\frac{1}{4}$ cup coarsely chopped yellow onion
   (about 1 very small onion)

$\frac{1}{4}$ cup coarsely chopped green bell pepper
   (about $\frac{1}{4}$ medium-size pepper)

$\frac{1}{2}$ cup coarsely chopped raw broccoli

$\frac{1}{2}$ teaspoon dried leaf basil, crumbled

$\frac{1}{2}$ teaspoon dried leaf oregano, crumbled

**PER SERVING**

118 calories
....
5 g fat (1 g saturated)
....
59 mg cholesterol
....
181 mg sodium
....

*⅛ teaspoon freshly ground black pepper*

*Pinch ground nutmeg*

*¼ cup coarsely shredded low-fat Cheddar cheese*

*2 large eggs plus 2 large egg whites*

*1 cup evaporated skim milk*

*2 tablespoons low-fat sour cream*

1. Preheat oven to 350°F.

2. Lay turkey bacon in ungreased 17 x 11 x 1-inch baking pan, set uncovered in oven, and bake 5 minutes. Turn strips and continue baking until nicely browned—about 5 minutes more. Remove from oven and reserve. Leave oven on.

3. Meanwhile, coat 10-inch pie pan with nonstick cooking spray. Center tortilla on bottom of pie pan, pressing edges about ¼ inch up sides of pan. Set aside.

4. Heat olive oil in large heavy skillet over moderately high heat until ripples appear on skillet bottom—1½ to 2 minutes. Add mushrooms, onion, bell pepper, broccoli, basil, oregano, black pepper, and nutmeg and sauté, stirring now and then, until vegetables are wilted—about 5 minutes.

5. Spread sautéed vegetables over tortilla crust. Coarsely chop reserved bacon and sprinkle evenly over vegetables, then scatter with cheese. Quickly combine eggs, egg whites, skim milk, and sour cream and pour evenly over all.

6. Bake uncovered until filling is set and knife inserted midway between center and edge comes out clean—25 to 30 minutes.

7. Transfer quiche to wire rack and cool 15 to 20 minutes, then cut into eight wedges and serve.

RECIPE FROM

*Gayla J. McAlary; Jenks, Oklahoma*

## MARTHA ALLISON

*Amarillo, Texas*

"Because my husband is a cardiologist," writes Martha, a registered nurse herself, "he is very disciplined about what foods he consumes. We both like Mexican food, especially veggie tacos. When he told me he wanted something more filling with a heartier taste, I experimented with different kinds of low-fat meats. The fat-free sausage was a hit. Last summer I added the mango sauce to give the dish a light, fresh taste and a little zip."

# Smoked Sausage Tacos with Mango-Chipotle Sauce

*Makes 4 servings*

Chipotles, *according to Rick Bayless, Chicago chef, cookbook author, and authority on Mexican cooking, are "smoke-dried cultivars of fresh jalapeños." And* adobo, *a staple of the Mexican kitchen, is a "vinegary, tomatoey, slightly sweet sauce." This recipe calls for canned* chipotles *in* adobo *sauce. Texas viewer Martha Allison's original recipe uses one* chipotle *and one tablespoon* adobo *sauce. "Mucho fiery!" said our New York recipe-tester Karen Pickus, who loves heat but doesn't like to burn. If you have an asbestos palate, go for it and use the amounts Martha suggests. Otherwise, halve or quarter those amounts.*

### SAUCE

*2 ounces low-fat cream cheese (Neufchâtel), softened*

*1* **chipotle** *pepper, seeded and coarsely chopped plus 1 tablespoon* **adobo** *sauce (from a 7-ounce can* **chipotles** *packed in* **adobo** *sauce) (see headnove above)*

*1 (8-ounce) container low-fat apricot-mango yogurt*

*1 cup moderately finely diced mango (for the easiest way to pit, peel, and dice mango, see Tips for Herbed Snapper with Warm Mango Salsa, page 7)*

### TACOS

*1 tablespoon olive oil*

*7 ounces (90 percent fat-free) smoked turkey sausage, sliced ¼ inch thick*

| PER SERVING |
|:---:|
| 308 calories |
| .... |
| 8 g fat (3 g saturated) |
| .... |
| 40 mg cholesterol |
| .... |
| 816 mg sodium |
| .... |

*1 large yellow onion, sliced into thin rings*

*1 large red bell pepper, cored, seeded, and cut lengthwise into strips*
   *¼ inch wide*

*6 ounces medium-size white mushrooms, trimmed and thinly sliced*

*½ cup water*

*1 tablespoon fresh lemon juice*

*1 tablespoon fresh lime juice*

*4 (8-inch) low-fat whole-wheat tortillas*

*¼ cup coarsely chopped fresh cilantro*

1. *For sauce:* Combine cream cheese, *chipotle* pepper, and *adobo* sauce in small non-metallic bowl. Gradually blend in yogurt, then fold in diced mango. Set aside.

2. *For tacos:* Heat olive oil in large heavy skillet over moderately high heat until ripples appear on skillet bottom—1½ to 2 minutes. Add sausage and brown, stirring frequently, for 3 minutes. Lift sausage to paper toweling to drain.

3. Add onion, bell pepper, mushrooms, water, and lemon and lime juices to skillet and bring quickly to a boil, stirring up browned bits on skillet bottom. Adjust heat so mixture bubbles gently, cover, and simmer until vegetables soften—about 5 minutes. With slotted spoon, lift vegetables to bowl and reserve.

4. Boil skillet liquid uncovered over moderately high heat, tilting pan this way and that, until only a glaze remains on skillet bottom—about 5 minutes.

5. Return reserved sausage to skillet, also reserved vegetables and all accumulated juices, and bring just to serving temperature.

6. To assemble tacos, place ½ cup sausage mixture on center of each tortilla, shaping first into a log, then spreading over half the tortilla and leaving narrow margin. Next, spread ¼ cup reserved sauce over sausage mixture on each tortilla and sprinkle with 1 tablespoon chopped cilantro.

7. Fold tortillas over, top with remaining sauce, dividing amount equally, and serve.

RECIPE FROM

*Martha Allison; Amarillo, Texas*

## KEITH SCARDINA

*Baton Rouge, Louisiana*

Owner and president of a refrigeration company, Keith grew up in a part of Louisiana where French influence is strong, so it's not surprising that he has a taste for Cajun cuisine. He was taught to cook by his mother and today likes to try out recipes for his wife Cindy and their four children. "I got the idea for cabbage soup from a Justin Wilson TV show," he recalls. "Since I just managed to catch the basic ingredients, I ad-libbed and came up with this recipe. My family all love it." The biggest challenge? "Finding a good-tasting low-fat sausage."

## Cabbage Soup with Turkey Sausage

*Makes 6 servings*

*Low-fat turkey sausage can deepen and enrich the flavor of soups without boosting the fat or calorie counts. This particular soup, chock-a-block with vegetables, makes a hearty meal.*

TIP: *The chef's way to chunk a half cabbage is to core it, lay it facedown on a cutting board, then to make four cuts each way—like a grid—spacing the cuts one inch apart.*

1 tablespoon olive oil

6 ounces low-fat turkey sausage

2 cups thinly sliced mushrooms (10 to 12 medium-size mushrooms)

1½ cups coarsely chopped yellow onion (about 1 large onion)

1 cup finely diced celery (about 2 medium-size ribs)

3 medium-size garlic cloves, minced

½ small cabbage (about 1 pound), cored and cut into 1-inch chunks (see headnote above)

1 teaspoon dried leaf thyme, crumbled

2 (15-ounce) cans low- or reduced-sodium tomatoes, with their liquid

2 (14.25-ounce) cans nonfat, low-sodium chicken broth

**PER SERVING**

186 calories
....
8 g fat (3 g saturated)
....
26 mg cholesterol
....
338 mg sodium
....

*2 tablespoons chopped fresh basil, or 2 teaspoons dried leaf basil, crumbled*

*2 tablespoons minced fresh Italian (flat-leaf) parsley*

*¼ teaspoon freshly ground black pepper*

1. Heat oil in very heavy soup kettle 2 minutes over low heat. Add sausage and sauté, turning often, until golden brown and cooked through—about 15 minutes. Lift sausage to paper toweling to drain.

2. Add mushrooms, onion, celery, and garlic to kettle, raise heat to moderately high, and sauté, stirring occasionally, until limp and golden—about 10 minutes.

3. Add cabbage and thyme to pot, and cook and stir until cabbage wilts—about 5 minutes.

4. Add tomatoes and chicken broth and bring quickly to a boil. Adjust heat so mixture bubbles gently, cover, and simmer 10 minutes.

5. Slice sausage very thin and add to soup along with basil, parsley, and pepper. Cover and simmer 5 minutes more.

6. Ladle into heated soup plates and serve.

RECIPE FROM

*Keith Scardina; Baton Rouge, Louisiana*

# MEAT

Ginger-Poached Filet of Beef with Vegetables and Horseradish Sauce 108

Fajitas Richard 111

Gazpacho Casserole 114

Veal Stew in the Style of Ossobuco 116

Broiled Marinated Lamb with Mediterranean Vegetables 119

Some Kind of Wonderful Venison 122

Roast Pork Tenderloin with Garlic and Apples 124

Spicy Pork Lo Murro 126

Romero Green Chili and Beans 128

Spicy Asian Pork Rolls 130

Pasta e Fagioli (Pasta and Bean Soup) 132

*New York, New York*

She began her television career by cooking off-camera for Julia Child, Marcella Hazan, Jacques Pépin, and nearly every other "foodie" who appeared on *Good Morning America*. Then one day Sara stepped in front of the camera herself, and guess what? A star was born. Today *GMA*'s food editor as well as hostess of an hour-long, weekday live cooking show on the Food Network and executive chef at *Gourmet* magazine, Sara graduated second in her class at the Culinary Institute of America in Hyde Park, New York. She grew up on New York City's historic Gramercy Park, the middle child of three, and earned her bachelor's degree at the University of Michigan. All of this before the CIA. Shortly afterward, she became the chef at a Boston restaurant and, on her days off, worked on the PBS television series *Julia Child & More Company*. At Julia's insistence, Sara apprenticed in France at Henri IV, a two-star Michelin restaurant in Chartres (the chef had visited Julia's TV set one day and Julia urged him to take Sara on). Returning to the United States, she continued to work in restaurants, first in Boston, then in New York, ending with a stint as *chef tournant* at the three-star La Tulipe in Greenwich Village. Sara and Julia remain great good friends today; in fact, Julia has appeared many times on Sara's Food Network show, *Cooking Live*. As for her personal life, Sara married her college sweetheart, Bill Adler, now a media consultant, and is the mother of two children—Ruthie, just entering her teens, and Sammy, nine.

# *Ginger-Poached Filet of Beef with Vegetables and Horseradish Sauce*

*Makes 6 servings*

*Few recipes are more elegant than this one, adapted, Sara Moulton says, from one created by Alessandro Stratta, formerly chef at the Phoenician in Scottsdale, Arizona, and now owner of his own Las Vegas restaurant. A few years ago, Alessandro entered a similar poached beef in a healthy menu contest sponsored by* Gourmet *and it was a finalist. For poaching her beef, Sara would use a chicken stock she'd made herself (from her freezer bank of chicken wings). And if you should happen to have homemade chicken stock, by all means use it. Otherwise, use canned chicken broth—the reduced-sodium, nonfat variety.*

NOTE: *Also see Sara's low-cal, low-fat Roast Pork Tenderloin with Garlic and Apples (page 124), and her slimming Angel Food Cake with Mocha Sauce (page 228).*

BEEF AND VEGETABLES

4 (14.25-ounce) cans reduced-sodium, nonfat
   chicken broth

½ pound fresh ginger, peeled and cut into slices
   ¼ inch thick

2 medium-size leeks (white part only), trimmed, washed
   well, and cut into ¼-inch dice

1½ pounds center-cut beef tenderloin, well trimmed
   of fat

6 medium-size carrots, trimmed, peeled, and cut on the diagonal into slices
   ¼ inch thick

3 cups small broccoli florets

SAUCE

½ cup low-fat sour cream

1 tablespoon drained prepared horseradish

1 teaspoon prepared English mustard

⅛ teaspoon freshly ground black pepper

PER SERVING

314 calories

····

12 g fat (5 g saturated)

····

80 mg cholesterol

····

204 mg sodium

····

1. *For beef and vegetables:* Bring chicken broth, ginger, and leeks to boiling in medium-size Dutch oven over moderately high heat. Adjust heat so broth bubbles gently, cover, and simmer 30 minutes.

2. Add beef, cover, and simmer very gently until medium-rare—20 to 25 minutes. A meat thermometer inserted in center of beef should register 130°F. Lift beef to heated large, deep platter, cover loosely with foil, and keep warm.

3. Strain poaching broth, discarding ginger and leeks, then return broth to Dutch oven. When beef has rested 15 minutes, bring broth quickly to boiling over high

heat. Add carrots and broccoli and boil uncovered just until crisp-tender—3 to 4 minutes.

4. *Meanwhile, prepare sauce:* Place all ingredients in small bowl and whisk to combine.

5. To serve, cut beef, slightly on an angle, into slices $\frac{1}{4}$ inch thick and arrange down center of heated platter. Wreathe carrots and broccoli around edge and spoon a little poaching broth over all. Pass sauce and remaining poaching broth in separate sauceboats.

RECIPE FROM

*Sara Moulton; New York, New York*

# RICHARD NORTHCUTT SACCARO

*Watchung, New Jersey*

This young attorney comes from a family who likes to cook and eat together. While attending law school in Florida, he worked on a fishing boat to help out with expenses, and "out of necessity," as he put it, made up all kinds of recipes using fresh fish. Back home in New Jersey, after passing the Florida Bar exam, he indulged his liking for Tex-Mex cuisine by experimenting with and finally perfecting a low-fat, colorful version of one of his all-time favorites—beef fajitas.

# Fajitas Richard

*Makes 6 servings*

*Fajitas are fussy, it's true. But they're an entire meal twirled up in a tortilla.*

NOTE: *You can substitute chicken cutlets for beef but you should pound them thin between sheets of plastic wrap (to keep them from tearing), then cut crosswise into strips $1/2$ to $3/4$ inch wide.*

**BEEF AND BEEF MARINADE**
$3/4$ *pound top round, trimmed of fat and sliced across the grain as thin as possible*

1 *teaspoon olive oil*

1 *tablespoon fresh lime juice*

$1/2$ *teaspoon dried leaf oregano, crumbled*

$1/2$ *teaspoon ground cumin*

$1/8$ *teaspoon salt*

$1/8$ *teaspoon freshly ground black pepper*

**VEGETABLES AND VEGETABLE MARINADE**
1 *large red onion, peeled and thinly sliced*

1 *medium-size green bell pepper, cored, seeded, and cut lengthwise into strips $1/2$ inch wide*

**PER SERVING**

399 calories

18 fat (5 g saturated)

39 mg cholesterol

518 mg sodium

*1 medium-size red bell pepper, cored, seeded, and cut lengthwise into strips*
   *$^{1}/_{2}$ inch wide*

*1 medium-size orange bell pepper, cored, seeded, and cut lengthwise into*
   *strips $^{1}/_{2}$ inch wide*

*1 medium-size yellow bell pepper, cored, seeded, and cut lengthwise into strips*
   *$^{1}/_{2}$ inch wide*

*2 teaspoons olive oil*

*$^{1}/_{2}$ teaspoon dried leaf oregano, crumbled*

*$^{1}/_{2}$ teaspoon ground cumin*

*$^{1}/_{8}$ teaspoon salt*

*$^{1}/_{8}$ teaspoon freshly ground black pepper*

FAJITAS
*6 (8-inch) flour tortillas*

*6 tablespoons nonfat tomato salsa*

*1 large ($^{1}/_{2}$-pound) firm-ripe avocado, peeled, pitted, quartered, each quarter*
   *thinly sliced, then tossed with 1 tablespoon fresh lime juice*

*6 tablespoons coarsely chopped fresh cilantro (about 1 small bunch)*

*6 tablespoons low-fat sour cream (optional)*

1. Preheat broiler. Coat broiler pan with nonstick cooking spray and set aside.

2. *For beef and beef marinade:* Place beef in large bowl, add all remaining ingredients, and toss well. Let marinate at room temperature 15 minutes.

3. *For vegetables and vegetable marinade:* Place all ingredients in large bowl, toss well, and marinate at room temperature 15 minutes.

4. Spread beef on broiler pan so pieces do not touch and broil 3 inches from heat until beef is only slightly pink inside—4 to 5 minutes. Transfer beef to heated plate, cover loosely to keep warm.

5. Spread vegetables evenly on broiler pan and broil 3 inches from heat, tossing gently every few minutes, until soft and touched with brown—about 15 minutes.

6. *For fajitas:* Spread tortillas on large baking sheet, set in broiler 3 inches from heat, and broil just until soft and lightly browned—about 1 minute.

7. To assemble, place tortillas browned sides down on counter and spoon 1 tablespoon salsa down the middle of each. Next, divide broiled beef and vegetables, avocado, cilantro, and, if desired, sour cream equally among the 6 tortillas.

8. Roll tortillas up (not too tight or filling will ooze out), halve, and serve.

RECIPE FROM

*Richard Northcutt Saccaro; Watchung, New Jersey*

A retired school librarian, Doris was born and brought up in St. Louis, where she still lives with her husband, a retired physics teacher. This mother of four and grandmother of eight holds strong beliefs about cooking: "Eating is more than fuel for the body," she says. "It should be soul-satisfying as well. I enjoy the creative aspect of cooking and the idea of giving sustenance to people—*real* sustenance with healthy food in a happy, serene environment." Experimenting with this gazpacho recipe was fun. She knew all the ingredients went well together but it took some "fiddling" to get it right.

# Gazpacho Casserole

*Makes 4 servings*

*This is the sort of recipe that was hugely popular in the fifties and sixties, perfect for a party buffet when doubled or tripled. In those days, no one much minded if the fat and calorie counts were over the moon. But in this Age of Fitness, the leaner a recipe, the better. This slimmed-down casserole is one you can enjoy with a clear conscience.*

*1 tablespoon olive oil*

*½ pound very lean ground beef round*

*1 cup coarsely chopped green bell pepper
(about 1 medium-size pepper)*

*1 cup coarsely chopped yellow onion
(about 1 medium-large onion)*

*3 medium-size cloves garlic, minced*

*1 (14.5-ounce) can low-sodium stewed tomatoes, with their liquid*

*½ cup low-sodium vegetable juice*

*¾ cup uncooked long-grain white rice*

*1 cup water*

*1 tablespoon Worcestershire sauce*

| PER SERVING |
| :---: |
| 350 calories |
| .... |
| 10 g fat (3 g saturated) |
| .... |
| 24 mg cholesterol |
| .... |
| 303 mg sodium |
| .... |

*½ teaspoon dried leaf thyme, crumbled*

*½ cup coarsely shredded low-fat Cheddar cheese*

1. Preheat oven to 450°F.

2. Heat olive oil in small Dutch oven over moderately high heat until ripples appear on pan bottom—1½ to 2 minutes. Add ground beef and cook, stirring and breaking up large chunks, for 3 minutes. Add bell pepper, onion, and garlic and cook and stir 3 minutes.

3. Add all remaining ingredients except cheese and bring to a boil. Adjust heat so mixture bubbles gently, cover, and simmer 15 minutes, stirring occasionally.

4. Turn into ungreased 1-quart casserole and sprinkle cheese evenly on top.

5. Bake uncovered until cheese melts and casserole is bubbly—about 10 minutes. Serve at once.

RECIPE FROM

*Doris Fridley; St. Louis, Missouri*

# ARTHUR SICKLE

*Cheshire, Connecticut*

"I learned to cook from my mother and grandmother, two great cooks who ran their own catering business," writes this manager of a data processing department. "As an adult, I have learned from my extensive collection of cookbooks and the great food shows on television. I tried ossobuco at our favorite local Italian restaurant; it reminded me of a chicken fricassee dish my family has made for years. I set out to reproduce it, but with a healthier approach, and served the resulting dish to my parents—got raves on my first attempt. I think the seasonings and sautéed aromatic vegetables make the flavor stand out."

# Veal Stew in the Style of Ossobuco

*Makes 8 servings*

*Veal shanks, the traditional cut for this Italian classic, are loaded with fat, the marrow inside the bones contributing the lion's share. This recipe uses lean veal shoulder, trimmed of fat, and fat-free chicken broth.*

**STEW**

1 cup finely diced yellow onion (about 1 medium-size onion)

1/3 cup finely diced celery (about 1 small rib)

3/4 cup finely diced carrot (about 1 medium-large carrot)

2 small cloves garlic, finely minced

1 teaspoon dried leaf thyme, crumbled

3 tablespoons flour

1/2 teaspoon salt

1/4 teaspoon freshly ground black pepper

2 pounds boneless lean veal shoulder, trimmed of fat and cut into 1/2-inch chunks

2 tablespoons olive oil

1/2 cup dry white wine such as an Italian Soave or pinot grigio

**PER SERVING**

344 calories

....

7 g fat (2 g saturated)

....

98 mg cholesterol

....

583 mg sodium

....

1 (28-ounce) can peeled whole Italian plum tomatoes, drained and coarsely
    chopped

2 (14.25-ounce) cans reduced-sodium, nonfat chicken broth

$\frac{1}{4}$ cup coarsely chopped fresh Italian (flat-leaf) parsley

MASHED POTATOES
4 large Yukon Gold potatoes (about 2$\frac{1}{2}$ pounds), peeled and cut into 1$\frac{1}{2}$-inch
    chunks

$\frac{1}{3}$ cup finely chopped chives (about 1 medium-size bunch)

$\frac{1}{2}$ cup skim milk

2 tablespoons low-fat sour cream

$\frac{1}{4}$ teaspoon salt

$\frac{1}{8}$ teaspoon freshly ground black pepper

1. Preheat oven to 350°F.

2. *For stew:* Spray medium-size Dutch oven well with nonstick cooking spray and set over moderately high heat for 1 minute. Add onion, celery, and carrot and sauté, stirring often, until vegetables begin to soften—about 3 minutes. Add garlic and thyme and cook and stir 1 minute more. Scoop vegetables into large bowl and reserve.

3. Place flour, salt, and pepper in large plastic bag and shake to combine. Pat veal chunks dry, then dredge a few chunks at a time by shaking in seasoned flour in bag. Shake excess flour from each batch.

4. Add 1 tablespoon olive oil to Dutch oven and heat over moderately high heat until ripples appear on pan bottom—1$\frac{1}{2}$ to 2 minutes. Add half the dredged veal and brown well on all sides—5 to 7 minutes. Lift browned veal to bowl with vegetables. Add remaining tablespoon oil to Dutch oven, brown remaining veal the same way, and add to bowl.

5. Pour wine into Dutch oven and boil, scraping up browned bits, until reduced by half—about 2 minutes. Add tomatoes and chicken broth, return reserved veal and vegetables to pot, and bring to a boil. Mix in 2 tablespoons parsley.

6. Cover, transfer to oven, and braise, stirring every half hour, until veal is fork-tender—about 1$\frac{1}{2}$ hours.

7. Spoon three-fourths of vegetables in Dutch oven and $\frac{1}{2}$ cup kettle liquid into food processor or electric blender and cool 15 minutes.

8. *For mashed potatoes:* Boil potatoes in just enough water to cover in covered medium-size saucepan until tender—about 12 minutes. Drain well, add remaining ingredients, and mash until fluffy. Keep warm.

9. To finish stew, pulse cooled vegetable mixture in food processor until smooth —about $1\frac{1}{2}$ minutes. Stir back into Dutch oven and bring stew quickly to serving temperature.

10. To serve, divide mashed potatoes among eight heated dinner plates, centering on plates, and with the back of a spoon, make well in each potato mound. Ladle stew over all and sprinkle lightly with remaining 2 tablespoons parsley.

RECIPE FROM

*Arthur Sickle; Cheshire, Connecticut*

# KAREN PICKUS

*New York, New York*

As *Good Morning America*'s Chef/Food Stylist, Karen played a major role in the Cut the Calories Cook-Off. And for this book, she tested each and every recipe. A graduate of the Culinary Institute of America in Hyde Park, New York, Karen was also a Pastry Fellow at the International Pastry Arts Center and an assistant to renowned Swiss chef Albert Kumin. Karen's food styling can be seen today in major cookbooks and magazines, also on the Food Network as well as on *Good Morning America (GMA)*. She has cooked off-camera for nearly every on-camera food celebrity you can name, including Julia Child. Karen's restaurant experience includes positions at New York City's Rainbow Room atop Rockefeller Center, at Maurice Restaurant at New York's Hotel Parker Meridien, and at the three-star La Tulipe in Greenwich Village. On *GMA*, the rhythm of live television dictates that no matter what the circumstances, come air time, everything must be ready, visually exciting, and mouth watering. Karen is a whiz at knowing just what needs to be done and pulling it all together. She can dig into her professional grab bag of experience and make every recipe come alive. No small talent.

## Broiled Marinated Lamb with Mediterranean Vegetables

*Makes 4 servings*

*Karen marinates her lamb before grilling to intensify the flavors and tenderize the meat. If you can marinate the meat overnight, so much the better. If not, give it the full 4 hours.*

NOTE: *Also see Karen's Chocolate Pudding with Pralined Pecans (page 200).*

## LAMB AND MARINADE

1 (2-inch-thick) boneless piece leg of lamb
  (about 1 pound), trimmed of all fat

1 teaspoon olive oil

3 large cloves garlic, minced

2 tablespoons fresh lemon juice

2 teaspoons finely chopped fresh rosemary, or ¾ teaspoon
  dried leaf rosemary, crumbled

1 teaspoon finely grated lemon zest

½ teaspoon dried leaf oregano, crumbled

⅛ teaspoon salt

⅛ teaspoon freshly ground black pepper

## VEGETABLES

1 tablespoon olive oil

1 cup coarsely diced yellow onion (about 1 medium-large onion)

3 large cloves garlic, minced

½ teaspoon dried leaf thyme, crumbled

¼ teaspoon salt

⅛ teaspoon freshly ground black pepper

1 cup (½-inch dice) eggplant (about ½ small eggplant)

1 cup moderately coarsely diced red bell pepper (about 1 medium-size
  pepper)

¼ cup water

1 cup moderately coarsely diced yellow squash (about 1 medium-size squash)

1 cup moderately coarsely diced zucchini (about 1 medium-size zucchini)

1 cup moderately coarsely diced, cored, seeded tomato (about 1 medium-size
  tomato)

¼ cup coarsely chopped fresh basil

¼ cup coarsely chopped fresh mint

PER SERVING

261 calories

....

12 g fat (3 g saturated)

....

64 mg cholesterol

....

277 mg sodium

....

1. *For lamb and marinade:* Place lamb and all remaining ingredients in 1-gallon self-sealing plastic bag, set in refrigerator, and marinate 4 hours or, better yet, overnight, turning bag over several times as lamb marinates.

2. Preheat broiler and line broiler pan with aluminum foil. Remove lamb from plastic bag, place on broiler pan, then broil 3 inches from heat for 7 minutes. Turn lamb and broil flip side until instant-read thermometer inserted into thickest part of lamb registers 130°F—about 7 minutes more (this will give you juicily pink lamb). Remove lamb from broiler, cover loosely with foil, and let stand 20 minutes.

3. *Meanwhile, prepare vegetables:* Heat oil in very large heavy skillet over moderately high heat until ripples appear on skillet bottom—1 1/2 to 2 minutes. Add onion and cook, stirring frequently, until it begins to turn golden—about 3 minutes.

4. Stir in garlic, thyme, salt, black pepper, eggplant, and red pepper and cook and stir 1 minute. Add water, cover, and cook 3 minutes. Add yellow squash, zucchini, and tomato, cover, and cook 3 minutes more. Remove skillet from heat.

5. Scoop 1/2 cup vegetable mixture into electric blender or food processor and cool 5 minutes. Keep remaining vegetables in skillet covered. Pulse 1/2 cup vegetable mixture until smooth—about 30 seconds—then stir back into skillet. Mix in basil and mint, cover, and let stand 10 minutes while you slice lamb.

6. Carve lamb on the diagonal into slices 1/8 inch thick, then arrange on heated platter and, if you like, drizzle with broiler pan drippings.

7. To serve, spoon vegetables onto platter alongside lamb.

RECIPE FROM
*Karen Pickus; New York, New York*

# DEBBIE PAIXÃO

*Burlington, New Jersey*

Debbie gives credit to her dad, mom, aunts, and grandmothers for teaching her to cook when she was a child growing up in New Jersey. "My father was a hunter so we always had plenty of venison, and as I grew I always tried different ways to cook it," she recalls. "I'm always looking to make things taste better and more interesting, and when it comes to cooking, whatever is in my kitchen at the time is fair game. I like this dish because it's easy to make and because my husband loves it—he took one bite and said, 'This is some kind of wonderful!'"

# Some Kind of Wonderful Venison

*Makes 4 servings*

*Unless you have a hunter in the family or a fancy butcher who can get you farm-raised venison, you'll have to substitute beef for venison. The best cut to use is eye round because it approximates the leanness of venison. Only the cooking time changes, which we note in the recipe below.*

NOTE: *Cremini are the brown mushrooms that look for all the world like the ubiquitous white variety. They are, in fact, youthful portobellos and will grow to giant size.*

**MARINADE AND VENISON**

1/2 cup dry red wine

3 tablespoons olive oil

2 tablespoons reduced-sodium soy sauce

1 tablespoon water

4 large cloves garlic, thinly sliced

1 small shallot, thinly sliced

1-inch cube fresh ginger, peeled and thinly sliced

1/2 teaspoon sugar

1/8 teaspoon freshly ground black pepper

3/4 pound tenderloin of venison or 4 (3-ounce, 1/2-inch thick) slices beef eye round

| PER SERVING |
| --- |
| 282 calories |
| .... |
| 13 g fat (2 g saturated) |
| .... |
| 72 mg cholesterol |
| .... |
| 428 mg sodium |
| .... |

SAUCE

*Venison marinade*

*1 pound medium-size cremini mushrooms, trimmed and thinly sliced*

*¼ cup moderately finely chopped sun-dried tomatoes (not oil-pack)*

*4 large cloves garlic, finely chopped*

*⅛ teaspoon freshly ground black pepper*

*1 tablespoon minced fresh parsley*

1. *For marinade and venison:* Place wine, 2 tablespoons olive oil, and all remaining ingredients except venison in sturdy jumbo-size plastic zipper bag; seal and shake to combine.

2. Add venison, press out air, reseal, and turn this way and that to coat. Set in refrigerator for at least 4 hours, turning bag every now and then.

3. When ready to proceed, preheat oven to 400°F. Also reserve marinade to use in sauce.

4. Heat remaining 1 tablespoon olive oil in large heavy ovenproof skillet over moderately high heat until ripples appear on skillet bottom—1½ to 2 minutes. Add venison and brown about 6 minutes on each side. Note: If using beef, brown 3 to 4 minutes on a side.

5. Transfer venison (but not beef) to oven and roast uncovered until meat thermometer inserted in center of venison registers 150°F. Note: If using beef, transfer browned beef to heated platter, cover loosely with foil, and keep warm.

6. When venison tests done, lift to heated platter, cover loosely with foil, and keep warm while you prepare sauce.

7. *For sauce:* Strain marinade into skillet, set over moderately high heat, and cook, scraping up browned bits, 1 to 2 minutes. Add mushrooms, tomatoes, garlic, and pepper, reduce heat to low, and simmer uncovered until flavors marry—about 10 minutes.

8. To serve, cut venison on the bias into 8 slices and overlap on platter (if using beef, simply overlap slices). Ladle sauce over all, sprinkle with parsley, and serve.

RECIPE FROM

*Debbie Paixão; Burlington, New Jersey*

# Roast Pork Tenderloin with Garlic and Apples

*Makes 4 servings*

Sara Moulton, whose recipe this is, likes her roast pork juicy with tinges of pink—perfectly safe—which means an internal temperature of around 150°F when it's taken from the oven. If you let the roast stand 20 minutes before serving, the internal temperature will rise to 160°F—this is called carry-over cooking. If you like well-done pork, continue roasting until an instant-read thermometer, inserted in the thickest part of the roast, registers 160°F. After standing twenty minutes, the internal temperature will be 170°F and the meat, alas, less succulent.

NOTE: *Also see Sara's Ginger-Poached Filet of Beef with Vegetables and Horseradish Sauce (page 108) and her Angel Food Cake with Mocha Sauce (page 228).*

**2 medium-size yellow onions, peeled and quartered**

**3 large cloves garlic, peeled**

**1 tablespoon olive oil**

**¾ pound well-trimmed pork tenderloin**

**¼ cup dry white wine**

**¾ cup apple juice**

**1½ cups reduced-sodium, nonfat chicken broth**

**2 medium-size Granny Smith apples, peeled, cored, and each cut into 12 wedges**

| PER SERVING |
| --- |
| 238 calories |
| .... |
| 7 g fat (2 g saturated) |
| .... |
| 57 mg cholesterol |
| .... |
| 87 mg sodium |
| .... |

1. Preheat oven to 400°F.

2. Bundle onions and garlic in heavy-duty aluminum foil, set in oven, and roast until softened—about 40 minutes.

3. Meanwhile, heat olive oil in large heavy ovenproof skillet (not iron) over moderately high heat until ripples appear on skillet bottom—1½ to 2 minutes. Add pork and brown well on all sides; this will take 5 to 7 minutes. Transfer pork to platter and set aside.

4. Skim excess fat from skillet, add wine, and boil 1 minute, scraping up browned bits on skillet bottom. Wine should be reduced by half.

5. Add apple juice and chicken broth and bring quickly to a boil. Add apples, adjust heat so mixture bubbles gently, and simmer uncovered until apples are just tender—3 to 5 minutes. With slotted spoon, lift apples to bowl and reserve.

6. Return pork and accumulated juices to skillet, then unwrap roasted onions and garlic and add to skillet. Transfer to oven and roast uncovered until quick-read thermometer, inserted in thickest part of pork, registers 150°F.—15 to 20 minutes. Transfer pork to platter, cover loosely with foil, and let stand 20 minutes.

7. Cool skillet mixture 5 to 10 minutes, then purée in electric blender or food processor until completely smooth—about 1 minute. Return to skillet, add reserved apples, and bring to a quick boil.

8. To serve, slice pork thin, slightly on the bias, arrange down center of heated platter, then spoon apples and sauce on top.

RECIPE FROM
*Sara Moulton; New York, New York*

*Sewell, New Jersey*

Growing up in South Philadelphia, Joann taught herself to cook. "I learned early on that diets do not work for me," she says. "I cook low fat, eat what I want in moderation, and exercise as often as I can." Because her days are busy (married to a computer programmer, she's a part-time computer technician, a part-time substitute teacher, and full-time mother of a teenage son), she prefers recipes that are versatile and quick like this pork dish. She explains: "My mother-in-law made a similar dish using pieces of pork with lots of fat. When I tried the recipe, I used boneless pork loin to eliminate fat, added chicken broth and fresh herbs to make a richer sauce. My family and friends love it!"

# Spicy Pork Lo Murro

*Makes 4 servings*

*Now that much of the fat has been bred out of hogs, pork is almost as much the dieter's friend as chicken or turkey breast. Cooked this way, it remains succulent and moist. Joann Murro, who created this recipe, often serves it over linguine. Do so, if you like, but be aware that 1 cup of cooked linguine will add 197 calories, 1 gram fat (0 gram saturated), 0 milligram cholesterol, and 1 milligram sodium to each serving.*

NOTE: *This recipe calls for well-trimmed pork chops, which means that all visible fat has been removed. Many good butchers will do this for you before they weigh the chops.*

4 (3-ounce) well-trimmed boneless pork loin chops

1/8 teaspoon salt

1/8 teaspoon freshly ground black pepper

1 tablespoon olive oil

1 cup coarsely chopped red bell pepper
(about 1 medium-size pepper)

1/2 cup thinly sliced carrot (about 1 medium-size carrot)

1 cup coarsely chopped yellow onion (about 1 medium-large onion)

**PER SERVING**

234 calories

····

9 g fat (2 g saturated)

····

48 mg cholesterol

····

314 mg sodium

····

*¼ pound mushrooms, stemmed and thinly sliced*

*2 medium-size cloves garlic, minced*

*3 bottles small, pickled hot red cherry peppers, stemmed, seeded, and thinly sliced*

*¼ cup pickled cherry pepper liquid (from bottled peppers above)*

*½ cup dry red wine*

*1 cup reduced-sodium, nonfat chicken broth blended with 2 teaspoons cornstarch*

*2 tablespoons chopped fresh Italian (flat-leaf) parsley*

*1 teaspoon chopped fresh thyme (preferably lemon thyme), or ½ teaspoon dried leaf thyme, crumbled*

1. Season pork chops with salt and black pepper.

2. Heat olive oil in large heavy skillet over moderately high heat until ripples appear on skillet bottom—1½ to 2 minutes. Add pork chops and brown 3 minutes on each side; lift chops to large plate and set aside.

3. Add bell pepper and carrot to skillet and sauté, stirring often and scraping up browned bits on skillet bottom—about 3 minutes. Add onion and sauté, stirring now and then—about 3 minutes more. Add mushrooms and garlic and sauté, stirring occasionally, for 3 minutes longer.

4. Add cherry peppers and cherry pepper liquid, stir well, then add wine. Bring to a boil, then boil uncovered 1 minute. Reduce heat to moderate, add broth-cornstarch mixture, and cook, stirring constantly, until mixture bubbles and thickens—about 2 minutes.

5. Return pork chops to skillet along with any accumulated juices, sprinkle with parsley and thyme, cover, and simmer over low heat until pork is cooked through—about 8 minutes.

6. Serve at once, accompanied, if you like, by hot drained linguine (see headnote).

RECIPE FROM

*Joann Murro; Sewell, New Jersey*

Born and brought up in Youngstown, Ohio, this forty-seven-year-young grandmother of two has just started her own electronic medical billing company. Patty loves to cook, especially anything spicy and Italian, and as a result has had to watch her weight. The forty pounds she lost have stayed off thanks to getting more exercise and lightening up favorite recipes like this Romero Green Chili and Beans. The original, Patty says, "was handed down through my husband's family and used lard and fatty meats. I substituted lower-fat ingredients and my husband swears my version's better." To round out the recipe, Patty uses tomatoes and onions fresh from her vegetable garden.

# Romero Green Chili and Beans

### Makes 8 servings

*Chili, to most people, is the fiery red stuff made with ground beef and kidney beans. Green chili, a New Mexico classic, couldn't be more different. It's made with pork, not beef, and the beans (pintos) are not stirred into the pot. They're cooked separately, then bedded in the bottom of each bowl before the chili is ladled on top.*

TIP: *When handling chili peppers, take care not to rub your face, especially your eyes. And wash your hands well with warm soapy water after the chili detail is done. Some pros wear surgical rubber gloves to protect their hands from the fire of the chilies.*

NOTE: *If you use salt-free, low-fat organic pinto beans, you'll trim the per serving fat content by 1 gram, reduce the calorie count to 359, and reduce the sodium to 678 millgrams.*

CHILI

2 (12-ounce) pork tenderloins, trimmed of fat and sliced $\frac{1}{2}$ inch thick

4 tablespoons flour mixed with $\frac{1}{8}$ teaspoon freshly ground black pepper (seasoned flour)

3 tablespoons olive oil

$2\frac{1}{2}$ cups coarsely chopped yellow onions (about 2 medium-large onions)

8 large cloves garlic, minced

*1 (28-ounce) can diced tomatoes, with their liquid*

*4 (4-ounce) cans whole green chilies, drained well, seeded,
and cut into 1-inch pieces*

*2 cups water*

BEANS

*1 tablespoon olive oil*

*1¼ cups coarsely chopped yellow onions (about 2 medium-large onions)*

*3 (15-ounce) cans pinto beans, rinsed and drained*

*¼ teaspoon salt*

1. *For chili:* Place tenderloin slices in large shallow bowl, add seasoned flour, and toss well to coat.

2. Heat 1 tablespoon olive oil in very large heavy saucepan over moderately high heat until ripples appear on pan bottom—about 1½ minutes. Add onions and garlic and cook, stirring occasionally, until soft—about 5 minutes. Scoop into large bowl and reserve.

3. Add another 1 tablespoon oil to pan, again heat until ripples appear on pan bottom, then add half the pork and cook, stirring often, until no longer pink—10 to 12 minutes. Add to bowl with onions and garlic. Add final 1 tablespoon oil to pan, heat as before, add remaining pork, cook as you did first batch, and add to bowl.

4. Scrape up but do not remove browned bits on pan bottom. Return pork, onions, and garlic to pan, add tomatoes, chilies, and water and bring quickly to a boil. Adjust heat so mixture bubbles gently, cover, and simmer until pork is tender—1 to 1¼ hours.

5. *When chili is about half done, prepare beans:* Heat olive oil in large heavy skillet over moderately high heat until ripples appear on pan bottom—about 1½ minutes. Add onions and cook, stirring occasionally, until soft—about 5 minutes.

6. Add beans and salt, reduce heat to low, and cook, tossing mixture now and then, until beans are steaming hot—about 15 minutes.

7. To serve, divide beans among eight large soup plates and smother with chili.

RECIPE FROM

*Patty Carson/Romero; New Castle, Colorado*

# MARY BETH KEREKES

*Boston, New York*

Mary Beth has two young children, a husband in the U.S. Coast Guard, and a heritage of good European cooking—her mother and her grandmother Zavislan taught her to cook and she also often uses the recipes of her other grandmother, now deceased. She created this recipe for pork rolls when, after the birth of her son, she realized she needed to lose the extra pounds she had gained during pregnancy. "I used low-starch Asian vegetables to provide color, texture, and taste," she explains, "then flash-blanched the veggies and cooked the rice in broth for flavor with no added fat."

# Spicy Asian Pork Rolls

*Makes 4 servings*

*You can make this recipe with chicken or turkey cutlets instead of pork—the method doesn't change and the flavor is nearly the same.*

NOTE 1: *The calorie count may seem high—not really, because this is a one-dish dinner. No accompaniments necessary.*

NOTE 2: *For this recipe you'll need a skillet with a heatproof handle or a flameproof casserole that can move from stovetop to oven.*

1 (14.25-ounce) can reduced-sodium, nonfat chicken broth

1 tablespoon peeled and finely minced fresh ginger

6 medium-size cloves garlic, finely minced

1 tablespoon low-sodium soy sauce

1½ teaspoons hoisin sauce

¼ teaspoon dry mustard

4 medium-size scallions, trimmed and cut into
   1½-inch lengths (include some green tops)

1 cup matchstick strips of carrots (about 2 medium-size carrots)

| Per Serving |
| :---: |
| .... |
| 424 calories |
| .... |
| 9 g fat (3 g saturated) |
| .... |
| 64 mg cholesterol |
| .... |
| 310 mg sodium |
| .... |

*1½ cups matchstick strips of celery (about 3 medium-size celery ribs)*

*1 cup thinly sliced, trimmed mushrooms (about 6 medium-size mushrooms)*

*1½ cups matchstick strips fresh or frozen snow peas*

*1 (8-ounce) can bamboo shoots, drained and cut into matchstick strips*

*1 cup uncooked converted rice*

*4 (3-ounce) slices boneless pork loin, trimmed of fat and pounded to a thickness of ⅛ inch*

1. Preheat oven to 350°F.

2. Bring broth, ginger, garlic, soy and hoisin sauces, and mustard to a boil in a large heavy skillet with a heatproof handle or flameproof 2-quart casserole over moderately high heat. Add scallions, carrots, celery, mushrooms, snow peas, and bamboo shoots and cook, stirring now and then, until vegetables are crisp-tender—about 2 minutes. Using slotted spoon, transfer vegetables to bowl and reserve.

3. Add rice to broth, reduce heat to moderately low, cover, and simmer 5 minutes.

4. Meanwhile, spoon 1½ tablespoons reserved vegetables on flattened pork slices, placing 1 inch from narrow end. Roll vegetables up in pork.

5. Stir remaining reserved vegetables into rice mixture. Place pork rolls, seam sides down, on top of rice.

6. Cover, transfer to oven, and bake until pork is well done—about 30 minutes. Serve at once.

RECIPE FROM

*Mary Beth Kerekes; Boston, New York*

# VINCENT V. FORMISANO

*Weymouth, Massachusetts*

This forty-nine-year-old carpenter and contractor, a Massachusetts native of Italian extraction, came by his cooking ability naturally. When he was a child, the Formisano family had four restaurants in Rhode Island and Massachusetts, and little Vincent spent hours in those restaurant kitchens absorbing the atmosphere. Today he has little false modesty about his considerable skill with a skillet. "I love to cook," he says. "I never have any problem cooking. This recipe has been in the family for years and every time I make it, it will come out perfect! On a cold night, with Italian bread, it's a full meal."

# Pasta e Fagioli
# (Pasta and Bean Soup)

*Makes 8 servings*

*Although beloved all over Italy, this thick, husky soup is a particular specialty of the Veneto, the northeast corner of the country where Venice is located.*

NOTE: *If you can find* pancetta *(lean, rolled Italian bacon), by all means use it in this recipe. You will need 3 tablespoons finely chopped* pancetta.

2 slices smoky lean bacon, finely chopped
   (see Note above)

1 cup coarsely chopped yellow onion
   (about 1 medium-large onion)

1 cup diced carrots (about 2 medium-size carrots)

1 cup finely chopped celery (about 2 medium ribs)

4 small cloves garlic, minced

2 tablespoons minced fresh Italian (flat-leaf) parsley

4 medium-size whole bay leaves

1 (6-ounce) can tomato paste

**PER SERVING**

456 calories
....
8 g fat (2 g saturated)
....
9 mg cholesterol
....
720 mg sodium
....

*2 cups water*

*1 (15-ounce) can cannellini (white kidney beans), rinsed and drained*

*1 (15-ounce) can red kidney beans, rinsed and drained*

*1 (19-ounce) can chickpeas, rinsed and drained*

*¼ teaspoon freshly ground black pepper*

*1 (16-ounce) package elbow macaroni, cooked and drained according to package directions*

*½ cup freshly grated Parmesan cheese*

1. Cook bacon in large heavy saucepan or soup pot over moderate heat, stirring often, until golden brown and almost all drippings cook out—4 to 5 minutes.

2. Add onion, carrots, celery, and garlic, reduce heat to low, and cook, stirring now and then, until vegetables wilt—about 5 minutes.

3. Stir in parsley, bay leaves, tomato paste, water, cannellini, red kidney beans, chickpeas, and pepper, adjust heat so mixture bubbles gently, cover, and simmer until vegetables are tender—about 20 minutes.

4. Ladle half of soup into large bowl, taking care to leave bay leaves in pan, cool 15 minutes, then purée in batches in food processor. Return puréed soup to pan, cover, and simmer 10 minutes.

5. Mix hot drained macaroni into soup, cover, and simmer 5 minutes. Discard bay leaves and stir in cheese.

6. Ladle into heated soup plates and serve.

RECIPE FROM

*Vincent V. Formisano; Weymouth, Massachusetts*

# MEATLESS ENTREÉS

Sweet Potato Burritos 136

Black Bean–Mango Burritos 138

Roasted Corn and Black Bean Enchiladas with Red Chili Sauce 140

Quick Tortilla Pizzas 142

Mushroom Veggie Burgers 144

Portobello Que Bella 146

Dieter's Delight Casserole 148

Eggplant Pirogues 150

Penne Pasta with Eggplant, Tomatoes, and Olives 152

Sunny Penne Pasta with Seven Vegetables 154

Pasta di Cucina with Broccoli Rabe 156

Fast and Easy Fusilli with Red Pepper Cream Sauce 158

Basil-Lemon Bowties 160

Risotto-Stuffed Artichokes 162

Southwest Couscous Salad 164

Mexican Black Bean and Quinoa Lasagne with Ancho Chili Sauce 166

Teresina's Minestrone 169

Hearty Broccoli-Potato Soup 171

Caramelized Onion Soup with Lemon-Corn Chutney 173

# DANA RICHARDSON

*Durham, North Carolina*

A social worker specializing in crisis work, Dana has an eclectic approach to cuisine (Japanese, Thai, Italian) and attributes her interest in cooking to the influence of "a dear friend, Kate, who is eighty-seven." Now that she's the mother of a three-year-old and working part time, Dana finds she can't afford to dine out as often as she did formerly. "I've learned that I can enjoy many restaurant dishes for less money if I cook them myself. I collect all the ingredients I feel may be in a recipe I've tasted in a restaurant, and keep at it until I've accomplished something that tastes great. My family loves these burritos!"

## *Sweet Potato Burritos*

*Makes 4 servings*

*Yummy! Kids adore these!*

TIP: *To save time, microwave the sweet potatoes. Here's how: Pierce potatoes deeply in several places with a kitchen fork, place one inch apart on floor of microwave oven, and microwave on High until soft—about 8 minutes. Let stand in turned-off oven 3 minutes, cool until easy to handle, and proceed with recipe.*

*2 small sweet potatoes (about 10 ounces each), scrubbed but not peeled*

*½ teaspoon ground cumin*

*⅛ teaspoon ground nutmeg (or better yet, freshly grated)*

*⅛ teaspoon ground cinnamon*

*8 (6-inch) corn tortillas*

*½ cup rinsed and drained canned black beans*

*½ cup moderately finely diced red onion (about ½ medium-size onion)*

*½ cup moderately finely shredded Monterey jack cheese*

*2 cups thinly sliced romaine (about ½ medium-size head)*

*¼ cup low-fat sour cream*

**PER SERVING**

315 calories

....

7 g fat (4 g saturated)

....

18 mg cholesterol

....

281 mg sodium

....

1. Preheat oven to 350°F. Spread piece of foil on middle oven rack, arrange potatoes on foil, not touching, and bake until a fork pierces them easily—about 1 hour. Remove foil and potatoes from oven but leave oven on.

2. Cool potatoes until easy to handle, then scoop flesh into large bowl. Add cumin, nutmeg, and cinnamon, mash well, and set aside.

3. Coat large baking sheet with nonstick cooking spray and set aside. Also spray both sides of each tortilla. Spread 1 tablespoon mashed sweet potato on one side of each tortilla, leaving $1/2$-inch margins all around. Scatter 1 tablespoon black beans on each tortilla, then 1 tablespoon each diced onion and shredded cheese.

4. Fold tortillas in half, pressing edges lightly to seal and turning tortillas over, if necessary, to keep them from unfolding.

5. Arrange tortillas, not touching, on prepared baking sheet and bake uncovered until tortillas are crisp and filling hot—about 15 minutes.

6. Top each tortilla with $1/4$ cup romaine and $1/2$ tablespoon sour cream and serve at once.

RECIPE FROM

*Dana Richardson; Durham, North Carolina*

*Mammoth Lakes, California*

Stephanie, who moved west from Dubuque, Iowa, describes herself as an artist and photo stylist. She and her husband, a computer systems administrator for a ski area, have "three furry children: Emma (dog), Pete (cat), and Zoie (cat)." A preference for vegetarian fare led to Stephanie's inspired combination of black beans and fruit salsa. "It seemed a great, simple match," she says. "I love colorful presentations, hence the additions of cilantro, mangos, and tomato and yogurt on top. This is one of the prettiest dishes I serve and our new 'old standby' when company is coming. It's always a hit!"

# Black Bean–Mango Burritos

*Makes 6 servings*

*This vegetarian main dish is as filling as it is colorful. It's quick and easy, too, especially if you let everyone build his or her own burrito. Only the mango requires a bit of attention.*

6 (7-inch) low-fat flour tortillas

1 tablespoon olive oil

1 cup coarsely chopped yellow onion
   (about 1 medium-large onion)

2 medium-size cloves garlic, minced

1 teaspoon ground cumin

1/8 teaspoon freshly ground black pepper

Pinch red pepper flakes

Dash hot red pepper sauce

1 (15-ounce) can black beans, rinsed and drained

1 1/2 cups diced mango (about 1 large mango; for the easy way to pit, peel, and
   dice mango, see headnote for Herbed Snapper with Warm Mango Salsa,
   page 7)

1 tablespoon light brown sugar

1 tablespoon fresh lemon juice

| PER SERVING |
| --- |
| 225 calories |
| .... |
| 5 g fat (1 g saturated) |
| .... |
| 3 mg cholesterol |
| .... |
| 445 mg sodium |
| .... |

*¹⁄₂ cup coarsely shredded low-fat Cheddar cheese*

*¹⁄₂ cup low-fat plain yogurt*

*1 cup diced, cored, unpeeled tomato (about 1 medium-size tomato)*

*¹⁄₂ cup coarsely chopped fresh cilantro*

1. Preheat oven to 350°F. Wrap stack of tortillas in aluminum foil, set in oven, and warm 5 to 7 minutes.

2. Meanwhile, heat olive oil in large heavy skillet over moderately high heat until ripples appear on skillet bottom—1¹⁄₂ to 2 minutes. Add onion and sauté, stirring often, until limp—about 3 minutes. Add garlic, cumin, black pepper, red pepper flakes, red pepper sauce, and black beans. Cook and stir just until heated through—about 2 minutes. Set off heat but keep warm.

3. Heat mango, brown sugar, and lemon juice in small nonreactive skillet over moderately high heat just until mango softens and juices appear—about 1 minute.

4. To assemble burritos, place ¹⁄₃ cup black bean mixture down center of each tortilla, then sprinkle with cheese, dividing total amount evenly. Roll tortillas up and place seam sides down on six heated dinner plates.

5. Dividing all amounts equally, top tortillas with yogurt, then mango mixture, then diced tomatoes and chopped cilantro. Serve at once.

RECIPE FROM

*Stephanie Donovan; Mammoth Lakes, California*

## PAGE K. BOOTH
### *Richmond, Virginia*

"About two years ago, I became a vegetarian," writes this young vice-president of a real estate title insurance company. "I was constantly challenged with finding tasty low-fat meals that provided the vitamins and proteins I needed while satisfying my husband's hearty appetite. We both work forty-plus hours a week and love Mexican foods that are fast and easy to prepare. This dish is very colorful, tastes great, and has become one of our favorites. I've been cooking since the age of five and learned from my maternal grandmother that if all good things go into a new creation, it has to come out good—unless you burn it."

# Roasted Corn and Black Bean Enchiladas with Red Chili Sauce

### *Makes 4 to 6 servings*

*These enchiladas contain no meat so unless you're a vegetarian who eats no animal products at all, these are the enchiladas for you. They contain low-fat sour cream and Cheddar, but everything else is "vegetable." Still, these enchiladas don't lack for flavor. In fact, they're plenty spicy.*

SAUCE
1 (10-ounce) can diced tomatoes with green chilies, drained

1 (10-ounce) can enchilada sauce (preferably low-sodium)

$1/4$ cup coarsely chopped fresh cilantro

1 teaspoon ground cumin

ENCHILADAS
1 tablespoon olive oil

1 cup coarsely chopped red onion (about 1 medium-size onion)

2 small cloves garlic, finely minced

1 cup frozen whole-kernel corn, separated but not thawed

EACH OF 4 SERVINGS

427 calories

13 fat (7 g saturated)

35 mg cholesterol

1,359 mg sodium

EACH OF 6 SERVINGS

284 calories

9 g fat (4 g saturated)

23 mg cholesterol

912 mg sodium

1 teaspoon ground cumin

$\frac{1}{2}$ teaspoon red pepper flakes

$\frac{1}{4}$ teaspoon freshly ground black pepper

1 (15-ounce) can black beans, rinsed and drained

1 (4.5-ounce) can chopped green chilies, rinsed and drained

$\frac{1}{2}$ cup moderately finely shredded low-fat Cheddar cheese

$\frac{1}{3}$ cup low-fat sour cream

$\frac{1}{4}$ cup coarsely chopped fresh cilantro

10 (7-inch) low-fat flour tortillas

1. Preheat oven to 350°F. Coat 13 x 9 x 2-inch baking dish with nonstick cooking spray and set aside.

2. *For sauce:* Pulse all ingredients in food processor 30 seconds, transfer to small saucepan, and set aside.

3. *For enchiladas:* Heat olive oil in large heavy skillet over moderately high heat until ripples appear on skillet bottom—$1\frac{1}{2}$ to 2 minutes. Add onion and garlic and sauté, stirring now and then, until beginning to brown—about 4 minutes.

4. Mix in corn, cumin, red pepper flakes, and black pepper and continue cooking uncovered, stirring occasionally, until corn begins to caramelize—about 4 minutes.

5. Remove from heat and stir in black beans, chilies, $\frac{1}{4}$ cup shredded Cheddar, sour cream, and cilantro.

6. Spoon $\frac{1}{4}$ cup black bean mixture onto center of each tortilla, shaping into log, and roll up tight.

7. Arrange enchiladas, seam sides down, in prepared baking dish, then spread with 1 cup reserved sauce in saucepan and sprinkle with remaining $\frac{1}{4}$ cup shredded Cheddar. Reserve remaining sauce.

8. Bake uncovered until bubbling—about 20 minutes. When enchiladas are almost done, set pan of reserved sauce over moderate heat, and bring quickly to serving temperature.

9. Serve enchiladas as soon as they come from the oven, transfer sauce to sauceboat, and pass separately.

RECIPE FROM
*Page K. Booth; Richmond, Virginia*

## KAREN BORCH

*Albuquerque, New Mexico*

Born in Minnesota and today a working artist in New Mexico, Karen once won a set of enamel cookware in a Norwegian recipe contest. This self-taught cook enjoys baking breads and pastries and invented her tortilla-pizza combination because, as she says, "It satisfied all my criteria: it's fast, easy, nutritious—has fiber, veggies, protein, carbs, and vitamins—and best of all, it has great taste. My family loves it, especially teens and hungry grown men."

# Quick Tortilla Pizzas

*Makes 4 servings*

*Perfect for a party! Here's how: Just triple or quadruple the recipe, bake in batches, and keep the hot pizzas coming. Served with a big green salad, these pizzas are also ideal for a light lunch.*

4 (8-inch) flour tortillas

¾ cup low-fat, low-sodium marinara sauce

1 cup very thinly sliced mushrooms
    (about 4 medium-large mushrooms)

¼ cup diced green bell pepper (about ¼ large pepper)

2 tablespoons coarsely chopped pitted black olives

1 large clove garlic, finely minced

¼ cup moderately finely chopped yellow onion (about ½ small onion)

¾ cup coarsely shredded low-fat mozzarella cheese

⅛ teaspoon salt

2 tablespoons coarsely chopped fresh basil (no substitute)

1 tablespoon minced fresh parsley

PER SERVING

244 calories
....
8 g fat (3 g saturated)
....
11 mg cholesterol
....
574 mg sodium
....

1. Preheat oven to 450°F. Line two large baking sheets with aluminum foil and set aside.

2. Heat tortillas, one by one, in a hot 10-inch iron skillet over moderate heat until crisp, 30 to 60 seconds on each side.

3. Arrange 2 tortillas on each baking sheet, then spread 3 tablespoons marinara sauce on each, leaving $1/2$-inch margins all round. Next, divide mushrooms, green pepper, olives, garlic, and onion among the 4 tortillas, sprinkling each evenly on top. Finally, scatter 3 tablespoons shredded cheese evenly on each tortilla.

4. Bake tortillas uncovered until cheese melts—about 10 minutes.

5. Sprinkle tortillas with salt, basil, and parsley, again dividing amounts evenly, and serve.

RECIPE FROM

*Karen Borch, Albuquerque, New Mexico*

# BEVERLY GOLDBERG

## *Stratford, Connecticut*

"Friends and family cannot believe these burgers are meatless," reports this busy fifty-six-year-old advertising representative who also teaches English as a Second Language to adults. She's found that not only do the burgers look and taste "real," they are also great substitutes for meatballs in soup and pasta dishes, and can easily be converted into meatless meat loaf. Her inspiration for the recipe came from her love of portobello mushrooms and her determination to create a burger with little or no fat—staying slim is important to Beverly, who enjoys performing onstage in community theater musicals.

# *Mushroom Veggie Burgers*

### *Makes 4 servings*

*Portobello mushrooms are so meaty, so juicy you'd swear these burgers were made with beef.*

NOTE: *The nutrient counts given here are for burgers* without *the optional ketchup and mustard. If you use them, you'll up the per serving calorie count by 28 and the per serving sodium count by 377 milligrams. The fat and cholesterol content don't change.*

| PER SERVING |
| :---: |
| 277 calories |
| .... |
| 7 g fat (1 g saturated) |
| .... |
| 0 mg cholesterol |
| .... |
| 753 mg sodium |
| .... |

1 tablespoon olive oil

1½ cups moderately finely chopped yellow onion
    (about 1 large onion)

3 small cloves garlic, finely minced

4 cups coarsely chopped portobello mushrooms
    (about 2 large mushrooms)

¼ teaspoon salt

⅛ teaspoon freshly ground black pepper

1 cup Italian-flavor bread crumbs

2 large egg whites

4 whole-wheat hamburger buns, split

4 tablespoons ketchup (optional)

*4 tablespoons prepared mustard (optional)*

*4 lettuce leaves*

*4 thin slices red onion*

*4 thin slices tomato*

1. Heat olive oil in 12-inch nonstick skillet over moderately high heat 1 minute. Add chopped onion and garlic and sauté, stirring occasionally, until limp and golden—about 3 minutes.

2. Add mushrooms and sauté, stirring now and then, until mushrooms soften and brown—about 4 minutes. Transfer mushroom mixture to large bowl and cool 10 minutes.

3. Using wooden spoon, mix salt, pepper, and bread crumbs into mushroom mixture. Add egg whites and mix thoroughly.

4. Scoop up mixture by $1/2$-cup measure, then using hands, shape into four patties about $3/4$ inch thick.

5. Wipe out skillet, spray with nonstick vegetable spray, and set over moderate heat. Add patties and brown 3 minutes on each side.

6. If you like, spread one cut side of each bun with ketchup and the second cut side with mustard. Lay lettuce leaf on bottom half of each bun, top with burger, red onion slice, and tomato slice, then top half of bun. Serve at once.

RECIPE FROM

*Beverly Goldberg; Stratford, Connecticut*

Laurie, an Army brat, grew up in Fort Huachuca, Arizona, and now lives in Portland with her husband, a TV news reporter, and their two teenage children. "I worry about those Fatal three *F*s—being female, fat, and forty," she jokes, "so creating meatless entrées is a challenge I enjoy. Mushrooms are a natural meat substitute that provide bulk without fat and absorb the flavors around them while providing their own wonderful earthy flavor. Marrying mushrooms with garlic and fresh herbs and adding spinach for nutritional value seemed like a good direction," she says. Laurie next blended in creamy low-fat goat cheese and surrounded it all with a fillo crust. The result? "A great entrée" family and friends adore!

## *Portobello Que Bella*

*Makes 12 servings*

*Four kinds of mushrooms go into this party-perfect casserole together with spinach and two types of goat cheese. They're layered into a baking dish with leaves of fillo, not brushed with melted butter or olive oil but sprayed instead with olive oil–flavored nonstick cooking spray. That's a terrific way to cut fat and calories without sacrificing an ounce of flavor.*

Olive oil–flavored nonstick cooking spray

¾ pound portobello mushrooms, trimmed and very coarsely chopped

½ pound fresh oyster mushrooms, trimmed and very coarsely chopped

½ pound fresh shiitake mushrooms, trimmed and fairly thickly sliced

½ pound medium-size fresh white mushrooms, trimmed and fairly thickly sliced

2 large cloves garlic, finely minced

1 medium-size leek, trimmed, washed well and thinly sliced

1 cup tender young spinach leaves, washed and spun dry

| PER SERVING |
| :---: |
| 107 calories |
| .... |
| 4 g fat (2 g saturated) |
| .... |
| 11 mg cholesterol) |
| .... |
| 251 mg sodium |
| .... |

*½ cup coarsely chopped fresh parsley*

*4 ounces feta cheese, crumbled*

*2 ounces chèvre, crumbled*

*¼ teaspoon salt*

*¼ teaspoon freshly ground black pepper*

*8 (18 x 14-inch) frozen fillo leaves in single stack (from a 1-pound package)*

1. Preheat oven to 350°F. Coat 13 x 9 x 2-inch baking dish well with olive oil–flavored nonstick cooking spray.

2. Pulse all four kinds of mushrooms, garlic, leek, spinach, and parsley in food processor 3 minutes. Scrape down work bowl sides, add feta, chèvre, salt, and pepper and pulse until smooth—about 1 minute more.

3. Cut 8 fillo leaves in half so you have 16 (9 x 14-inch) half leaves, place on counter, and cover with damp tea towel. Working quickly, coat each of 8 half leaves with olive oil–flavored nonstick cooking spray and place in bottom of prepared baking dish.

4. Smooth mushroom filling over fillo. Spray remaining 8 half leaves the same way, lay on top of filling, then spray top leaf.

5. Bake uncovered until fillo is flaky and golden brown—about 40 minutes. Cool 10 minutes, cut into 12 pieces, and serve.

RECIPE FROM

*Laurie Christopher; Portland, Oregon*

Born and brought up on a Virginia farm, Mary Lu now lives in Blue Ridge Mountain country where she teaches art at a middle school and her husband works as a professional craftsman. "This recipe evolved as a vegetarian alternative to cabbage rolls," she told us, "which I find time-consuming because stuffing the leaves is difficult. Most people don't realize that mine is a meatless dish and would never consider it diet food because it tastes very rich and is very filling. In fact, a lot of people tell me they can't believe they are eating cabbage and loving it!"

# Dieter's Delight Casserole

*Makes 6 to 8 servings*

*Few casseroles are more accommodating than this one and few are more healthful. The only faintly tedious chore is slicing the cabbage, but if you processor-slice it, the job's done in no time.*

NOTE: *Most bottled pasta sauces are loaded with salt, so aim for one that is low in sodium or at least has had the sodium reduced.*

½ *small (1-pound) cabbage, halved, cored, and each half sliced ⅛ inch thick*

½ *cup water*

¼ *pound mushrooms, stemmed and thinly sliced*

1 *(1-pound) container low-fat cottage cheese or part-skim ricotta cheese*

1 *cup coarsely shredded low-fat Swiss cheese*

1 *cup brown rice, cooked according to package directions*

¼ *cup chopped fresh Italian (flat-leaf) parsley*

⅛ *teaspoon freshly ground black pepper*

1 *(26-ounce) bottle tomato-based pasta sauce (preferably low- or reduced-sodium)*

EACH OF 6 SERVINGS

355 calories

...............

9 g fat (2 g saturated)

...............

18 mg cholesterol

...............

355 mg sodium

...............

EACH OF 8 SERVINGS

266 calories

...............

7 g fat (2 g saturated)

...............

13 mg cholesterol

...............

266 mg sodium

...............

1. Preheat oven to 375°F.

2. Boil cabbage in water in small covered saucepan over moderate heat until tender—7 to 8 minutes. Drain (there will be very little liquid) and set aside.

3. Meanwhile, combine mushrooms, cottage cheese, $\frac{1}{2}$ cup Swiss cheese, cooked rice, parsley, and pepper in large bowl.

4. Spread cabbage evenly over bottom of ungreased 13 x 9 x 2-inch baking dish. Smooth mushroom mixture on top, then cover with pasta sauce.

5. Bake uncovered until bubbly—about 30 minutes. Sprinkle remaining $\frac{1}{2}$ cup Swiss cheese evenly on top and bake uncovered just until cheese melts—about 5 minutes more.

6. Remove casserole from oven and let stand 10 minutes, then cut into squares and serve.

RECIPE FROM

*Mary Lu Lewis; Harrisonburg, Virginia*

# VICKI NIOLET

*Bay St. Louis, Mississippi*

"When you live in a little town one hour away from New Orleans," writes this artist and gallery shop owner, "you are saturated with the food and attitudes of the 'Big Easy.' Refugee cooks import those wonderful seafood dishes that make New Orleans so popular, and the laidback atmosphere excuses the few extra pounds you might gain. This recipe is one that I've come up with to satisfy my cravings without the lethal aspects of that old enemy, butter." The wife of a pilot and the mother of three grown children, Vicki suffers from diabetes and has to watch her weight constantly. She recently shed twenty pounds and has kept almost all of them off thanks to a diet devoid of sugar and low in carbohydrates. "It seems to be a very healthy diet."

## *Eggplant Pirogues*

*Makes 4 servings*

*A pirogue is the South Louisiana fishing boat beloved by Cajuns. Hollowed-out eggplants make perfect edible pirogues that can be filled with a variety of stuffings. The one here is mostly vegetable. However, you could substitute 1½ to 2 cups coarsely diced cooked shrimp, crab, or crawfish for the broccoli florets.*

2 small (12-ounce) eggplants

1 tablespoon olive oil

1 cup coarsely chopped yellow onion
    (about 1 medium-large onion)

3 large cloves garlic, minced

½ pound mushrooms, stemmed and thinly sliced

¼ cup coarsely chopped fresh basil

½ teaspoon dried leaf oregano, crumbled

⅛ teaspoon salt

⅛ teaspoon freshly ground black pepper

¼ cup water

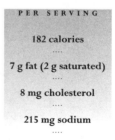

**PER SERVING**

182 calories
....
7 g fat (2 g saturated)
....
8 mg cholesterol
....
215 mg sodium
....

150

*2 cups small broccoli florets, blanched 1 minute and drained*

*½ cup finely shredded low-fat mozzarella cheese*

TOPPING
*¼ cup plain dry bread crumbs blended with 1 tablespoon freshly grated*
  *Romano cheese*

1. Preheat oven to 400°F.

2. Halve each eggplant lengthwise, then using melon baller, scoop out centers leaving shells ¼ inch thick. Cut scooped-out eggplant into ½-inch dice and set aside.

3. Heat oil in very large heavy skillet over moderately high heat until ripples appear on skillet bottom—1½ to 2 minutes. Add onion and cook, stirring frequently, until it begins to brown—3 to 5 minutes.

4. Add garlic, mushrooms, basil, oregano, salt, and pepper and cook and stir until mushrooms wilt—about 2 minutes. Stir in diced eggplant and water, cover, and cook until eggplant is tender—about 5 minutes.

5. Transfer all to medium-size bowl, then mix in broccoli and mozzarella cheese. Dividing amount evenly, fill eggplant shells (pirogues) with mixture.

6. Place stuffed pirogues in ungreased 13 x 9 x 2-inch baking dish and pour ½ cup water around them.

7. Cover with aluminum foil and bake until pirogues are soft—about 25 minutes.

8. Remove pirogues from oven and preheat broiler. Sprinkle topping evenly over pirogue stuffing.

9. Set pirogues in broiler 3 inches from heat and broil until topping browns lightly—3 to 4 minutes. Serve at once.

RECIPE FROM

*Vicki Niolet; Bay St. Louis, Mississippi*

# ERIN COOPEY
*Mountain View, California*

"I developed this recipe in the summer of '97," said Erin, a corporate concierge in the Silicon Valley. "I was teaching English in Japan and although I am an adventurous eater, Japanese food is unusual and at times I was desperate for something familiar and Western. I had only two gas burners and a toaster oven to cook with and most imported foods were outrageously priced at the local stores, so pasta—relatively inexpensive—was an obvious choice. I combined seasonal produce from Japan with a few imports (black olives and Parmesan) and finished the dish with a little balsamic vinegar. The Scottish woman down the hall joined me for dinner and loved it!"

# Penne Pasta with Eggplant, Tomatoes, and Olives

*Makes 4 servings*

*This is the recipe to prepare when locally grown young eggplants and sun-ripened tomatoes are in season. If you pick an eggplant that's young enough, it will be firm, devoid of bitterness, and its seeds will barely be visible. Older specimens must be salted, weighted, and rid of their bitter juices. Save yourself the time and trouble by using a baby (or adolescent) eggplant.*

TIP: *Bring a large kettle of lightly salted water to a boil at the outset, then toss in the penne at the same time that you add the tomatoes to the skillet (step 2). This way, the pasta will be done at about the same time as the eggplant, tomatoes, and olives. If the pasta needs a few minutes more, no problem. The eggplant mixture will wait for the pasta, but not vice versa.*

>    *1 tablespoon olive oil*
>    *½ cup diced red onion (about 1 small onion)*
>    *2 small cloves garlic, minced*

*1 cup diced yellow bell pepper (about 1 medium-size pepper)*

*1 small (12-ounce) eggplant, trimmed and cut into ½-inch dice but not peeled*

*¼ teaspoon salt*

*¼ teaspoon red pepper flakes*

*¼ teaspoon freshly ground black pepper*

*1½ cups coarsely chopped, seeded, unpeeled red-ripe tomatoes (about 3 medium-size tomatoes)*

*1 (8-ounce) package penne, cooked and drained according to package directions*

*¼ cup coarsely chopped fresh Italian (flat-leaf) parsley*

*⅓ cup thinly sliced, pitted ripe olives*

*¼ cup balsamic vinegar*

*¼ cup freshly grated Parmesan cheese*

| PER SERVING |
| --- |
| 350 calories |
| .... |
| 9 g fat (2 g saturated) |
| .... |
| 5 mg cholesterol |
| .... |
| 380 mg sodium |
| .... |

1. Heat olive oil in large heavy skillet over moderately high heat until ripples appear on skillet bottom—1½ to 2 minutes. Add onion and garlic and sauté, stirring now and then, until soft—about 2 minutes.

2. Mix in bell pepper, eggplant, salt, red pepper flakes, and black pepper, reduce heat to low, cover, and cook, stirring occasionally, 10 minutes. Add tomatoes, cover, and cook until eggplant softens—about 5 minutes more.

3. Dump hot drained penne into large heated bowl, add skillet mixture along with parsley, olives, vinegar, and cheese. Toss well and serve at once.

RECIPE FROM

*Erin Coopey; Mountain View, California*

*Coventry, Rhode Island*

Nanette, a native of Massachusetts, taught herself to cook with the help of cookbooks and cooking shows on television, and today enjoys preparing new recipes for husband Mike and teenage daughters Marie and Kate. Explaining how she happened to dream up this dish, she told us, "I just got bored with the same old things for dinner! It was in the summer when I thought of it, and I had all the ingredients already in the house. I tested the recipe on my in-laws, who are very health-conscious—and also Italian—and they liked it a lot."

# *Sunny Penne Pasta with Seven Vegetables*

*Makes 6 servings*

*You might call this a warm pasta salad. The heat of the pasta intensifies the flavor of the vegetables, which have been fairly finely cut but not cooked. You can substitute a pound of diced, cooked chicken breast for the cannellini, but the recipe won't be vegetarian.*

*Sequence is critical here: Have all ingredients ready to receive the hot pasta as soon as it's drained.*

1 (15-ounce) can cannellini, Great Northern, navy,
  or pea beans, rinsed and drained

1 cup thinly sliced mushrooms
  (5 to 6 medium-size mushrooms)

1 cup moderately finely diced red bell pepper
  (about 1 medium-size pepper)

1 cup moderately finely diced yellow bell pepper
  (about 1 medium-size pepper)

1 cup thinly sliced carrots (about 2 small carrots)

½ cup moderately finely chopped red onion (about ½ small onion)

2 small cloves garlic, minced

**PER SERVING**

152 calories

....

5 g fat (2 g saturated)

....

7 mg cholesterol

....

464 mg sodium

....

$\frac{1}{4}$ cup moderately finely chopped sun-dried tomato (not oil-packed)

2 tablespoons well-drained small capers

1 tablespoon olive oil

2 tablespoons minced fresh Italian (flat-leaf) parsley

2 teaspoons chopped fresh basil

$\frac{1}{4}$ teaspoon freshly ground black pepper

$\frac{1}{2}$ cup freshly grated Parmesan cheese

1 (16-ounce) package penne, cooked and drained according to package directions

1. Place all ingredients except penne in large shallow heatproof bowl and toss well.

2. Dump hot drained penne into bowl, toss again, and serve.

RECIPE FROM

*Nanette Gallagher; Coventry, Rhode Island*

## JOANNE M. FRIEDMAN

*Newton, New Jersey*

Joanne teaches special ed in high school, raises horses in her spare time, and credits her mom, her dad, and "the cooking channel" with awakening her interest in experimenting with new recipes. She created this pasta dish on a night when she wanted to cook something light that would allow her to use olive oil, a recent recommendation of her physician. "I had all the necessary ingredients on hand and putting them together was so easy that I was pleasantly surprised at my family's positive reaction," she recalls. "I still cook it at least twice a week." (See also Joanne's recipe for Italian Ricotta Pie, page 194.)

# *Pasta di Cucina with Broccoli Rabe*

*Makes 4 servings*

*Fettuccine is the perfect backdrop for broccoli rabe's bitter bite. To save time, we use canned artichoke hearts and we don't soak the dried tomatoes. We also cook the broccoli rabe right along with the pasta—saves dishwashing, too.*

NOTE: *Use fresh basil only for this recipe; every good supermarket stocks it year round.*

1 (8-ounce) package fettuccine

2 tablespoons olive oil

5 medium-size cloves garlic, finely minced

1 (13.75-ounce) can water-packed artichoke hearts, drained well

1/4 cup coarsely chopped sun-dried tomatoes (not oil-pack) (see headnote above)

2 tablespoons well-drained small capers

1/4 teaspoon freshly ground black pepper

1/2 pound broccoli rabe, trimmed and cut into 1-inch chunks

1 tablespoon coarsely chopped fresh basil

| PER SERVING |
| --- |
| 330 calories |
| 15 g fat (3 g saturated) |
| 5 mg cholesterol |
| 776 mg sodium |

*1 tablespoon coarsely chopped fresh Italian (flat-leaf) parsley*

*¼ cup freshly grated Parmesan cheese*

1. Begin cooking fettuccine according to package directions in very large pot of boiling water.

2. Meanwhile, heat 1 tablespoon olive oil in large heavy skillet over moderate heat for 1 minute. Add garlic, artichoke hearts, sun-dried tomatoes, capers, and pepper, and sauté lightly just until heated through—about 1 minute. Remove from heat, cover loosely, and keep warm.

3. Two minutes before fettuccine is al dente, add broccoli rabe and boil 2 minutes longer.

4. Drain fettuccine and broccoli rabe well, dump into large heatproof bowl, add remaining 1 tablespoon olive oil and artichoke mixture, and toss well.

5. Divide fettuccine mixture among four large heated plates, sprinkle each portion with chopped basil and parsley and grated cheese, dividing all amounts evenly. Serve at once.

RECIPE FROM

*Joanne M. Friedman; Newton, New Jersey*

## CARMEL M. SALANDRA

*Williamsville, New York*

Carmel, a homemaker and mother of three adult daughters, has never been on a diet—instead, she says, she "eats healthy" and tries to prepare foods that are low in calories for herself and her husband, an aerospace engineer. Her fusilli recipe is typical of the kind of cooking she prefers. "I love creamy foods," Carmel confesses, "but I know how caloric they are." Using a lower-fat cream cheese, she discovered, gave her "a tasty sauce on the first try."

# Fast and Easy Fusilli with Red Pepper Cream Sauce

*Makes 4 servings*

*With this recipe, choreography is everything. Put the fusilli on to cook when you begin the sauce so that the two are done at the same time.*

NOTE: *A chiffonade is something that's been finely slivered, in this case fresh basil leaves. The easiest way to do the job? Stack 5 or 6 large leaves, roll them up tight, then slice straight across the roll, spacing the cuts ⅛ inch apart or less.*

2 (12-ounce) jars roasted red peppers, drained well

3 tablespoons low-fat cream cheese (Neufchâtel)

½ cup evaporated skim milk

½ teaspoon salt

¼ teaspoon freshly ground black pepper

⅛ teaspoon ground hot red pepper (cayenne)

1 tablespoon olive oil

½ cup chopped yellow onion (about 1 small onion)

3 medium-size cloves garlic, finely minced

1 teaspoon grated lemon zest

1 tablespoon fresh lemon juice

| PER SERVING |
| :---: |
| 370 calories |
| .... |
| 9 g fat (3 g saturated) |
| .... |
| 14 mg cholesterol |
| .... |
| 854 mg sodium |
| .... |

*1 (8-ounce) package fusilli, cooked and drained according to package directions*

*¼ cup freshly grated Parmesan cheese*

*¼ cup firmly packed fresh basil chiffonade (see Note)*

1. Purée red peppers in food processor 2 minutes. Add cream cheese, evaporated milk, salt, black pepper, and cayenne, and process until completely smooth—about 2 minutes longer.

2. Heat olive oil in large heavy skillet over moderate heat 1 minute. Add onion and garlic, and cook, stirring occasionally, until translucent but not brown—about 5 minutes.

3. Add red pepper purée and bring to a simmer. Add lemon zest and juice and cook, stirring, just until steaming—about 2 minutes.

4. To serve, ladle 1 cup fusilli on each of four large heated serving plates. Top each portion with ½ cup pepper cream sauce and 1 tablespoon each grated cheese and basil chiffonade.

RECIPE FROM

*Carmel M. Salandra; Williamsville, New York*

Marsha's profession—event marketing with a major business publication— keeps her on the go and makes her appreciate recipes that are quick and trustworthy. Born in New Jersey, where her grandmother taught her the basics of good cooking, she now lives in Manhattan and credits the Food Network with raising her culinary skills to new levels. Following the Weight Watcher's program, she lost ten pounds and has kept most of it off by creating recipes for flavorful low-fat entrées such as this pasta, which "came together satisfactorily after only a few tries."

# Basil-Lemon Bowties

*Makes 4 servings*

*Marsha Green, who created this lovely light entrée, says it was inspired by her love of fresh basil, also by a lemon fettuccine that's no longer available. For this recipe, however, she favors farfalle (pasta bowties). You should cook the pasta while you prepare the sauce so both are ready at the same time. If you plan things properly, Marsha says, the recipe takes just "thirty minutes front door to dinner table."*

NOTE: *This recipe calls for half a cup of basil chiffonade. For directions on how to prepare it, see the headnote for Fast and Easy Fusilli with Red Pepper Cream Sauce, page 158.*

1 tablespoon olive oil

1 medium-size clove garlic, minced

1 (8-ounce) package medium-size bowties, cooked
   and drained according to package directions

1 tablespoon fresh lemon juice

1 teaspoon finely grated lemon zest

$^{1}/_{2}$ cup firmly packed fresh basil chiffonade
   (see Note above)

$^{1}/_{2}$ teaspoon salt

**PER SERVING**

216 calories

····

7 g fat (2 g saturated)

····

5 mg cholesterol

····

509 mg sodium

····

*¼ teaspoon freshly ground black pepper*

*¼ cup freshly grated Parmesan cheese*

1. Heat oil in very large heavy skillet over low heat 1 minute. Add garlic and sauté, stirring often, 1 minute. Turn off heat.

2. Add well-drained bowties and toss well until coated with garlic/oil mixture. Add lemon juice and zest, basil, salt, and pepper, and toss until basil wilts.

3. Divide pasta among four large heated plates, top each portion with 1 tablespoon grated cheese, and serve.

RECIPE FROM

*Marsha D. Green; New York, New York*

*Owosso, Michigan*

This self-taught personal chef, who has three sons aged eleven, thirteen, and fifteen, prepares weekly meals for clients and specializes in imaginative low-fat dishes using vegetables and fruits in season whenever possible. "I created this recipe during artichoke season, which lasts such a short time that I fill artichokes with everything I can think of to take advantage of it," Shawn explains. "One of my clients is on a diet for heart disease and I wanted to create something, low in fat for him and his family. Versatile risotto seemed a perfect match for the artichokes."

# Risotto-Stuffed Artichokes

*Makes 4 servings*

*Not every rice makes good risotto. Indeed, you need short-grain rice, the Italian arborio, for example, if the risotto is to cook up creamy yet have grains that are slightly al dente. Fortunately, nearly every good supermarket now stocks arborio rice (sometimes it's simply called "risotto rice"). Look for it.*

NOTE 1: *For the toasted cheese–bread crumbs, mix ¼ cup soft white bread crumbs with 2 tablespoons freshly grated Parmesan cheese, spread in a large baking pan, and bake uncovered at 350°F until golden brown—8 to 10 minutes.*

NOTE 2: *To toast pignoli (pine nuts), see headnote for Chicken Cutlets with Roasted Red Peppers Clelia Style, page 52.*

TIPS: *The easiest way to remove the choke (thistly center) from an artichoke is to spread the leaves and then use a melon baller to reach down inside and scoop out all the prickly parts. To tell if an artichoke is done, pierce the bottom with a sharp-pronged fork. If it goes in easily, the artichoke is tender. Another way: Pull on a leaf near the base. If it loosens, the artichoke is done.*

> *4 large (8-ounce) artichokes, trimmed, points of leaves snipped off, and chokes removed (see Tips above)*
> *1 (14.25-ounce) can reduced-sodium, nonfat chicken broth*

1 tablespoon fresh lemon juice

1 teaspoon finely grated lemon zest

1 medium-size clove garlic, finely minced

1 tablespoon olive oil

1 cup uncooked arborio rice (see headnote)

1 cup moderately finely diced red bell pepper
  (about 1 medium-large pepper)

1 medium-size shallot, finely minced

2 tablespoons toasted pignoli (pine nuts) (see Note 2)

2 tablespoons freshly grated Parmesan cheese

1/4 cup toasted cheese–bread crumbs (see Note 1)

**PER SERVING**

448 calories

....

9 g fat (3 g saturated)

....

7 mg cholesterol

....

415 mg sodium

....

1. Pour water to a depth of 1/2 inch in a very large stainless steel or enameled metal kettle and bring to a boil over moderately high heat. Trim bottoms of artichokes so they will stand straight, then ease into kettle, one by one, placing right side up. As soon as water returns to a boil, adjust heat so it bubbles gently, cover, and cook artichokes until tender—about 30 minutes.

2. While artichokes cook, bring chicken broth, lemon juice and zest, and garlic to a simmer in a small saucepan over moderate heat. Reduce heat to low and keep broth mixture hot.

3. Heat olive oil in large heavy saucepan over moderately high heat until ripples appear on pan bottom—1 1/2 to 2 minutes. Add rice, bell pepper, and shallot and sauté, stirring now and then, until lightly golden—about 5 minutes.

4. Add 1/2 cup hot broth mixture, stirring often, until completely absorbed. Add remaining broth mixture 1/2 cup at a time, cooking and stirring after each addition until all liquid is absorbed; this will take about 20 minutes. Stir toasted pignoli and cheese into risotto.

5. Drain artichokes well by standing upside down on several thicknesses of paper toweling. Then spoon 1/2 cup hot risotto into center of each artichoke.

6. Arrange stuffed artichokes on large heated platter, sprinkle with toasted cheese–bread crumbs, and serve at once.

**RECIPE FROM**
*Shawn Merkel; Owosso, Michigan*

*Eagar, Arizona*

Born in Guam and brought up in Tucson, Arizona, Margaret taught herself to cook with the help of magazines, cookbooks, and advice from television personalities— especially Julia Child. She recalls that she "yo-yo dieted" for twenty years, losing fifteen pounds and then regaining it, until she learned how to keep her weight down through behavioral modification. "You must change your eating habits to be healthy!" she says. Today she favors a Mediterranean cuisine using fish, vegetables, grains, and olive oil. This salad, a masterful blend of black beans, corn, and couscous, is an example of a recipe that started more simply and evolved over time.

# *Southwest Couscous Salad*

*Makes 4 servings*

*Couscous, sometimes called "Moroccan pasta," may be the cook's best friend—its blandness makes it endlessly versatile and it requires no cooking, only a 5- to 10-minute soak in boiling water. Thus, this vegetarian salad couldn't be quicker. It packs plenty of flavor, too, and doesn't lack for color.*

TIPS: *For maximum flavor, use Haas avocados. And to keep the slices from darkening, either brush with or dip into fresh lime or lemon juice.*

*1 cup couscous*

*½ teaspoon ground cumin*

*½ teaspoon dried leaf oregano, crumbled*

*¼ teaspoon salt*

*1 cup boiling water*

*1 (15-ounce) can black beans, rinsed and drained*

*1 cup frozen corn kernels, thawed and drained*

*½ cup diced red onion (about 1 medium-small onion)*

*¼ cup diced red bell pepper (about ¼ medium-size pepper)*

**PER SERVING**

393 calories

....

9 g fat (1 g saturated)

....

0 mg cholesterol

....

395 mg sodium

....

*¼ cup coarsely chopped fresh cilantro*

*¼ cup thinly sliced scallions (include some green tops) (about 2
    medium-size scallions)*

*1 tablespoon finely diced, seeded jalapeño pepper (about 1 small pepper)*

*2 tablespoons fresh lime juice*

*1 tablespoon olive oil*

*1 medium-size romaine, separated into leaves or thickly sliced*

*½ medium-size firm-ripe avocado (preferably Haas), peeled, cut into 8 slices,
    and lightly brushed with fresh lime juice*

*1 large firm-ripe tomato, cored and cut into 12 wedges but not peeled*

1. Combine couscous, cumin, oregano, and salt in large heatproof bowl. Pour in
boiling water, cover, and let stand until all water is absorbed—about 10 minutes.

2. Fluff couscous with fork, then mix in beans, corn, onion, bell pepper, cilantro,
scallions, and jalapeño. Add lime juice and olive oil and toss well.

3. Bed romaine on large platter, mound couscous mixture on top, then surround
with avocado slices and tomato wedges. Serve immediately.

RECIPE FROM

*Margaret Coalter; Eagar, Arizona*

*Cherry Hill, New Jersey*

This enterprising private chef teaches clients to cook in their own homes and provides catering services, specializing in southwestern vegetarian cuisine. Having lost thirty pounds by the unique method of "walking through Europe" (combined with becoming vegetarian), Barry understands the challenges and advantages of meatless cooking. To make this low-fat, dairy-free lasagne, he layers a casserole dish with corn tortillas, quinoa ("an ancient Inca grain that is nutty in flavor and very high in protein"), black beans, and a red sauce compounded of ancho chilies, garlic, oregano, and cumin.

# Mexican Black Bean and Quinoa Lasagne with Ancho Chili Sauce

*Makes 6 to 8 servings*

*To the ancient Incas, the ivory-colored beads of quinoa (prounced KEEN-wah) were "the Mother Grain," a sustainer of life in hard times in the high Andes. Except for a green-peanutlike aftertaste, quinoa is as bland as rice. Unlike rice, however, it packs a lot of protein. Most organic groceries and health food stores stock quinoa and some of the better supermarkets also carry it.*

TIP: *To make the sauce, you must handle ancho chili peppers (nothing more than dried poblanos and now widely available). The sweetest of the dried chilies and only mild to medium-hot, anchos can still cause you grief if you should rub your face—and especially your eyes—while working with them. So, do as the pros do and wear surgical rubber gloves.*

SAUCE
*2 large ancho chili peppers (see Tip above)*
*1 cup boiling water*
*1 (28-ounce) can crushed tomatoes*
*1/4 cup minced garlic (an entire medium-size bulb)*

*1 teaspoon dried leaf oregano, crumbled*

*¼ teaspoon ground cumin*

*⅛ teaspoon freshly ground black pepper*

L A S A G N E
*¾ cup uncooked quinoa (see headnote),*
*rinsed three times in cool water*

*1½ cups water*

*Pinch salt*

*12 (6-inch) no-salt-added corn tortillas*

*½ cup thinly sliced scallions (include some green*
*tops) (6 to 8 medium-size scallions)*

*1 (15-ounce) can black beans, rinsed and drained*

*¼ cup coarsely chopped fresh cilantro*

E A C H   O F   6   S E R V I N G S

305 calories

3 g fat (0.4 g saturated)

0 mg cholesterol

359 mg sodium

E A C H   O F   8   S E R V I N G S

229 calories

3 g fat (0.3 g saturated)

0 mg cholesterol

269 mg sodium

1. Preheat oven to 400°F. Coat 13 x 9 x 2-inch baking dish with nonstick cooking spray and set aside.

2. *For sauce:* Soak ancho chilies in boiling water 10 minutes. Cool and drain, reserving soaking water. Remove stems, seeds, and strings inside chilies and add to soaking water. Drop chilies into food processor and set aside.

3. Strain chili soaking water into second ungreased 13 x 9 x 2-inch baking dish, add tomatoes, garlic, oregano, cumin, and black pepper. Stir well, then roast uncovered for 30 minutes. Remove from oven (but leave oven on) and cool 15 minutes. Add to food processor with chilies and pulse about 1 minute until smooth; set ancho sauce aside.

4. *For lasagne:* Place quinoa, water, and salt in medium-size heavy saucepan and bring to a boil over moderately high heat. Adjust heat so water bubbles gently, then boil quinoa uncovered until all water is absorbed—about 15 minutes.

5. To assemble lasagne, cover bottom of prepared baking dish with 6 tortillas, overlapping as needed. Layer quinoa on top, spread with half the reserved ancho sauce, and sprinkle evenly with all the scallions. Cover with remaining 6 tortillas, again overlapping as needed, spoon black beans evenly over all, and spread with remaining ancho sauce.

6. Cover with aluminum foil, placing dull side up, and bake until bubbly—about 20 minutes.

7. Lift off aluminum foil and let lasagne stand at room temperature 10 minutes. Sprinkle with cilantro, cut into squares, and serve.

RECIPE FROM

*Barry Cohen; Cherry Hill, New Jersey*

## MARY E. DITTO

### Oak Park, Illinois

"For sixty-five summers my mother, Teresina, prepared this minestrone with fresh-picked vegetables from my father Angelo's garden," Mary, a retired school-teacher, wrote us. "She had impeccable taste and used only the best produce. Onions had to be cooked to the transparent stage and garlic minced and arranged on top of the Swiss chard. The pasta was cooked separately and timed precisely. She carefully tended, but never tasted during the cooking." Now Mary and her grown children make the soup for their children and their children's friends, and it's always hungrily devoured.

## Teresina's Minestrone

### Makes 4 servings

If you can find vine-ripe Italian plum (Roma) tomatoes, by all means use them for this husky Italian vegetable soup. For one cup, you'll need four peeled, seeded, and coarsely chopped plum tomatoes.

TIP 1: The fastest way to peel tomatoes is to drop them into a large pan of boiling water, count twenty seconds, then lift from the boiling water and "shock" or plunge into cold water for a few seconds. The skins will loosen magically and you can slip them right off. To seed plum tomatoes, halve lengthwise, then scoop out seeds with your fingers.

TIP 2: The most efficient way to slice Swiss chard is to stack 8 to 10 leaves, then slice straight across at 1-inch intervals.

1 tablespoon olive oil

1 large yellow onion, thinly sliced the long way so you
  have strips instead of circles

1 cup finely diced celery (about 2 medium-size celery ribs)

1 large clove garlic, minced

1 (10-ounce) bunch fresh Swiss chard, trimmed of stalks,
  then leaves cut into strips 1 inch wide (see Tip 2)

**PER SERVING**

207 calories
....
6 g fat (2 g saturated)
....
5 mg cholesterol
....
314 mg sodium
....

1 cup coarsely chopped, peeled, and seeded vine-ripe Italian plum (Roma) tomatoes, or 1 cup canned crushed tomatoes (preferably low-sodium)

2 (8-ounce) cans low-sodium tomato sauce

3 cups water

2 tablespoons coarsely chopped fresh Italian (flat-leaf) parsley

1 teaspoon dried leaf basil, crumbled

$1/8$ teaspoon freshly ground black pepper

$1/2$ cup shelled fresh or solidly frozen green peas

$1/2$ cup ditalini pasta, cooked and drained according to package directions

$1/4$ cup freshly grated Parmesan cheese

1. Heat olive oil in medium-size Dutch oven over moderately high heat until ripples appear on pan bottom—$1^{1}/2$ to 2 minutes. Add onion, celery, and garlic and cook, stirring often, until vegetables soften—about 5 minutes.

2. Add Swiss chard and cook and stir until chard wilts—about 2 minutes. Add tomatoes, tomato sauce, water, parsley, basil, and pepper and bring to a boil. Adjust heat so mixture bubbles gently and simmer uncovered, stirring occasionally, until flavors mellow and marry—about 15 minutes.

3. Stir in peas, ditalini, and Parmesan and simmer uncovered, stirring occasionally, 5 minutes more.

4. Ladle into four heated soup plates and serve.

RECIPE FROM

*Mary E. Ditto; Oak Park, Illinois*

## KIM A. GILLILAND

*Grove City, Pennsylvania*

Kim vividly recalls creating the special soup she still loves today: "I was living alone in a small apartment in Rhode Island on a cold night that called for soup—only I didn't have any canned. I searched through recipes, couldn't find anything appealing, so makeshifted with some staples I had in the kitchen. I never measure, just threw it together and voilà!" Today Kim lives in the town where she was born, with her dentist husband (for whom she works as office manager), three adult stepchildren, three dogs, two cats, a guinea pig, and a ferret.

# Hearty Broccoli-Potato Soup

*Makes 6 servings*

*Choose red-skin potatoes for this soup and don't peel them—the skins add nice color.*

NOTE: *The broccoli, both florets and stems, should be cut quite small—no more than $1/2$ inch across—if they are to cook quickly and retain their bright green color.*

| | |
|---|---|
| 1 tablespoon olive oil | **PER SERVING** |
| 1 cup finely chopped yellow onion (about 1 medium-large onion) | 194 calories |
| 3 medium-size cloves garlic, minced | 3 g fat (0.4 g saturated) |
| 4 medium-size red-skin potatoes, cut into $1/2$-inch cubes but not peeled (about $3^1/2$ cups cubed potatoes) | 5 mg cholesterol |
| 2 tablespoons flour | 261 mg sodium |
| $1/4$ teaspoon salt | |

$1/4$ teaspoon salt

$1/4$ teaspoon freshly ground black pepper

2 (14.25-ounce) cans nonfat, low-sodium chicken or vegetable broth

1 (12-ounce) can evaporated skim milk

$1^1/4$ pounds broccoli, trimmed, divided into small florets, and stems peeled and cut into $1/2$-inch chunks (about 4 cups prepared broccoli) (see Note above)

*1 tablespoon minced fresh Italian (flat-leaf) parsley*

*1 tablespoon chopped fresh basil (no substitute)*

1. Heat olive oil in very large heavy saucepan over moderately high heat until ripples appear on pan bottom, about 1½ minutes. Add onion and garlic and cook, stirring occasionally, until soft, about 5 minutes.

2. Add potatoes, flour, salt, and pepper, stirring well to mix. Slowly add chicken broth and evaporated milk, stirring all the while. Bring quickly to a boil, again stirring.

3. Reduce heat to low, cover, and simmer until potatoes are tender, about 20 minutes.

4. Add broccoli, parsley, and basil and simmer uncovered, stirring now and then, until broccoli is crisp-tender, about 10 minutes.

5. Ladle into heated soup bowls and serve.

RECIPE FROM

*Kim A. Gilliland; Grove City, Pennsylvania*

The GMA family with the winners of the contest: Charlie Gibson, winner Sandy Greene, Diane Sawyer, winner Jan Curry, chef Sara Moulton, Antonio Mora, and Tony Perkins. CREDIT: IDA ASTUTE

*Above:* Entrée winner Sandy Greene's Oven-Fried Chicken with Andouille Sausage. CREDIT: JOANNE HAYES    *Below:* Dessert winner Jan Curry's Caramel Cheesecake with Praline Sauce. CREDIT: JAN CURRY

*Above:* Finalist Poolsin Krisanauwatara's Spicy Salmon Salad. CREDIT: POOLSIN KRISANAUWATARA
*Below:* Finalist Joan Churchill's Grilled Halibut with Rum Sauce, Great Greens and Olives. CREDIT: JOAN CHURCHILL

*Above:* Finalist Clelia Graceffa Egan's Chicken Cutlets with Roasted Red Peppers Clelia Style. CREDIT: CLELIA GRACEFFA EGAN

*Below:* Finalist Sarah Tackett's Turkey Salsa Meatloaf. CREDIT: SARAH TACKETT

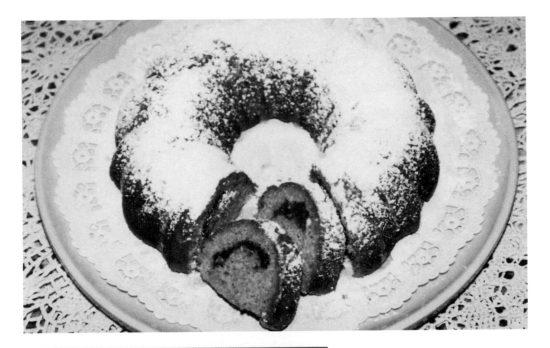

*Above:* Finalist Sherry Sirch's "Not" Cream Cheese Cake. CREDIT: JOANNE HAYES
*Below:* Kristin Renzema's Double Chocolate Hazelnut Cheesecake.
CREDIT: KRISTIN RENZEMA

*Above:* Lisa Stift's Feta-Stuffed Chicken with Cucumber Dill Sauce. CREDIT: JOANNE HAYES
*Below:* Rachel Brown's French Cream, Skinnied Down and Gussied Up.

CREDIT: RACHEL BROWN

Margaret Shelton's "It's My Chocolate Cake." CREDIT: MARGARET SHELTON

*Bakersfield, California*

Dru, whose husband Mike is a California produce grower and shipper, describes her own job as "executive staff cook." This means, she explains, that during harvest season she cooks for her husband's crew at the ranch as well as for other produce farmers in the surrounding area. A typical lunch Dru might serve on such occasions would include soup, salad, and entrée for twenty to twenty-five hungry men. "My onion soup was a winner," she recalls, "probably because I used fresh onions and corn that were brought to me by the local growers straight from the field."

# *Caramelized Onion Soup with Lemon-Corn Chutney*

*Makes 4 servings*

*This unusual onion soup is ready to eat in less than 45 minutes—and that includes making the chutney.*

NOTE: *Each portion is topped with a slice of toasted French bread. To make, cut four slices ½ inch thick, coat one side with butter-flavored nonstick cooking spray, then sprinkle each with ¼ teaspoon finely chopped fresh rosemary (or a pinch dried). Place in pie tin and toast 5 minutes in a 350°F oven. Turn slices and toast 5 minutes longer. That's all there is to it.*

**SOUP**

1 tablespoon unsalted butter

3 large yellow onions (about 1½ pounds), halved lengthwise, then each half thinly sliced

2 tablespoons flour

2 (14.25-ounce) cans reduced-sodium, nonfat beef or vegetable broth

1 (12-ounce) can evaporated skim milk

¼ teaspoon freshly ground black pepper

4 (½-inch-thick) slices toasted French bread (see Note)

**PER SERVING**

304 calories
....
4 g fat (2 g saturated)
....
11 mg cholesterol
....
321 mg sodium
....

173

CHUTNEY

1 cup frozen whole-kernel corn, thawed and drained

$\frac{1}{2}$ medium-size red bell pepper, cored, seeded, and finely diced

$\frac{1}{2}$ medium-size red onion, finely diced

4 medium-size scallions, trimmed and thinly sliced (include some green tops)

2 tablespoons fresh lemon juice

$\frac{1}{8}$ teaspoon freshly ground black pepper

1. *For soup:* Melt butter in large heavy saucepan over moderate heat, add onions, and sauté, stirring now and then, until richly golden—about 15 minutes.

2. Blend in flour, then slowly whisk in beef broth and evaporated milk. Raise heat to moderately high and cook, whisking constantly, until mixture thickens slightly. Adjust heat so mixture bubbles gently, and simmer uncovered until mixture thickens and flavors mellow—about 25 minutes.

3. *Meanwhile, prepare chutney:* Mix all ingredients in small bowl and set aside.

4. Season soup with pepper, ladle into heated soup bowls, and float a slice of toasted French bread in each. Top toast with chutney, dividing amount equally, and serve at once.

RECIPE FROM
*Dru Kovacevich; Bakersfield, California*

# Desserts

# CHEESECAKES

Caramel Cheesecake with Praline Sauce *(Grand Prize Winner, Desserts)*     178

"Not" Cream Cheese Cake *(Finalist, Desserts)*     180

Double Chocolate Hazelnut Cheesecake     182

Paul's Chocolate Cheesecake     184

Black Forest Cheesecake     186

Orange Cheesecake     189

# JAN CURRY

### Raleigh, North Carolina

Jan is a set designer married to a scenic designer. Although she recalls watching Julia Child's cooking classes on television when she was still in high school, she's basically a self-taught cook who enjoys baking and creating low-fat recipes with "the most natural ingredients possible." Challenging Jan's artistic talents was this sumptuous cheesecake. "A chocolate version of the cheesecake has been a family favorite for years," she told us. "I changed it to caramel—my favorite flavor—and added a praline sauce to dress it up. It took several tries to get it just right, much to the delight of my faithful taste testers." Jan's patience paid off. Her Caramel Cheesecake with Praline Sauce won the Grand Prize in the Dessert category of *Good Morning America*'s Cut the Calories Cook-Off. And that's not all. Barely six months later, Jan's snow-dusted English stone village, a gingerbread construction of awesome detail, won the 1999 Grand Prize in the Gingerbread House Competition staged each year by the Grove Park Inn Resort in Asheville, North Carolina. *Good Morning America* covered that event.

### GRAND PRIZE WINNER, DESSERTS

## Caramel Cheesecake with Praline Sauce

*Makes an 8-inch cheesecake, 12 servings*

*For this "best of show," Jan Curry teamed two favorite flavors—caramel and praline. But she managed to keep the fat and calories well within bounds. Evaporated skim milk, a godsend to anyone trying to shed a few pounds, forms the base of the sauce, its creaminess and slight caramel flavor contributing to a deceptive richness.*

CRUST
2½ tablespoons graham cracker crumbs

1 tablespoon sugar

FILLING
1 cup low-fat (1 percent) cottage cheese

2 (8-ounce) packages low-fat cream cheese (Neufchâtel), softened

PER SERVING

245 calories
....
9 g fat (6 g saturated)
....
47 mg cholesterol
....
263 mg sodium
....

178

1¼ cups firmly packed light brown sugar

1 tablespoon water

2 teaspoons vanilla extract

¼ cup unsifted all-purpose flour

1 large egg plus 1 large egg white

SAUCE

⅓ cup evaporated skim milk

2½ tablespoons firmly packed light brown sugar

1 teaspoon vanilla extract

1 tablespoon coarsely chopped pecans

1. Preheat oven to 325°F. Coat 8-inch springform pan with nonstick cooking spray (preferably butter-flavored) and set aside.

2. *For crust:* Combine crumbs and sugar, sprinkle evenly over bottom of prepared pan, and set aside.

3. *For filling:* Pulse cottage cheese in food processor until completely smooth—about 1½ minutes. Add cream cheese, sugar, water, and vanilla and pulse 1 minute more. Add flour and pulse 30 seconds, scraping down work bowl sides twice. Add egg and egg white and pulse 30 seconds to combine, again scraping down work bowl sides.

4. Taking care not to dislodge crumbs, pour filling into pan and smooth top.

5. Bake uncovered 45 minutes; turn oven off and leave cheesecake in oven 30 minutes longer—just until cheesecake springs back when lightly touched.

6. Transfer cheesecake to wire rack and cool in upright pan to room temperature. Cover with plastic wrap and refrigerate for at least 4 hours.

7. *For sauce:* Bring milk, sugar, and vanilla to a boil in a very small heavy saucepan over moderate heat. Reduce heat to low, then cook, stirring constantly, until flavors marry—1 to 1½ minutes. Remove from heat and mix in pecans. Cool to room temperature.

8. To serve, cut cheesecake into 12 wedges and ladle a little sauce on each plate alongside.

RECIPE FROM
*Jan Curry; Raleigh, North Carolina*

## SHERRY SIRCH

*Kamloops, British Columbia, Canada*

"I've been playing with this cheesecake recipe for five years now and finally have got it right," says Sherry, a tax preparer who credits her mother and a high school home ec class for teaching her to cook. "I found the idea of using cottage cheese instead of cream cheese in an old handwritten recipe book of my mom's. I added my favorite ingredients, took out some things I didn't want, and altered the measurements to get a nice consistency. If you don't tell your guests this recipe is low in fat, they won't figure it out."

FINALIST, DESSERTS

# "Not" Cream Cheese Cake

*Makes an 8-inch cheesecake, 12 servings*

*Sherry Sirch, the lady from Canada who sent us this recipe, usually bakes it in a 9 x 9 x 2-inch ovenproof glass baking dish. And that works well. But using an 8-inch springform pan makes for a showier cheesecake.*

CRUST

*1 cup graham cracker crumbs*

*2 tablespoons unsalted butter, at room temperature*

FILLING

*2 cups part-skim ricotta cheese*

*2 (5-ounce) cans evaporated skim milk*

*⅔ cup sugar*

*3 (¼-ounce) envelopes plain gelatin softened in ¼ cup cold water*

*3 teaspoons vanilla extract*

*2 teaspoons finely grated lemon zest*

TOPPING

*1 cup canned cherry pie filling or canned blueberries in syrup, with their liquid*

| PER SERVING |
| :---: |
| 187 calories |
| .... |
| 6 g fat (3 g saturated) |
| .... |
| 19 mg cholesterol |
| .... |
| 115 mg sodium |
| .... |

1. Preheat oven to 350°F.

2. *For crust:* Blend crumbs and butter in 8-inch springform pan and press firmly over bottom and one-fourth of the way up sides. Bake crust uncovered until golden—8 to 10 minutes. Remove from oven and cool to room temperature.

3. *For filling:* Pulse ricotta cheese in food processor 1 minute. Scrape down work bowl sides, then pulse until completely smooth—about 30 seconds more.

4. Heat milk and sugar in small heavy saucepan over moderate heat until mixture steams—4 to 5 minutes. Add softened gelatin, vanilla, and lemon zest and whisk until gelatin dissolves completely—about 2 minutes. Cool mixture 8 to 10 minutes.

5. Add gelatin mixture to ricotta cheese in food processor and pulse until completely smooth—about 30 seconds—scraping down work bowl sides at half time.

6. Pour filling into cooled crust, set uncovered in refrigerator, and chill until set—at least 2 hours. Note: You can cover cheesecake with plastic wrap before you chill it if you take care not to let the plastic touch the filling and ruin the surface.

7. Cut cheesecake into wedges, spoon topping over each portion, dividing amount evenly, and serve.

RECIPE FROM

*Sherry Sirch; Kamloops, British Columbia, Canada*

## KRISTIN RENZEMA

*Warren, Oregon*

Kristin, who describes herself as "a part-time portrait photographer and a full-time mom," likes to make desserts for her young daughter and her husband, an electrical engineer. Despite her fondness for cheesecake she felt guilty about eating it until, through trial and error, she hit upon this version using lower-fat cream cheese and an Oregon favorite, hazelnuts. "I kept baking 'trials' and sending them with my husband to his workplace for taste testing. His coworkers liked them all!" Kristin said. She herself considered her final version "a little custardy but very good." Her family can't believe it's low fat.

## Double Chocolate Hazelnut Cheesecake

*Makes a 9-inch cheesecake, 14 servings*

*One effective way to slash cheesecake calories is to minimize the crust—here it's a bottom coat of crumbs and finely chopped nuts. The filling is easily slimmed down, too. Simply substitute low-fat cream cheese, part-skim ricotta, and low-fat sour cream for the full fat.*

TIP: *Dutch process cocoa has deeper chocolate flavor than its American counterparts.*

CRUST
½ scant cup chocolate graham cracker crumbs
    (about 3 whole crackers)

1 tablespoon melted unsalted butter

2 tablespoons finely chopped blanched hazelnuts

FILLING
2 (8-ounce) packages low-fat cream cheese (Neufchâtel),
    cubed

1½ cups firmly packed part-skim ricotta cheese

1 cup sugar

½ cup unsweetened Dutch process cocoa powder

6 tablespoons hazelnut liqueur

3 teaspoons vanilla extract

| PER SERVING |
| --- |
| 254 calories |
| .... |
| 14 g fat (8 g saturated) |
| .... |
| 52 mg cholesterol |
| .... |
| 230 mg sodium |
| .... |

*1 large egg plus 1 large egg white*

*3 tablespoons miniature semisweet chocolate chips*

TOPPING
*½ cup low-fat sour cream*

*1½ tablespoons sugar*

*2 teaspoons unsweetened Dutch process cocoa powder*

*2 tablespoons finely chopped blanched hazelnuts*

1. Preheat oven to 350°F. Coat bottom and sides of 9-inch springform pan with nonstick cooking spray and set aside.

2. *For crust:* Mix crumbs, melted butter, and hazelnuts until uniformly crumbly, then pat firmly over bottom of prepared pan. Bake uncovered 7 minutes. Remove pan from oven and set on wire rack while you prepare filling. Also reduce oven temperature to 300°F.

3. *For filling:* Pulse cream cheese, ricotta, and sugar 1 minute in food processor. Scrape down work bowl sides, add cocoa, liqueur, vanilla, egg and egg white, and pulse 1 minute. Scrape bowl and pulse 1 minute more until smooth. Add chocolate chips and pulse quickly to combine.

4. Pour filling over crust in springform pan and bake uncovered until nearly set and filling jiggles only slightly when pan is nudged—about 50 minutes.

5. *Meanwhile, prepare topping:* Combine sour cream, sugar, and cocoa and set aside.

6. When cheesecake has baked 50 minutes, carefully smooth topping over surface and sprinkle with hazelnuts. Bake uncovered 10 minutes more.

7. Transfer cheesecake to wire rack and cool to room temperature in upright pan, then cover loosely with plastic wrap and chill several hours before serving.

RECIPE FROM
*Kristin Renzema; Warren, Oregon*

## PAUL PROVENZANO

*Missouri City, Texas*

In addition to cooking, this talented Texan's skills and interests include hunting, fishing, taxidermy, writing cookbooks and westerns, and raising, training, and judging retriever dogs. He especially enjoys cooking wild game—"everything from ducks, geese, quail, pheasants, and turkey to venison, elk, and moose"—but also dabbles in desserts. Having sampled a chocolate cheesecake at his brother's house, he decided to create a low-fat version that could be eaten without guilt, and after three tries, came up with this winner. Having lost forty pounds, Paul keeps his weight in check by sticking to a low-fat, low-sugar diet.

# *Paul's Chocolate Cheesecake*

*Makes a 9-inch cheesecake, 12 servings*

*Cocoa goes into the cheesecake proper and mini chocolate chips go on top together with toasted roughly chopped pecans.*

NOTE: *To toast the nuts, chop and spread in an ungreased pie pan, then set in a preheated 350°F oven for 7 to 8 minutes until golden brown, stirring occasionally. Keep an eye on the nuts, however—they burn easily.*

### CRUST
1 cup graham cracker crumbs

2 tablespoons unsalted butter, at room temperature

### FILLING
2 (8-ounce) packages low-fat cream cheese (Neufchâtel), softened

6 tablespoons sugar

1 large egg plus 2 large egg whites, lightly beaten

6 tablespoons unsweetened cocoa powder

3 teaspoons vanilla extract

1 (12-ounce) can evaporated skim milk

**PER SERVING**

333 calories

....

14 g fat (8 g saturated)

....

54 mg cholesterol

....

291 mg sodium

....

TOPPING

*¹/₂ cup nonfat plain yogurt*

*3 tablespoons sugar*

*2 tablespoons toasted, coarsely chopped pecans (see Note)*

*2 tablespoons miniature semisweet chocolate chips*

1. Preheat oven to 350°F.

2. *For crust:* Blend crumbs and butter in 9-inch pie plate and press firmly over bottom and up sides. Bake crust uncovered until golden—about 8 minutes. Remove from oven and set aside but leave oven on.

3. *For filling:* Pulse cream cheese and sugar in food processor 1 minute. Scrape down work bowl sides, add egg/egg white mixture and cocoa, and pulse 1 minute more. Again scrape down work bowl sides. Pulse in vanilla, then with machine running, slowly add milk. When all milk is in, churn until completely smooth—about 1 minute more.

4. Taking care not to dislodge crust, pour in filling.

5. Bake cheesecake uncovered until filling is just set—about 30 minutes.

6. *For topping:* Combine yogurt and sugar in small bowl and very gently spread on top of hot cheesecake. Sprinkle evenly with toasted pecans and chocolate chips, return to oven, and bake until yogurt sets—about 5 minutes more.

7. Transfer cheesecake to wire rack and cool in upright pan to room temperature, then refrigerate at least 2 hours before cutting into wedges and serving.

RECIPE FROM

*Paul Provenzano; Missouri City, Texas*

## CHAMEIN T. CANTON

*Amityville, New York*

"I came up with this recipe out of necessity," Chamein told us, "because you cannot be a true New Yorker without cheesecake! The problem is, how can you have your cake and eat it too if you're on a low-fat diet? This recipe combining chocolate, cherries, and cheesecake was my solution. It's a family favorite for all—whether dieting or not." Chamein, mother of twelve-year-old twins, paralegal, and psychologist, has lost an impressive sixty pounds on a low-fat, high-protein regimen and maintains the loss by sticking to desserts like this one.

# *Black Forest Cheesecake*

*Makes a 10-inch cheesecake, 16 servings*

*Part-skim ricotta and low-fat cream cheese bring the fat and calorie counts down within reason. In addition, we've made the whipped topping optional. Use a commercial low-fat whipped topping, if you like. Better yet, use the Skinny Whipped Topping we've developed especially for this cookbook (page 275).*

TIP: *This cheesecake bakes in a hot water bath, and unless you have a water-tight spring-form pan, the type used by pastry chefs, you must wrap the pan snugly in heavy-duty aluminum foil to keep the water from leaking into the pan and ruining the cheesecake. The best way to go about it is to tear off two 18- to 20-inch lengths of foil and then lay them on the counter at right angles to each other. Center the pan on the foil strips where they intersect, then smooth the strips tight across bottom and up sides of the pan, creasing as needed but taking care not to puncture or tear the foil. Bring the ends of the foil straight up, then roll down until only about ¹/₂ inch above the rim of the pan. This should water-proof your springform pan.*

**CRUST**
*1 (6-ounce) package chocolate graham crackers*

*1 tablespoon sugar*

*2 tablespoons unsalted butter, at room temperature*

FILLING

1 (15-ounce) container part-skim ricotta cheese

2 (8-ounce) packages low-fat cream cheese (Neufchâtel), softened

1 cup sugar

1/4 cup unsweetened cocoa powder

2 tablespoons (that's right, **tablespoons**) vanilla extract

2 large eggs plus 2 large egg whites

1 (12-ounce) can cherry pie filling

1/4 cup reserved crumbs (from crust mixture above)

OPTIONAL TOPPING
*Skinny Whipped Topping (page 275)*

| PER SERVING |
| :---: |
| 273 calories |
| .... |
| 12 g fat (7 g saturated) |
| .... |
| 59 mg cholesterol |
| .... |
| 240 mg sodium |
| .... |

1. Preheat oven to 350°F. Coat foil-wrapped 10-inch springform pan (see Tip) with nonstick cooking spray (preferably butter-flavored) and set aside.

2. *For crust:* Pulse graham crackers to crumbs in food processor, add sugar, and pulse quickly to combine. Spoon out 1/4 cup crumbs and reserve to sprinkle over finished cheesecake. Add butter to crumbs remaining in processor and pulse briskly until uniformly crumbly. Dump crumb mixture into prepared pan, then press firmly over bottom and halfway up sides. Set aside. Also wipe processor work bowl and blade clean.

2. *For filling:* Pulse ricotta in food processor until smooth—about 1 minute. Add cream cheese, sugar, cocoa, and vanilla and pulse 1 minute more, scraping work bowl sides down at half time. Add eggs and egg whites and pulse 30 seconds. Scrape down work bowl sides and pulse until completely smooth—about 30 seconds more.

3. Pour into prepared crust, set cheesecake in large shallow roasting pan, and pour enough hot water into pan to come one-third of the way up sides of springform pan.

4. Bake uncovered until filling is just set and springs back when touched—about 1 hour. Very carefully lift cheesecake from hot water bath, taking care not to let hot water scald you, and set on large wire rack. Cool cheesecake to room tem-

perature and carefully remove foil wrapper.

5. Cover cheesecake with plastic wrap and refrigerate overnight.

6. Spread cherry pie filling over top of cheesecake, then sprinkle with reserved crumb mixture.

7. To serve, cut into wedges and, if you like, drift each portion with a tablespoon or two of whipped topping.

RECIPE FROM

*Chamein T. Canton; Amityville, New York*

# DAWNA HOERNER

*Miamisburg, Ohio*

This orange cheesecake, Dawna says, is her "most requested dessert." And that's a lot of desserts because this fifty-two-year-old who's lived in five South American countries and thirteen states, is a personal chef—"a chef for hire with my own business," she explains. (Dawna's twenty-four-year-old son is also a chef.) Dawna developed this particular orange cheesecake because "I love cheesecake and wanted a fast, easy way to make it *from scratch*. This one is so good I've made it for weddings. With low-fat substitutes, it even tastes good on a diet!" Dawna, it turns out, is as handy with a camera as she is with a whisk—her orange cheesecake photograph was so glamorous it was one of the food shots *Good Morning America* chose to decorate the set the day the grand prize winners were announced. "Too bad I didn't win, too," she quips. Well, as far as family and friends are concerned, Dawna's orange cheesecake takes top honors every time.

## Orange Cheesecake

*Makes a 9-inch cheesecake, 8 servings*

*Delicious and richly orangey. In fact, oranges in four forms are used: frozen orange juice concentrate (a fast and easy way to build flavor), orange marmalade (to glaze), orange liqueur (to thin the glaze), and for the crowning touch, a ring of mandarin orange sections.*

**CRUST**

*1 cup graham cracker crumbs*

*2 tablespoons unsalted butter, at room temperature*

**FILLING**

*1 (8-ounce) package low-fat cream cheese (Neufchâtel), softened*

*¼ cup sugar*

*½ cup low-fat sour cream*

*3 tablespoons frozen orange juice concentrate*

**PER SERVING**

252 calories

· · · ·

11 g fat (6 g saturated)

· · · ·

32 mg cholesterol

· · · ·

238 mg sodium

· · · ·

*3 teaspoons vanilla extract*

*3 large egg whites*

TOPPING

*2 tablespoons orange marmalade blended with 1 tablespoon Grand Marnier or other orange liqueur*

*1 (11-ounce) can mandarin orange sections, drained well*

1. Preheat oven to 350°F.

2. *For crust:* Blend crumbs and butter in 9-inch springform pan, pat firmly over bottom, and set aside.

3. *For filling:* Churn cream cheese, sugar, sour cream, orange juice concentrate, vanilla, and egg whites in food processor 2 minutes. Scrape down work bowl sides and churn until completely smooth—about 1 minute more.

4. Taking care not to dislodge crust, pour filling into pan and smooth top.

5. Bake uncovered until just set—about 20 minutes. Transfer cheesecake to wire rack and cool to room temperature in upright pan.

6. *For topping:* With back of tablespoon, spread marmalade mixture over top of cheesecake, then ring mandarin orange sections decoratively around edge.

7. Cut into 8 wedges and serve.

RECIPE FROM

*Dawna Hoerner; Miamisburg, Ohio*

# PIES AND PUDDINGS

Peach and Almond Custard Tart                          192

Italian Ricotta Pie                                    194

Lee's Low-Fat Peanut Butter Pie                        196

Carol's Tirami Sù                                      198

Karen's Chocolate Pudding with Pralined Pecans         200

Low-Fat Chocolate-Banana Bread Pudding                 202

Bread Pudding                                          204

French Cream, Skinnied Down and Gussied Up             206

Lower-Calorie Rice Pudding                             208

Date Pudding                                           210

Banana Flan with Exotic Sauce                          212

Upside-Down Peach Pudding Cake                         214

## CELESTE SKOGERBOE

*Bemidji, Minnesota*

Celeste was born and brought up on a potato and grain farm in the Red River Valley, married a physician, had three children, and taught school until her retirement. Now involved in the demanding life of volunteer work in church and community, she loves to entertain and wishes she had time to do more of it. "My sister always asks me, 'How do you think of these things?' when I come up with a new recipe," she says. "Well, the idea for this one came when I decided to make a peach tart with the almonds and almond flavoring we all love."

# Peach and Almond Custard Tart

*Makes an 8-inch tart, 8 servings*

*If you make many tarts, you should invest in a set of tart tins with removable bottoms—this recipe calls for an 8-inch one. They're inexpensive, they give your pies a professional finish, and because their fillings are shallower than those baked in conventional pie pans, their crusts are less likely to be soggy. This one, in fact, is downright crunchy. With fresh peach slices spiraled on top, this tart's a beauty. It's also deceptively rich.*

TIPS: *The zip-quick way to peel a peach? Blanch 30 to 60 seconds in boiling water, then slip off the skin. To toast sliced almonds, spread in a pie pan and bake uncovered at 350°F, shaking pan occasionally, until uniformly golden brown—6 to 8 minutes.*

CRUST
*1 cup graham cracker crumbs*

*2 tablespoons melted unsalted butter*

*1 large egg white, lightly beaten*

FILLING
*¼ cup sugar*

*2 tablespoons cornstarch*

*1 (12-ounce) can evaporated skim milk*

*1 large egg yolk, lightly beaten*

PER SERVING

200 calories
....
6 g fat (2 g saturated)
....
36 mg cholesterol
....
148 mg sodium
....

*1 tablespoon fresh lemon juice*

*1 teaspoon finely grated lemon zest*

*1 teaspoon vanilla extract*

*½ teaspoon almond extract*

TOPPING
*2 large firm-ripe peaches (about 1 pound), peeled, pitted, thinly sliced, and
    dipped in lemon juice*

*2 tablespoons toasted sliced almonds (see Tips)*

1. Preheat oven to 350°F. Coat 8-inch tart tin with removable bottom with non-stick cooking spray and set aside.

2. *For crust:* Mix crumbs, melted butter, and beaten egg white until uniformly moist, then pat firmly over bottom and up sides of prepared tart tin. Bake uncovered until golden brown—10 to 11 minutes. Remove from oven, set on wire rack, and cool to room temperature.

3. *For filling:* Combine sugar and cornstarch in small heavy saucepan. Blend milk and egg yolk, then whisk into sugar mixture. Bring to boiling over moderate heat, then boil 1 minute, stirring constantly. Off heat, add lemon juice and zest, vanilla and almond extracts.

4. Pour into baked crust, lay plastic wrap flat on surface of filling, and refrigerate several hours until set.

5. *For topping:* Carefully remove plastic wrap from filling, spiral peach slices on top, and sprinkle with toasted sliced almonds.

6. Cut into 8 wedges and serve.

RECIPE FROM
*Celeste Skogerboe; Bemidji, Minnesota*

# JOANNE M. FRIEDMAN

*Newton, New Jersey*

This versatile cook (see her for Pasta di Cucina with Broccoli Rabe recipe, page 156) faced a tricky problem when her father requested a special dessert for his birthday. Ricotta pie, for many years a family favorite at her Italian grandmother's house in Philadelphia, was the obvious choice. But because her father had recently been put on a strict diabetic diet, she had to make changes in the old recipe. "The most difficult part was including just enough fat to keep the texture traditional while still maintaining the low-fat level and finding a sugar substitute that would hold up in baking," she recalls. Her dad was delighted with the result.

## *Italian Ricotta Pie*

*Makes a 9-inch pie, 10 servings*

*Whether made with sugar or sugar substitute (which Joanne uses because her father has diabetes), this pie bakes nicely and its filling is light and high.*

TIP: *To minimize the risk of spillage, set pie crust, still in its foil pan, in a standard 9-inch pie pan.*

*2 (9-inch) frozen deep-dish pie crusts, thawed*

*2 large eggs plus 4 large egg whites*

*3 cups part-skim ricotta cheese*

*1/2 cup granulated sugar or 3/4 cup aspartame sweetener made specifically for baking*

*1/3 cup coarsely chopped candied citron*

*3 teaspoons vanilla extract*

*1 tablespoon skim milk*

**PER SERVING (WITH SUGAR)**

320 calories

15 g fat (5 g saturated)

65 mg cholesterol

313 mg sodium

**PER SERVING (WITH SUGAR SUBSTITUTE)**

283 calories

15 g fat (5 g saturated)

65 mg cholesterol

313 mg sodium

1. Preheat oven to 400°F.

2. Prick bottom of one pie crust with fork, set in standard 9-inch pie pan, and bake uncovered just until crust begins to turn golden—about 10 minutes. Remove from oven and reduce oven temperature to 350°F. Spread second thawed pie crust on counter, then cut into strips 1 inch wide. Cover with plastic wrap and set aside.

3. Whisk eggs and egg whites until frothy in large bowl. Using rubber spatula, mix in ricotta, sugar or aspartame, citron, and vanilla. Pour into baked pie crust, then lay strips of pastry on top in lattice pattern, cutting as needed to fit and making sure ends of strips touch crust all around. Brush lattice strips with skim milk.

4. Bake uncovered until filling is set and pastry golden brown—45 to 55 minutes.

5. Remove pie from oven, set on wire rack, and cool to room temperature before cutting.

RECIPE FROM

*Joanne M. Friedman; Newton, New Jersey*

## BOBBIE LEE HATFIELD

*Myrtle Beach, South Carolina*

Bobbie Lee and her husband Harold, both retired telephone company employees, have two adult sons and enjoy easy, simple, and nutritious meals. "In 1993 I was diagnosed with breast cancer," writes Bobbie Lee. "After surgery and chemo, I decided to change my lifestyle for the health of myself and my family and started cutting fats in my favorite recipes. I work with each recipe until the taste and texture are satisfactory, not telling my husband until it is completed. I quit making changes only when I get a thumbs-up from him."

# Lee's Low-Fat Peanut Butter Pie

*Makes a 9-inch pie, 10 servings*

*Now that low-fat graham cracker crumb crusts are available, this recipe couldn't be easier.*

NOTE: *Instead of using commercial low-fat whipped topping in this recipe, we've substituted low-fat cream cheese whipped until silky smooth with evaporated skim milk. Our taste-testers pronounced the results "heavenly."*

1 (12-ounce) can evaporated skim milk

1 (¼-ounce) envelope plain gelatin

1 (8-ounce) package low-fat cream cheese (Neufchâtel), softened

½ cup confectioners (10X) sugar

¾ cup reduced-fat creamy peanut butter

3 teaspoons vanilla extract

1 (9-inch) prepared low-fat graham cracker crust

| PER SERVING |
| :---: |
| 264 calories |
| .... |
| 13 g fat (5 g saturated) |
| .... |
| 17 mg cholesterol |
| .... |
| 275 mg sodium |
| .... |

1. Whisk milk and gelatin together in medium-size heavy saucepan set over low heat. Whisk constantly until mixture boils and gelatin dissolves completely—about 2 minutes. Transfer to heatproof bowl and cool 15 minutes.

2. Meanwhile, beat cream cheese and 10X sugar at low mixer speed in large bowl

until smooth—about 1 minute. Scrape down sides of bowl, add peanut butter and vanilla, and beat 1 minute more. Again scrape down sides of bowl.

3. With mixer still at low speed, slowly add milk-gelatin mixture and beat until very smooth—about 2 minutes, scraping down sides of bowl at half time.

4. Set pie crust in 10-inch pie pan or on small baking sheet (this is to catch any spills), then carefully pour in peanut butter filling (it will come right to top of crust).

5. Set uncovered in refrigerator and chill several hours until set.

6. Cut into wedges and serve.

RECIPE FROM

*Bobbie Lee Hatfield; Myrtle Beach, South Carolina*

## CAROL ROSS
*Boyne City, Michigan*

"My husband and I loved the *tirami sù* at a local restaurant," says Carol, a retired speech/drama teacher who now keeps busy as a watercolorist and stone carver. "I decided to reproduce the recipe in low fat. Re-creating the creaminess of the original mascarpone cheese was the hardest part. And because I am an artist, the visual picture of the food is important, so I decided the dessert had better presentation if made like a Charlotte Russe. On a tour of northern Italy my husband dined on *tirami sù* six times—all the recipes in the different regions were excellent, but my low-calorie one could have fooled any of the chefs!"

# Carol's Tirami Sù

*Makes 16 servings*

*Translated literally,* tirami sù *means "pick-me-up." The original, writes John Mariani in* The Dictionary of Italian Food and Drink, *"was created in the 1960s at El Toulà restaurant in Treviso, Italy," and is made with a buttery cheese called mascarpone. This slimmed-down version substitutes part-skim ricotta cheese and churns it to silky smoothness in a food processor.*

**SHELL**
*36 lady fingers, halved crosswise*
*¼ cup strong black coffee (preferably espresso)
    mixed with 2 tablespoons Amaretto (almond liqueur)*

**FILLING**
*2 (8-ounce) packages low-fat cream cheese (Neufchâtel),
    softened*
*3 tablespoons granulated sugar*
*2 (8-ounce) containers nonfat coffee-flavored yogurt*
*3 tablespoons unsweetened cocoa powder*
*2 tablespoons cornstarch*
*2 teaspoons instant espresso granules*

**PER SERVING**

231 calories
....
11 fat (6 g saturated)
....
118 mg cholesterol
....
206 mg sodium
....

*1½ cups part-skim ricotta cheese*

*2 tablespoons confectioners (10X) sugar*

*1 tablespoon unsweetened cocoa powder*

1. *For shell:* Stand 24 lady finger halves, cut sides in, around edge of 9-inch spring-form pan, then cut and piece half of remaining lady fingers to cover bottom of pan; reserve balance of lady fingers. Brush espresso-Amaretto mixture evenly over lady-finger shell to moisten. Set shell aside.

2. *For filling:* Pulse cream cheese and granulated sugar in food processor 1 minute, scraping down work bowl sides after 30 seconds. Add yogurt, cocoa, cornstarch, and espresso granules and pulse until completely smooth—about 1 minute, again scraping down work bowl sides at half time. Transfer filling to bowl and reserve. Also wipe food processor work bowl and blade clean.

3. *For topping:* Pulse ricotta in food processor until completely smooth—about 2 minutes, scraping down work bowl sides twice. Add 10X sugar and pulse just to combine.

4. Pour half of filling into lady-finger shell, add half of topping mixture, smoothing to edges, then cover with remaining lady fingers, cutting and piecing as needed. Spoon remaining filling over lady fingers and "frost" with remaining topping.

5. Cover with plastic wrap and chill at least 4 hours.

6. Just before serving, dust topping with 1 tablespoon cocoa.

RECIPE FROM

*Carol Ross; Boyne City, Michigan*

# Karen's Chocolate Pudding with Pralined Pecans

*Makes 6 servings*

*Karen is Karen Pickus,* Good Morning America's *Chef/Food Stylist, who tested all the recipes for this cookbook. This particular recipe, her own creation, is her young daughter Marjolaine's favorite because it combines her favorite tastes and textures—chocolatey, nutty, creamy. To complement the smoothness of the pudding, Karen adds the crunch of pralined pecans. Also see Karen's recipe for Broiled Marinated Lamb with Mediterranean Vegetables (page 119).*

## PUDDING
1/4 cup unsweetened Dutch process cocoa powder

3 tablespoons cornstarch

1/3 cup sugar

3 cups skim milk

1 ounce unsweetened chocolate, finely chopped

2 teaspoons vanilla extract

## PECANS
1 teaspoon egg white

1/3 cup coarsely chopped pecans

1 1/2 teaspoons sugar

1/8 teaspoon salt

## TOPPING
1 recipe Skinny Whipped Topping (page 275)

| PER SERVING |
| --- |
| 271 calories |
| .... |
| 8 g fat (2 g saturated) |
| .... |
| 5 mg cholesterol |
| .... |
| 116 mg sodium |
| .... |

1. *For pudding:* Whisk together cocoa, cornstarch, and sugar in medium-size heavy saucepan, then slowly whisk in milk. Set over moderately high heat and bring quickly to boiling. Reduce heat to moderately low and cook, whisking constantly, until thickened—about 2 minutes.

2. Remove from heat, add chocolate and vanilla, and whisk until chocolate melts completely about 1 minute.

3. Divide pudding among six ungreased $\frac{1}{2}$-cup ramekins. If you want to serve puddings warm, cool 45 minutes. If you want to serve them cold, refrigerate several hours.

4. *Meanwhile, prepare pecans:* Preheat oven to 350°F. Place egg white in ramekin and whisk with fork until frothy. Place nuts on ungreased large baking sheet, add egg white, and stir until nuts are completely covered. Sprinkle with sugar and salt and stir until nuts are evenly coated.

5. Spread nuts on baking sheet and bake uncovered until lightly toasted—about 5 minutes. Remove from oven and cool to room temperature.

6. To serve, spoon Skinny Whipped Topping on chocolate pudding, dividing total amount evenly, then sprinkle with pralined pecans.

RECIPE FROM

*Karen Pickus; New York, New York*

## ZIVA SANTOP

*Agoura Hills, California*

Ziva, a native of Johannesburg, South Africa, taught herself to cook. Although she likes cooking (and eating) chocolate desserts, a vegetarian diet combined with exercise and calorie control keeps her weight under control. "My family loves bread pudding but because of health problems we have tended to stay away from desserts," she says. "Now that numerous low-fat products are available, it's easier to create tasty low-fat desserts. Since chocolate and banana go well together, I decided to combine them to create this bread pudding."

# *Low-Fat Chocolate-Banana Bread Pudding*

*Makes 6 servings*

*Nonfat yogurt, low-fat cocoa, evaporated skim milk, and egg whites may be the dieter's best friends. Teamed with bananas, rum, cinnamon, and nutmeg, they lighten up an old favorite without sacrificing an ounce of goodness.*

1½ cups nonfat plain yogurt

½ cup evaporated skim milk

½ cup low-fat cocoa powder

4 large egg whites

½ cup firmly packed dark brown sugar

¼ cup granulated sugar

2 tablespoons dark rum

3 teaspoons vanilla extract

1 teaspoon ground cinnamon

½ teaspoon freshly grated nutmeg

¼ teaspoon salt

¼ cup semisweet chocolate chips

2 medium-size ripe bananas

| PER SERVING |
| --- |
| 333 calories |
| .... |
| 4 g fat (2 g saturated) |
| .... |
| 2 mg cholesterol |
| .... |
| 344 mg sodium |
| .... |

*3 cups day-old firm-textured white bread, cut into ½-inch cubes*
  *(about 6 slices)*

*1 teaspoon confectioners (10X) sugar*

1. Preheat oven to 350°F. Coat 9 x 5 x 3-inch loaf pan with nonstick cooking spray and set aside.

2. Combine all ingredients except bananas, bread cubes, and 10X sugar in large bowl.

3. Peel bananas, chunk, then purée 2 minutes in food processor or electric blender at high speed. Scrape down work bowl sides and churn 1 minute longer until completely smooth.

4. Blend banana purée into pudding mixture, fold in bread cubes, and let stand 20 minutes at room temperature.

5. Pour pudding mixture into prepared pan and bake uncovered until pudding is completely set and a cake tester inserted in center comes out clean—about 1 hour and 10 minutes. Transfer pudding to wire rack and cool in upright pan for 20 minutes—pudding should still be warm.

6. Sift 10X sugar on top of pudding and serve.

RECIPE FROM
*Ziva Santop; Agoura Hills, California*

Diane, a homemaker and mother of two, is married to an attorney and works part time as a cashier at a local grocery store. She attributes her cooking skills to her mother and to the chefs she worked with in earlier restaurant jobs. Diane's approach to cooking is like her approach to dieting: simple and sensible. To lose twenty-two pounds, she started the day with a good breakfast, drank a can of diet formula for lunch, had a sensible dinner, and walked forty-five to fifty minutes in the evenings. To create this deceptively rich-tasting pudding, she started with a basic recipe and simply cut back on fat.

# *Bread Pudding*

*Makes 6 servings*

*What makes this bread pudding special is that the only sweetener is maple syrup—pure maple syrup, not pancake syrup with ersatz maple flavoring. It's also made with egg whites only and no fat, which explains the low nutrient counts all round.*

TIP: *For best results, use a firm-textured or home-style bread, not the squishy stuff.*

*6 large egg whites*

*1¾ cups evaporated skim milk*

*½ cup plus 6 tablespoons pure maple syrup
(see headnote above)*

*3 teaspoons vanilla extract*

*1 teaspoon ground cinnamon*

*½ teaspoon ground nutmeg*

*6 slices firm-textured white bread, cut into ½-inch cubes (do not remove crusts)*

**PER SERVING**

295 calories

....

1 fat (0 g saturated)

....

3 mg cholesterol

....

335 mg sodium

....

1. Pulse egg whites, milk, ½ cup maple syrup, vanilla, cinnamon, and nutmeg in food processor until foamy—about 30 seconds. Pour into medium-size bowl, fold in bread cubes, cover with plastic wrap, and refrigerate 4 hours.

2. Preheat oven to 350°F. Coat 9 x 5 x 3-inch loaf pan with nonstick cooking spray (preferably butter-flavored).

3. Pour pudding mixture into prepared pan and bake uncovered until knife inserted in center comes out clean—50 to 55 minutes. Remove from oven and cool in upright pan on wire rack 20 to 30 minutes.

4. To serve, cut into six slices—right in pan—arrange on dessert plates, and top each portion with 1 tablespoon of the remaining maple syrup.

RECIPE FROM

*Diane Schofield; Penfield, New York*

## RACHEL W. N. BROWN

*Mt. Sidney, Virginia*

"I first read about French Cream many years ago," writes Rachel, who owns a quilting shop and is married to a minister. "But the ingredients were extremely rich—cream cheese, whipping cream, sour cream. When I wanted something special for a holiday dessert, I began substituting one low-fat alternative at a time, and finally added the berry sauce, which completes the dish and makes a great presentation. I serve it often for dinner groups because it can be made ahead and looks as though it could be served in the finest restaurant. Our friends call it the 'uptown' look!"

# French Cream, Skinnied Down and Gussied Up

*Makes 8 servings*

*"Simply elegant" is a good way to describe this cool creamy dessert with its sauce of puréed berries.*

NOTE: *If you like, add a couple of teaspoons orange liqueur to the sauce—not in Rachel Brown's original recipe but a nice addition. It will up the calories only slightly.*

**FRENCH CREAM**

*1 (8-ounce) package low-fat cream cheese (Neufchâtel), softened*

*1 (8-ounce) container low-fat sour cream*

*1 (12-ounce) can evaporated skim milk*

*¾ cup sugar*

*1 (¼-ounce) envelope plain gelatin*

*3 teaspoons vanilla extract*

**SAUCE**

*1 (12-ounce) package frozen unsweetened mixed berries (strawberries, raspberries, and blueberries), partially thawed*

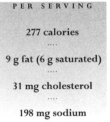

**PER SERVING**

277 calories

····

9 g fat (6 g saturated)

····

31 mg cholesterol

····

198 mg sodium

····

3 tablespoons sugar

$^1/_2$ teaspoon almond extract

ACCOMPANIMENT
1 pint red-ripe strawberries, hulled and quartered, or 1 pint fresh raspberries
   or blueberries

1. Coat eight $^1/_2$-cup custard cups or ramekins with nonstick cooking spray and set aside.

2. *For French cream:* Beat cream cheese in medium-size bowl at high electric mixer speed until smooth—about 2 minutes. Add sour cream and again beat until smooth—2 minutes more.

3. Combine evaporated milk and sugar in small heavy saucepan and sprinkle in gelatin. Set over moderate heat and heat, stirring often, just until sugar and gelatin dissolve—2 to 3 minutes.

4. Pour hot milk mixture into cream cheese mixture and beat at medium speed until completely smooth—about 2 minutes. Stir in vanilla.

5. Divide cream cheese mixture evenly among 8 prepared custard cups, set on baking sheet, cover with plastic wrap, and refrigerate overnight.

6. *For sauce:* Pulse mixed berries, sugar, and almond extract in electric blender or food processor until completely smooth—2 to $2^1/_2$ minutes.

7. To serve, dip custard cups quickly in very hot water, loosen around edges with tip of paring knife, then invert on eight dessert plates. Top each portion with sauce, dividing total amount evenly, then spoon strawberries alongside, again dividing amount evenly.

RECIPE FROM
*Rachel W. N. Brown; Mt. Sidney, Virginia*

In the community where Emily lives with her husband, a social worker, and three daughters, life includes frequent fellowship dinners at church. "There's always a tempting array of desserts," Emily says, "but several people are diabetic and unable to eat sugar. They would ask me what I had brought, and when I told them 'cake,' they would say they wished they could eat it. I made my family's favorite rice pudding one day and realized it could easily be made sugar-free and low-fat. Now I make it often and take it to church dinners and other socials. It means a lot to people who can't eat sugar to find something sweet that tastes as good as the real thing!"

# *Lower-Calorie Rice Pudding*
### *Makes 4 servings*

*What dieters so often crave is comfort food—something sweet and creamy like this easy rice pudding. The best rice to use for it is long-grain white rice. Emily Edens, whose recipe this is, makes her rice pudding with aspartame sweetener. We give you a choice: real sugar or sugar substitute.*

*1 cup water*

*½ cup uncooked long-grain white rice*

*3 cups skim milk*

*½ cup sugar or ¼ cup aspartame sweetener made specifically for baking*

*1 large egg plus 2 large egg whites, lightly beaten*

*½ cup golden seedless raisins*

*2 teaspoons vanilla extract*

*1 teaspoon ground cinnamon*

**PER SERVING (WITH SUGAR)**

342 calories

2 g fat (0.7 g saturated)

56 mg cholesterol

142 mg sodium

**PER SERVING (WITH SUGAR SUBSTITUTE)**

247 calories

2 g fat (0.7 g saturated)

56 mg cholesterol

142 mg sodium

1. Bring water to boiling in large heavy saucepan over moderately high heat. Add rice and cook uncovered, stirring occasionally, for 8 minutes.

2. Stir in milk and sugar (*but not aspartame sweetener*) and bring to a boil. Adjust heat so liquid barely bubbles, cover, and cook until rice is soft—about 1 hour. Watch pot closely and if rice threatens to stick, turn heat to lowest point, and if necessary, slide an insulator between pan and burner.

3. Using fork, mix beaten egg and egg whites into pudding and continue beating just until eggs cook—about 1 minute.

4. Stir in raisins and vanilla, and if using, aspartame sweetener.

5. Spoon into four dessert bowls, dust with cinnamon, and serve hot.

RECIPE FROM

*Emily Oaks Edens; Sanders, Kentucky*

## ALYS R. DISTERDICK

*Thousand Palms, California*

Born in Indiana and transplanted to California, Alys looks at least twenty years younger than her actual age, possibly because eating "plain food" has kept her weight within fifteen pounds of what it was in her teens (today at five feet, eight inches she weighs 147 pounds). Her deceptively simple recipe for date pudding is one she remembers seeing prepared by her mother, who taught her to cook. Although she has given the recipe, over the years, to a number of friends, Alys says she has never seen a similar recipe, or tasted a similar pudding.

*Makes 6 servings*

*A lovely old-fashioned recipe lightened up for today's times.*

NOTE: *For directions on how to toast chopped almonds, see the Note for Amaretto-Baked Pears in Pastry (page 254). Top, if you like, with a commercial low-fat whipped topping. Better yet, use our Skinny Whipped Topping.*

*¹/₂ cup coarsely chopped toasted almonds
  (see Note above)*

*1¹/₂ cups sifted all-purpose flour*

*1 cup coarsely chopped pitted dates*

*1 teaspoon baking soda*

*1 cup boiling water*

*2 teaspoons unsalted butter*

*²/₃ cup sugar*

*3 teaspoons vanilla extract*

OPTIONAL TOPPING
*Skinny Whipped Topping (page 275)*

| PER SERVING |
| --- |
| 337 calories |
| .... |
| 6 g fat (1 g saturated) |
| .... |
| 3 mg cholesterol |
| .... |
| 212 mg sodium |
| .... |

1. Preheat oven to 350°F. Coat 8 x 8 x 2-inch baking pan with nonstick cooking spray (preferably butter-flavored) and set aside.

2. Toss almonds with flour in small bowl and set aside. Place dates in medium-size heatproof bowl, mix in baking soda, boiling water, and butter, and let stand just until butter melts—3 to 4 minutes.

3. Using rubber spatula, mix in sugar, almond-flour mixture, and vanilla and stir only enough to combine.

4. Turn into prepared pan, spreading to corners, and bake uncovered until nicely browned and firm to the touch—35 to 40 minutes.

5. Transfer pudding to wire rack, cool in upright pan 20 minutes, then cut into six squares and serve warm. Drift each portion, if you like, with rounded table-spoon Skinny Whipped Topping.

RECIPE FROM

*Alys R. Disterdick; Thousand Palms, California*

Born in France, Brigitte received her first lessons in cooking from her mother, went on to study at the Cordon Bleu in Paris, and today is chef in a private home where she likes best to cook French and Chinese specialties and particularly enjoys offering "grande cuisine" with careful attention to presentation. "I tried to perfect a light dessert using bananas and found an exotic sauce to go with it," she says. "It is very easy, quick, and low in calories. And everyone loves it—my employers, my family, and all my friends."

# *Banana Flan with Exotic Sauce*

*Makes 6 servings*

*An unusual pudding that combines the flavors of India and the South Pacific. What makes the sauce exotic is the teaming of mango chutney, cardamom, ginger, vanilla, and Angostura bitters.*

**FLAN**

*6 medium-size ripe bananas (about 2½ pounds), peeled and sliced ½ inch thick*

*1 tablespoon fresh lime juice*

*⅓ cup cool brewed orange or mango tea*

*1 large egg plus 1 large egg white*

*2 tablespoons honey*

*2 tablespoons low-fat sweetened condensed milk*

**SAUCE**

*2 tablespoons flour*

*1 cup water*

*2 tablespoons sugar*

*1 (1-inch) piece fresh ginger, peeled and sliced ¼ inch thick*

*1 tablespoon finely chopped mango chutney*

*3 teaspoons vanilla extract*

| PER SERVING |
|:---:|
| 189 calories |
| .... |
| 2 g fat (0.6 g saturated) |
| .... |
| 36 mg cholesterol |
| .... |
| 54 mg sodium |
| .... |

*1 teaspoon Angostura bitters*

*½ teaspoon ground cardamom*

1. Preheat oven to 375°F. Coat six shallow (½-cup) ramekins with nonstick cooking spray (preferably butter-flavored) and set aside.

2. *For flan:* Pulse bananas and lime juice in food processor 1 minute. Scrape down work bowl sides, add remaining ingredients, and pulse 1 minute more.

3. Divide evenly among prepared ramekins, set in 13 x 9 x 2-inch baking pan, then pour enough hot water into pan to come one-third of the way up ramekins. Bake uncovered until tops of flans are firm—about 45 minutes. Transfer to wire rack, cool to room temperature, then cover and refrigerate overnight.

4. *For sauce:* Blend flour and water in small heavy saucepan, whisking until smooth. Add sugar and ginger, and bring to a quick boil over moderately high heat, whisking constantly. Adjust heat so mixture bubbles gently and cook 5 minutes longer, whisking all the while. Strain sauce, then mix in all remaining ingredients.

5. To serve, carefully loosen flans by running sharp paring knife around edge of ramekins, tapping lightly, and inverting onto dessert plates.

6. Spoon 2 tablespoons sauce around each flan and serve.

RECIPE FROM

*Brigitte Cox; Hobe Sound, Florida*

# DIANNE KAATZ

*Spokane, Washington*

Dianne is owner and director of a real estate and mortgage company. Born and brought up in British Columbia, she taught herself to cook and today enjoys preparing "anything that's fattening!" although despite that preference she has managed to lose about thirty pounds and keep half of it off. This versatile and easily prepared fruit pudding is one she adapted from an old Irish recipe, cutting down fat and using fresh fruits in season. It proved to be a great hit with her family.

# *Upside-Down Peach Pudding Cake*

*Makes 8 servings*

*Like many homey fruit puddings, this one's wonderfully versatile (substitute canned pitted plums or cherries for peaches, if you like) but it won't get A-plus for visuals. In the oven, it "bubbles and carries on like a science project," someone said, separating into three layers— a sweet crust, a thin custardy layer, and peaches, some under the crust and some showing. This pudding cake's even better with a topping of some sort. We recommend our Skinny Whipped Topping (per-tablespoon nutrient counts for the topping are given with that recipe on page 275) or a nonfat yogurt (frozen or otherwise), especially vanilla or lemon.*

NOTE: *You can spice the pudding up a bit by adding $^1/_2$ teaspoon each ground cinnamon and ginger and $^1/_4$ teaspoon ground nutmeg along with the flour in step 3.*

*1 tablespoon unsalted butter*

*1 cup sifted all-purpose flour*

*1 cup sugar*

*1 cup skim milk*

*1 teaspoon baking powder*

*$^1/_2$ teaspoon baking soda*

*$^1/_8$ teaspoon salt*

| PER SERVING |
| :---: |
| 202 calories |
| .... |
| 2 g fat (1 g saturated) |
| .... |
| 4 mg cholesterol |
| .... |
| 192 mg sodium |
| .... |

1 *(16-ounce) bag frozen unsweetened sliced peaches, separated but not thawed*

OPTIONAL TOPPING
*Skinny Whipped Topping (page 275)*

1. Preheat oven to 350°F.

2. Place butter in 13 x 9 x 2-inch baking pan and set in oven just long enough for butter to melt—1 to 2 minutes. Remove pan from oven, tilting this way and that to coat evenly with melted butter.

3. Next, add to pan in order listed but without stirring flour, sugar, milk, baking powder, baking soda, and salt. Whisk or fork briskly just enough to combine—batter should be lumpy. Fold in frozen peach slices, distributing evenly, or, if you prefer, simply lay them on top, again distributing evenly.

4. Bake uncovered until nicely browned—25 to 30 minutes.

5. Cool 15 minutes in upright pan on wire rack, then cut into squares and serve, topping each portion, if you like, with a rounded tablespoon Skinny Whipped Topping.

RECIPE FROM
*Dianne Kaatz; Spokane, Washington*

# CAKES AND COOKIES

Plain and Fancy Tea Cake *(Finalist, Desserts)*     218

Nonna's Raw Apple Cake     220

Heavenly Chocolate Pudding Cake with Hot Fudge–Kahlúa Sauce     222

It's My Chocolate Cake     224

Chocoholic's Carob Cake with Orange Marmalade and Carob Frosting     226

Sara Moulton's Angel Food Cake with Mocha Sauce     228

Spicy Whole-Wheat Angel Food Cake     230

Dream Shares     232

Caramel Apricot Brownies     234

Jennifer's Really Good Low-Fat Chocolate Chip Cookies     236

Peanut Butter–Chocolate Chip Cookies     238

Toffee Chip Cookies     240

Energy Cookies     242

Quick-as-a-Wink Lemon Balls     244

Lemon Meringue Cookies     246

## FLORENCE E. GOODMAN

*Beverly, Massachusetts*

This homemaker and mother of three was born in New York and credits Public School 82 in Queens (along with her grandmother) with teaching her how to cook. Some time ago Florence succeeded in losing forty pounds simply by disciplining herself to eat less, and has maintained that weight loss. Keeping up with medical recommendations concerning diets, she has revised all her favorite recipes to reduce salt, sugar, and "bad" fats. These new recipes, friends and relatives agree, produce dishes that taste better and are more digestible than the originals.

FINALIST, DESSERTS

# *Plain and Fancy Tea Cake*

*Makes an 8-inch Bundt cake, 14 servings*

*The size of the Bundt pan is critical to the success of this recipe. Make sure that it measures 8 inches across the top, then determine the volume by filling the pan to the brim with water (use a 1-pint or 1-quart measure to add water). The pan should hold 6 cups exactly, no more, no less.*

**BATTER**

*2 large egg whites, lightly beaten*

*1 teaspoon baking soda*

*1½ teaspoons baking powder*

*⅛ teaspoon salt*

*½ teaspoon ground nutmeg*

*3 teaspoons vanilla extract*

*2 tablespoons olive oil*

*1 cup granulated sugar*

*½ cup unsweetened applesauce*

*¾ cup nonfat plain yogurt*

*2 teaspoons finely grated orange zest*

**PER SERVING**

173 calories

....

3 g fat (0.4 g saturated)

....

0 mg cholesterol

....

182 mg sodium

....

*¼ cup fresh orange juice*

*1 cup sifted all-purpose flour*

*1 cup unsifted whole-wheat flour*

STREAK
*¼ cup firmly packed dark brown sugar*

*2 tablespoons finely ground walnuts*

*2 teaspoons ground cinnamon*

TOPPING
*2 teaspoons confectioners (10X) sugar*

1. With oven rack in middle position, preheat oven to 350°F. Coat 8-inch (6-cup) Bundt pan with nonstick cooking spray and set aside.

2. *For batter:* Place all batter ingredients except all-purpose and whole-wheat flours in large bowl in order listed, then whisk until smooth. Add the two flours and with large rubber spatula, fold in lightly. Don't overbeat or cake may be tough.

3. *For streak:* Combine all ingredients in small bowl.

4. Pour half the batter into prepared pan, sprinkle streak mixture evenly on top, then cover with remaining batter.

5. Bake on middle oven rack until cake is firm to the touch and pulls away from sides of the pan—40 to 45 minutes.

6. Cool cake in upright pan on wire rack 15 minutes. Shake pan lightly to loosen cake, invert on rack, and cool to room temperature.

7. Sift 10X sugar over cake, cut into 14 slim wedges, and serve.

RECIPE FROM

*Florence E. Goodman; Beverly, Massachusetts*

## ALBA BRAGOLI-HARDING
*Norfolk, Virginia*

Born in Italy and taught to cook in Tuscany by her mother and grandmother, Alba today has a son and two young grandchildren. When she's not practicing the unusual profession of courtroom sketch artist, she enjoys preparing Italian regional foods for her family. "This apple cake is my grandmother's recipe," she writes, "with the fat halved and applesauce added for moistness. Although in true Italian fashion I never measure anything, this recipe can stand variation quite well, also additions of raisins, walnuts, pine nuts, or chestnuts. My family loves it, especially in fall and winter."

# Nonna's Raw Apple Cake

*Makes a 10-inch tube cake, 14 servings*

*The best apples to use for this cake are Galas, Golden Delicious, Ida Reds, or Jonagolds because they're blessed with rich apple flavor and don't cook down to mush. Four cups of thinly sliced apples go into the batter and one cup is layered on top, giving the baked cake nice crunch.*

TIP: *Instead of coating the pan with nonstick spray, then dusting with flour, you can use one of the nonstick sprays that also contains flour, saving yourself an extra step.*

1¾ cups sifted all-purpose flour

2 teaspoons baking powder

5 cups peeled, cored, and thinly sliced apples
   (see headnote above) (about 5 small or 4 medium-size
   apples)

2 teaspoons ground cinnamon

1 cup plus 3 tablespoons sugar

6 tablespoons vegetable oil

2 large eggs plus 1 large egg white

| PER SERVING |
| --- |
| 214 calories |
| .... |
| 7 g fat (0.7 g saturated) |
| .... |
| 30 mg cholesterol |
| .... |
| 83 mg sodium |
| .... |

*¹⁄₂ cup unsweetened applesauce*

*¹⁄₃ cup fresh orange juice*

*3 teaspoons vanilla extract*

1. With oven rack in middle position, preheat oven to 350°F. Coat 10-inch tube pan with nonstick cooking spray, then dust with flour, tapping out excess. Set pan aside.

2. Whisk flour and baking powder together in shallow bowl to combine; set aside also.

3. Place sliced apples in large bowl, add cinnamon and 3 tablespoons sugar, and toss well. Let stand while you prepare cake batter.

4. Using hand electric mixer at low speed, beat remaining 1 cup sugar with oil until well blended—about 1 minute. Add eggs and egg white, applesauce, orange juice, and vanilla and continue beating at low speed until well combined—about 1 minute.

5. Fold in reserved flour mixture, then 4 cups sliced apples together with all accumulated juices. Pour into prepared pan, smoothing to edges, then arrange remaining 1 cup sliced apples decoratively on top.

6. Bake until cake pulls from sides of pan, is springy to the touch, and a cake tester inserted midway between edge and central tube comes out clean—about 1 hour and 10 minutes.

7. Cool cake in upright pan on wire rack 30 minutes, loosen around edge and central tube, and invert on wire rack. Turn cake right-side up so apples are on top and cool to room temperature before serving.

RECIPE FROM

*Alba Bragoli-Harding; Norfolk, Virginia*

## LESLIE S. COUICK

*Rock Hill, South Carolina*

A valued volunteer in church and community, Leslie still finds time to cook—a skill she learned from her grandparents. "It took me a couple of weeks and several baked cakes before I perfected this recipe," she explains. "My husband loves chocolate and I wanted a recipe that would be healthy and low in fat but also rich and satisfying. I incorporated prunes for added fiber and applesauce to replace fat. Fat-free chocolate sauce makes the recipe convenient and Kahlúa makes it divine!"

# Heavenly Chocolate Pudding Cake with Hot Fudge-Kahlúa Sauce

*Makes a 9-inch square cake, 12 servings*

*Puréed prunes and applesauce take the place of shortening in this lean and lovely cake. The substitution of cornstarch for some of the flour keeps it light.*

NOTE: *We've made ice cream an optional accompaniment, and the nutrient counts below do not include it. If you add low-fat ice cream, you will increase the per-person counts by 50 calories, 1 gram fat (0.3 gram saturated), 3 milligrams cholesterol, and 25 milligrams sodium.*

SHORTCUT: *Instead of melting hot fudge sauce in the top of a double boiler, you can do it six times faster in a microwave oven. Here's how: Scoop fudge topping into a 1-quart microwave-safe glass measure, cover with waxed paper, and microwave 30 seconds on High. Remove from oven, whisk until smooth, then add Kahlúa slowly, whisking all the while. Easy does it!*

**CAKE**

1½ cups sifted all-purpose flour

½ cup unsweetened cocoa powder

¼ cup cornstarch

1 teaspoon baking powder

½ teaspoon baking soda

¼ teaspoon salt

**PER SERVING**

277 calories

. . . .

2 g fat (0.5 g saturated)

. . . .

19 mg cholesterol

. . . .

335 mg sodium

. . . .

*¹⁄₂ cup firmly packed pitted prunes*

*¹⁄₂ cup unsweetened applesauce*

*6 tablespoons hot water*

*³⁄₄ cup sugar*

*1 large egg plus 2 large egg whites*

*1 cup nonfat buttermilk*

*3 teaspoons vanilla extract*

TOPPING
*1 (16-ounce) jar fat-free hot fudge topping (see Shortcut)*

*¹⁄₄ cup Kahlúa or other coffee or chocolate liqueur*

OPTIONAL ACCOMPANIMENT
*1¹⁄₂ pints low-fat coffee ice cream*

1. With oven rack in middle position, preheat oven to 350°F. Coat 9 x 9 x 2-inch baking dish with nonstick cooking spray and set aside.

2. *For cake:* Whisk flour, cocoa, cornstarch, baking powder, baking soda, and salt together in large bowl, make well in center, and set aside.

3. Purée prunes with applesauce and water in food processor by pulsing briskly. Scrape down work bowl sides, then churn mixture until absolutely smooth—about 5 minutes. Add sugar and pulse 1 minute, then add egg and egg whites and pulse until well blended—about 1 minute more.

4. Dump prune mixture into well in dry ingredients along with buttermilk and vanilla, and fold just until smooth. Don't overbeat or cake may be tough.

5. Pour batter into prepared baking dish, smoothing to edges, and bake until cake is springy to the touch and cake tester inserted in middle comes out clean—about 30 minutes. Cool cake to room temperature in upright pan on wire rack.

6. *Meanwhile, prepare topping:* Heat and stir fudge topping in double boiler over barely simmering water until melted—about 3 minutes. Remove from heat and blend in Kahlúa. Spread smoothly on cooled cake.

7. To serve, cut cake into 12 large squares and top each portion, if you like, with ¹⁄₄ cup ice cream.

RECIPE FROM
*Leslie S. Couick; Rock Hill, South Carolina*

*Chatham, Virginia*

This self-described rural Virginian, a former schoolteacher, mother of two sons, and grandmother of two granddaughters, enjoys quilting, golfing, gardening (both vegetables and flowers), collecting pottery, and cooking food that is "highly spiced, fancy, and tasty." In January 1998 she embarked on a structured diet program that allowed her no sugar and very little fat, and since that time has lost fifty-five pounds. Meanwhile, her taste for chocolate cake led her to work out a recipe low in fat, sugar, and calories. "Normally I use absolutely *no* flour," she explains, "so the hard part was getting the idea of making flour from oatmeal. After that I just added ingredients allowed on my diet."

# *It's My Chocolate Cake*

*Makes a 13 x 9 x 2-inch loaf cake, 15 servings*

*If you make this cake with aspartame sugar substitute, be sure to use the one that is* marked specifically for baking, *not the one in little packets that you use to sweeten coffee or tea. The two are not the same, and only the one designed for baking will work properly here.*

CAKE

2¼ cups unsifted oat flour

1½ cups nonfat dry milk powder

⅓ cup unsweetened cocoa powder

1½ teaspoons baking powder

1 teaspoon baking soda

½ teaspoon ground cinnamon

⅛ teaspoon salt

1 (23-ounce) jar unsweetened applesauce

⅔ cup granulated sugar, or ½ cup plus 2 tablespoons
    aspartame sweetener made specifically for baking
    (see headnote above)

PER SERVING
(WITH SUGAR)

224 calories

5 g fat (3 g saturated)

12 mg cholesterol

208 mg sodium

PER SERVING (WITH
SUGAR SUBSTITUTE)

182 calories

5 g fat (3 g saturated)

12 mg cholesterol

247 mg sodium

5 large egg whites, lightly beaten

3 teaspoons vanilla extract

FROSTING

1 (8-ounce) package low-fat cream cheese (Neufchâtel), softened

1 cup confectioners (10X) sugar, or ½ cup aspartame sweetener made specifically for baking

½ cup unsweetened cocoa powder

3 teaspoons vanilla extract

3 tablespoons skim milk

1. Preheat oven to 325°F. Coat 13 x 9 x 2-inch baking pan with nonstick cooking spray and set aside.

2. *For cake:* Combine oat flour, dry milk powder, cocoa, baking powder, baking soda, cinnamon, and salt in large mixing bowl. Add all remaining ingredients and, with wooden spoon, stir just enough to mix—no more or you may toughen the cake.

3. Pour batter into prepared pan, smoothing to edges, and bake until springy to the touch and cake tester inserted in middle of cake comes out clean—about 25 minutes.

4. Cool cake to room temperature in upright pan on wire rack.

5. *Meanwhile, prepare frosting:* With electric mixer at low speed, beat cream cheese, 10X sugar, cocoa, and vanilla in small bowl until smooth—about 1 minute. Slowly add skim milk and beat until a good spreading consistency—about 1 minute more.

6. Swirl frosting over top of cake, cut into 15 squares, and serve.

RECIPE FROM

*Margaret Shelton; Chatham, Virginia*

## AMY L. WASSERMAN
*Pelham, Massachusetts*

Amy, a collage illustrator who likes to cook gourmet vegan/vegetarian dishes, also creates tempting desserts. "When I cut meat out of my diet, I started to lose weight," she says. "More recently, I cut out sugar and have maintained my current slim weight." But when she was advised to lay off chocolate, Amy knew she'd have to find a substitute. "I had a carob cake recipe but it had a strong, bitter.carob flavor and a lot of fat too," she explained. "I found that decaf espresso did the trick for the flavor and that bananas can replace oil or fat in recipes. It took me only a few attempts to perfect the recipe."

# Chocoholic's Carob Cake with Orange Marmalade and Carob Frosting

*Makes a 9-inch, 2-layer cake, 14 servings*

*Carob powder, unlike cocoa, is very low in fat (23 percent lower, in fact) but its sugar content is nine times that of cocoa. This cake is made entirely without shortening. And maple syrup takes the place of refined sugar.*

**FOR PREPARING PANS**
*Nonstick cooking spray*

*2 tablespoons carob powder*

**CAKE**
*1½ cups sifted all-purpose flour*

*¾ cup carob powder*

*1 teaspoon baking powder*

*1 teaspoon baking soda*

*⅛ teaspoon salt*

*2 large very ripe large bananas, peeled and chunked*

*1 cup pure maple syrup*

*1 large egg plus 2 large egg whites*

*3 teaspoons vanilla extract*

*3 teaspoons instant espresso granules*

*1 cup nonfat buttermilk*

**PER SERVING**

234 calories
....
3 g fat (2 g saturated)
....
23 mg cholesterol
....
192 mg sodium
....

¾ *cup carob powder*

½ *cup confectioners (10 X) sugar*

*3 tablespoons unsalted butter, at room temperature*

½ *cup skim milk (about)*

FILLING
¼ *cup orange marmalade*

1. With oven rack in middle position, preheat oven to 350°F. Next, prepare pans: Coat two 9-inch layer cake pans with nonstick cooking spray, add 1 tablespoon carob powder to each, then tip pans this way and that to coat bottoms and sides evenly. Top out excess carob powder and set pans aside.

2. *For cake:* Whisk flour, carob powder, baking powder, baking soda, and salt together in large bowl and set aside.

3. Purée bananas by churning 3 minutes in food processor. Scrape down work bowl sides, add maple syrup, egg and egg whites, vanilla, and coffee granules and churn until completely smooth—about 1 minute more.

4. Pour banana mixture into large mixing bowl and, using large rubber spatula, mix in dry ingredients alternately with buttermilk, beginning and ending with dry ingredients and taking care not to overbeat or cake may be tough.

5. Divide batter between prepared pans and bake until cake tester inserted in center of cakes comes out clean—30 to 35 minutes. Cool layers in upright pans on wire racks to room temperature, then loosen carefully around edges and turn out on separate racks.

6. *For frosting:* With electric mixer at low speed, cream carob powder, 10X sugar, and butter until fluffy—about 2 minutes. With mixer still at low speed, add milk, 1 tablespoon at a time, until frosting is good spreading consistency.

7. *To assemble cake:* Using marmalade as filling, sandwich two layers together, then frost top and sides of cake. Cut into 14 wedges and serve.

RECIPE FROM

*Amy L. Wasserman; Pelham, Massachusetts*

# Sara Moulton's Angel Food Cake with Mocha Sauce

*Makes a 10-inch tube cake, 12 servings*

*More angel food cakes fail because of overbeaten egg whites than underbeaten ones. They should peak nicely, yes, but they should be glistening and moist, not dry. Also see Sara's two other low-fat, low-cal recipes: Ginger-Poached Filet of Beef with Vegetables and Horseradish Sauce (page 108) and Roast Pork Tenderloin with Garlic and Apples (page 124).*

**CAKE**

1 cup sifted cake flour

$1\frac{1}{2}$ cups superfine sugar

10 large egg whites

1 teaspoon cream of tartar

3 teaspoons vanilla extract

1 tablespoon fresh lemon juice

1 teaspoon finely grated lemon zest

**SAUCE**

1 tablespoon instant espresso crystals

3 tablespoons boiling water

2 ounces bittersweet chocolate, finely chopped

$\frac{3}{4}$ cup evaporated skim milk

$\frac{1}{3}$ cup granulated sugar

3 tablespoons unsweetened Dutch process cocoa powder

$1\frac{1}{2}$ tablespoons cornstarch

3 tablespoons light corn syrup

**PER SERVING**

226 calories

....

2 g fat (1 g saturated)

....

1 mg cholesterol

....

81 mg sodium

....

1. With rack in middle position, preheat oven to 325°F.

2. *For cake:* Sift flour with $\frac{1}{2}$ cup superfine sugar five times and set aside.

3. Beat egg whites and cream of tartar in large bowl at medium electric speed

228

until frothy. With mixer still at medium speed, add remaining 1 cup superfine sugar gradually, then continue beating until whites peak stiffly but are still moist and shiny.

4. Adding one-third of total amount at a time, slowly sift flour-sugar mixture into beaten whites and fold in lightly but thoroughly with large rubber spatula. Finally, fold in vanilla, lemon juice, and zest.

5. Pour batter into ungreased 10-inch tube pan and bake until cake is golden brown and springy to the touch—50 to 60 minutes.

6. Remove cake from oven and cool in upside-down pan to room temperature.

7. *As soon as cake has cooled, prepare sauce:* Combine espresso crystals and boiling water in small heatproof bowl, add chocolate and stir until melted; set aside.

8. Bring evaporated milk to boiling in small saucepan over moderate heat, then blend into espresso-chocolate mixture.

9. Wipe pan clean, then add sugar, cocoa, and cornstarch and combine, pressing out all lumps. Slowly whisk in espresso-chocolate mixture, then corn syrup. Bring to a quick boil over moderate heat, reduce heat to low, and cook, stirring constantly, until sauce thickens—1 to 2 minutes. Remove from heat.

10. To serve, loosen cake around edge of pan and central tube and invert on cake plate. Cut cake into 12 wedges using serrated bread knife and gentle seesaw motion. Place cake wedges on dessert plates and top each portion with 1 1/2 tablespoons warm sauce.

RECIPE FROM

*Sara Moulton; New York, New York*

## ARTHUR W. LUMSDEN
*Cheyenne, Wyoming*

"When I retired," writes this transplanted native of Westchester County, New York, "I decided to expand my baking abilities. Once I had become proficient at baking bread, I decided angel food cake would be fun and away I went. Through imagination, practice, and trial and error, I developed several flavors including butter-pecan, lemon, apricot, and raspberry. One day I thought: If whole-wheat flour is healthier than white, why not make a whole-wheat angel food cake? It was a success on the first try." A diabetic, Arthur himself partakes only of the bread he bakes—never the cakes. But he does love to share them!

# Spicy Whole-Wheat Angel Food Cake
### *Makes a 10-inch tube cake, 16 servings*

*Angel food cakes have a reputation for being the very devil to make. So who would have dreamed that you could make one with anything other than the silkiest cake flour? This recipe proves that even whole-wheat flour makes a fine, high-rising angel cake, and make a note, this one contains zero fat, zero cholesterol.*

TIP: *The egg whites will beat to greater volume if you first bring them to room temperature.*

1 cup unsifted whole-wheat flour

1½ cups sugar

1 teaspoon ground cinnamon

½ teaspoon ground ginger

¼ teaspoon ground nutmeg

14 large egg whites

1½ teaspoons cream of tartar

½ teaspoon salt

1½ teaspoons vanilla extract

| PER SERVING |
|:---:|
| 115 calories |
| .... |
| 0 g fat (0 g saturated) |
| .... |
| 0 mg cholesterol |
| .... |
| 121 mg sodium |
| .... |

1. Slide oven rack into middle position and preheat oven to 400°F.

2. Sift flour, 1 cup sugar, cinnamon, ginger, and nutmeg four times and place in large bowl.

3. Beat egg whites, cream of tartar, and salt in large electric mixer bowl at high speed until silvery. With mixer still at high speed, add remaining $1/2$ cup sugar and continue beating until meringue peaks stiffly—about 4 minutes. Beat in vanilla.

4. By hand, fold in flour mixture, $1/2$ cup at a time—easy does it!

5. Spoon batter into ungreased 10-inch angel food cake pan and bake until golden brown and springy to the touch—25 to 30 minutes.

6. Remove cake from oven and cool to room temperature in upside-down pan.

7. Carefully loosen cake around edge and central tube and turn out on cake plate. Cut into 16 wedges and serve.

RECIPE FROM
*Arthur W. Lumsden; Cheyenne, Wyoming*

Patricia thinks her interest in cooking must be genetic since both sides of the family produced "good German cooks specializing in thrifty, hearty dishes and lots of sweets." She recalls especially a "daffodil cake" her mother used to make ("all yellow and white swirls") that she tried unsuccessfully for years to duplicate: "It never tasted like Mother's and after a while I gave up. Then, when coffee flavor became so popular, I remembered the old daffodil favorite." She decided to make a sponge cake as nearly like it as possible, incorporating the swirls but using a coffee flavor. This simple but elegant dessert, when baked in small tube pans, can be cut in half and shared—hence its name.

# *Dream Shares*

*Makes a 10-inch tube cake, 12 servings*

*A most unusual cake with toasted spiced pecans coating the bottom of the pan and two batters, one yellow, one white, swirled together to create a marbleized effect. Yet there's nothing complicated about this low-fat, low-calorie dessert.*

*⅓ cup coarsely chopped pecans*

*¼ teaspoon ground cinnamon*

*½ cup plus ¼ teaspoon sugar*

*6 large egg whites*

*4 large egg yolks*

*3 tablespoons Kahlúa or other coffee liqueur*

*1½ cups sifted all-purpose flour*

| PER SERVING |
| :---: |
| 141 calories |
| .... |
| 4 g fat (1 g saturated) |
| .... |
| 71 mg cholesterol |
| .... |
| 30 mg sodium |
| .... |

1. Preheat oven to 350°F.

2. Toss pecans with cinnamon and ¼ teaspoon sugar in small bowl, then spread on large ungreased baking sheet, and bake 5 minutes. Remove from oven, cool, then scatter half of pecans over bottom of ungreased 10-inch tube pan. Set pan aside.

3. Beat egg whites in large bowl of electric mixer at high speed until frothy. With mixer still at high speed add $1/4$ cup sugar gradually, then continue beating until whites peak stiffly but are still moist and shiny.

4. Using same beaters, beat egg yolks and remaining $1/4$ cup sugar in second large bowl of electric mixer at high speed until thick and pale yellow. Add Kahlúa and beat only enough to combine.

5. Adding one-third of total amount at a time, slowly sift flour over beaten yolks and fold in lightly but thoroughly with large rubber spatula. Fold in half of beaten whites, then fold in remaining beaten whites, swirling to marbleize.

6. Pour batter into prepared pan, sprinkle remaining pecans on top, and bake until cake springs back when touched—about 30 minutes.

7. Remove cake from oven and cool in upside-down pan to room temperature.

8. To remove cake from pan, run metal spatula carefully around edge of pan and central tube. Invert on cake plate, cut into 12 wedges, and serve.

RECIPE FROM

*Patricia Waterman; Flower Mound, Texas*

Joseph, a writer, and his wife Jessica, an artist, both enjoy cooking (see her recipe for Southport Seafood Pie, page 26). As someone who shed twenty pounds and has managed not to regain them, Joseph had fun dreaming up this brownie recipe. "There are so many chocolate 'diet' brownies that I wanted something different," he explained. "I experimented with wholesome ingredients like puréed fruit and whole-grain flours. When the apricot brownies came out of the oven they simply cried out for caramel topping: 'CARAMEL! GIVE US CARAMEL!' I did, and they were right—it was a match made in apricot heaven."

# *Caramel Apricot Brownies*

*Makes 12 servings*

*This is a truly low-fat recipe because egg whites take the place of whole eggs and apricots double for butter. Finally, whole-wheat flour replaces refined white flour, pumping up the fiber.*

¾ **cup granulated sugar**

1½ **cups unsifted whole-wheat flour**

¼ **cup firmly packed light brown sugar**

½ **teaspoon baking soda**

½ **teaspoon salt**

⅛ **teaspoon ground nutmeg**

2 **large egg whites, lightly beaten**

3 **teaspoons vanilla extract**

½ **teaspoon cream of tartar**

1 **(5-ounce) can apricot halves in light syrup, drained and puréed**

6 **tablespoons nonfat vanilla-flavored yogurt**

¼ **cup fat-free caramel sauce**

| PER SERVING |
| --- |
| 153 calories |
| .... |
| 0.3 g fat (0 g saturated) |
| .... |
| 0 mg cholesterol |
| .... |
| 182 mg sodium |
| .... |

1. Preheat oven to 325°F. Coat 9 x 9 x 2-inch baking dish with nonstick cooking spray and set aside.

2. Spoon out 2 tablespoons granulated sugar and reserve. Combine remaining granulated sugar, flour, brown sugar, baking soda, salt, and nutmeg in large bowl and reserve.

3. Combine egg whites, vanilla, and cream of tartar in large bowl, then with mixer at low speed, gradually add reserved 2 tablespoons granulated sugar. Continue beating at low speed until meringue peaks stiffly but is not dry. Carefully fold in puréed apricots. Finally, fold in combined dry ingredients, taking care not to over-mix.

4. Spoon batter into prepared pan, spreading to corners, and bake until springy to the touch—about 30 minutes. Cool in pan on upright wire rack 1 hour.

5. To serve, cut into 12 squares, top each portion with ½ tablespoon yogurt, then drizzle with caramel sauce.

RECIPE FROM

*Joseph C. Gambino; Cañon City, Colorado*

*Tomahawk, Wisconsin*

In her thirty-four years, Jennifer has lived in California, New York, Germany, Arizona, Washington state, and North Carolina. Now, with husband Chris and seven-year-old son Alexander, she makes her home in Wisconsin. She created this cookie recipe to satisfy a serious craving. "I have the biggest sweet tooth in the world," she explains, "but every time I made chocolate chip cookies they tasted too greasy and made me feel really guilty. So I decided I would try adding and deleting things to reduce the fat, and after about twelve batches the recipe seemed right." Her sensible attitude toward food in general and cookies in particular has allowed Jennifer to lose fifteen pounds.

# Jennifer's Really Good Low-Fat Chocolate Chip Cookies

*Makes 2½ dozen*

*In these moist and chewy cookies, applesauce takes the place of half the shortening, significantly reducing fat and calories. You can substitute reduced-fat chocolate chips for the regular but you will lower the overall fat per cookie by a mere fifth of a gram and you will raise the amount of saturated fat by nearly half a gram (the difference in calories is negligible). So far reduced-fat chips are available only in the regular size, meaning there will be fewer chips per cookie.*

TIP: *If you whisk the flour, baking soda, and salt together in a large bowl, there's no need to sift them.*

1¾ cups unsifted all-purpose flour

1 teaspoon baking soda

¼ teaspoon salt

¼ cup (½ stick) unsalted butter (no substitute)

½ cup granulated sugar

| PER COOKIE |
| :---: |
| 92 calories |
| .... |
| 3 g fat (2 g saturated) |
| .... |
| 11 mg cholesterol |
| .... |
| 67 mg sodium |
| .... |

*¹⁄₃ cup firmly packed dark brown sugar*

*1 large egg plus 1 large egg white*

*¹⁄₂ cup old-fashioned rolled oats (not quick-cooking)*

*¹⁄₄ cup unsweetened applesauce*

*3 teaspoons vanilla extract*

*³⁄₄ cup miniature semisweet chocolate chips*

1. Preheat oven to 375° F. Coat three baking sheets with nonstick cooking spray and set aside.

2. Place flour, baking soda, and salt in large bowl and whisk briskly to combine; set aside.

3. Cream butter with granulated and brown sugars in large bowl at high speed with an electric mixer until light—2 to 3 minutes.

4. Beat in egg and egg white, then add remaining ingredients (including flour mixture). Beat at moderately low speed just enough to combine.

5. Drop dough from gently rounded tablespoon onto prepared baking sheets, spacing about 2 inches apart.

6. Bake until golden brown and irresistible smelling—8 to 10 minutes.

7. Cool cookies on baking sheets 1 to 2 minutes until they firm up a bit, then, using spatula, transfer to wire racks to cool. Store in airtight container.

RECIPE FROM

*Jennifer Regan-Mitchell; Tomahawk, Wisconsin*

## BRUNI SLINN

*Aurora, Colorado*

Bruni, who was born and brought up in New Jersey, now lives in Colorado where she is in private practice as a physical therapist. Because of her professional interest in physical fitness, she's aware that "diet" is "a lifelong ritual" and is careful herself to eat in moderation. "I like to experiment with recipes, so I tried to get peanut butter and chocolate chips as low-fat as I could," she told us. "This recipe is healthy, easy to put together, and uses only one bowl for quick cleanup. My husband loves these cookies!"

# Peanut Butter-Chocolate Chip Cookies

*Makes about 4 dozen*

*Two favorite flavors teamed in a single cookie. The difference here is that applesauce substitutes for some of the butter, and wheat germ and toasted wheat cereal add nutrients and fiber. Finally, miniature chocolate chips take the place of regular, spreading their chocolately goodness further.*

½ cup wheat germ

½ cup toasted cracked wheat cereal

1¼ cups unsifted all-purpose flour

1 teaspoon baking soda

¼ teaspoon salt

¼ cup unsweetened applesauce

6 tablespoons unsalted butter, softened

½ cup reduced-fat chunky peanut butter

½ cup sugar

1 large egg plus 1 large egg white

2 teaspoons vanilla extract

½ cup miniature semisweet chocolate chips

| PER COOKIE |
| :---: |
| 64 calories |
| .... |
| 3 g fat (1.5 g saturated) |
| .... |
| 8 mg cholesterol |
| .... |
| 57 mg sodium |
| .... |

1. Preheat oven to 350°F. Coat four baking sheets with nonstick cooking spray and set aside.

2. Combine wheat germ, cereal, flour, baking soda, and salt in large bowl and set aside also.

3. Using hand electric mixer at low speed, cream applesauce, butter, peanut butter, and sugar 1 minute. Beat in egg, egg white, and vanilla, then add combined dry ingredients and beat 1 minute. By hand, fold in chocolate chips.

4. Drop dough by rounded teaspoon onto prepared baking sheets, spacing $1^1/_2$ inches apart (you should get 12 cookies on each sheet). With hands, flatten each cookie to a thickness of about $^1/_4$ inch.

5. Bake until golden brown and irresistible-smelling—8 to 10 minutes. Transfer cookies at once to wire racks and cool to room temperature. Store in airtight cannister.

RECIPE FROM

*Bruni Slinn; Aurora, Colorado*

# MEGHAN McVEY

### *Bessemer, Michigan*

This young cook, just nineteen, is a sophomore at Bowling Green State University in Ohio. "In high school, I was constantly baking cookies for my family, friends, and sports teams," she writes, "but I was also trying to eat healthy so that I could stay in shape for sports. I thought of this recipe when I was baking cookies to send to my brother, who was away at college. I just threw in different ingredients and they ended up tasting really good! My brother called to tell me how good they were, and when I told him they were low fat, he couldn't believe it!"

# *Toffee Chip Cookies*
### *Makes 3½ dozen*

*This recipe calls for English toffee pieces, a relatively new product packaged by a major candy manufacturer—look for them beside the chocolate chips in the baking section of your supermarket. If you're unable to find them, buy English toffees and cut them into small pieces. But keep an eye on the label and reject toffees that are freighted with fat and calories. The nutrient counts given here are for cookies made with the ready-to-use toffee pieces.*

*½ cup granulated sugar*

*½ cup firmly packed dark brown sugar*

*6 tablespoons unsalted butter, softened*

*2 large egg whites, lightly beaten*

*3 teaspoons vanilla extract*

*2¼ cups unsifted all-purpose flour*

*1 teaspoon baking soda*

*⅓ cup miniature semisweet chocolate chips*

*⅓ cup English toffee baking pieces (see headnote above)*

| PER COOKIE |
| --- |
| 74 calories |
| .... |
| 3 g fat (1 g saturated) |
| .... |
| 6 mg cholesterol |
| .... |
| 44 mg sodium |
| .... |

1. Preheat oven to 350°F. Coat three baking sheets with nonstick cooking spray (preferably butter-flavored) and set aside.

2. Using hand electric mixer at low speed, cream granulated sugar, brown sugar, and butter 2 minutes. Add egg whites and vanilla and beat 1 minute more.

3. Quickly whisk flour with baking soda to combine, then add to creamed mixture and beat 30 seconds at low speed. By hand, fold in chocolate chips and toffee pieces.

4. Roll dough into 42 (1-inch) balls, place on prepared baking sheets, spacing $1\frac{1}{2}$ to 2 inches apart. With hands, flatten each cookie to a thickness of about $\frac{1}{4}$ inch.

5. Bake until golden—8 to 10 minutes. Transfer cookies at once to wire racks and cool to room temperature. Store in airtight container.

RECIPE FROM

*Meghan McVey; Bessemer, Michigan*

## IDA FLORENCE ALKIRE

*Seiling, Oklahoma*

One of eight children brought up on a farm in northwest Oklahoma, Ida Florence learned to cook as a youngster and went on to become manager of a school food service, where she worked until her retirement. "I learned that applesauce could be used to replace half the shortening in some baked products," she told us, "and since my husband likes cookies, I wanted one that was moist and pleasing to his taste. I toyed with a basic oatmeal cookie, making changes until I had a recipe we both liked. In my experimenting, some results were less desirable but nothing was wasted— I gave residue to the cats or pitched it over the back fence for the skunks or opossums."

# Energy Cookies

*Makes about 4 dozen*

*The "energy" comes from oatmeal and raisins, the punchy flavor from applesauce, orange juice concentrate, brown sugar, and cinnamon. Our taste-testers loved the cookies' chewiness!*

*1 cup unsifted all-purpose flour*

*½ cup unsifted whole-wheat flour*

*1 teaspoon baking powder*

*1 teaspoon baking soda*

*1 teaspoon ground cinnamon*

*¼ cup (½ stick) unsalted butter, softened*

*⅓ cup granulated sugar*

*⅓ cup firmly packed dark brown sugar*

*1 large egg plus 1 large egg white*

*½ cup unsweetened applesauce*

*½ cup frozen orange juice concentrate, thawed*

*2 cups quick-cooking rolled oats*

*1 cup seedless raisins*

| PER COOKIE |
| --- |
| 64 calories |
| 1 g fat (0.75 g saturated) |
| 7 mg cholesterol |
| 40 mg sodium |

3. Drop meringues from rounded teaspoon onto prepared baking sheets, spacing 2 inches apart. Set in oven, immediately turn oven off, and let cookies remain in the oven for 2 hours (you can even leave them in overnight).

4. Peel meringues off parchment and store in airtight container.

RECIPE FROM

*Jenny Sacks; New Orleans, Louisiana*

# FRUIT DESSERTS

Luscious Lemon-Berry Parfait *(Finalist, Desserts)*     250

Balsamic Berries with Vanilla Cream     252

Amaretto-Baked Pears in Pastry     254

Sweet Nachos with Fresh Raspberry Salsa     256

Crêpes Bombes Nanette     258

Celestial Fruit Mousse in Meringue Nests with Raspberry Sauce     260

Simply Marvelous Meringues     263

Angel Food Biscotti with Raspberry Coulis     265

Blueberry Crisp     267

Emeril's Roasted Peach Soup with a Peach and Raspberry Sorbet     269

Heavenly Roasted Fruit     271

Amaretto Strawberry Dessert     273

Skinny Whipped Topping     275

*White Salmon, Washington*

A native of St. Louis, Margee now lives in Washington state where her husband Randy works in construction management and she is golf shop manager at a local course. She also plays golf, power walks, bikes, and watches intake of calories and fats— a lifestyle that keeps her slim. Of her berry parfait recipe she writes: "Where we live all types of berries grow wild and bountiful, and berry-picking has become a family pastime. While I'm picking I'm usually thinking about what to do with all the berries. This creation came after a whole day of picking."

FINALIST, DESSERTS

# *Luscious Lemon-Berry Parfait*

*Makes 4 servings*

*This is actually a sort of trifle made with angel food cake (preferably homemade). Nonfat vanilla yogurt takes the place of custard, significantly trimming fat, cholesterol, and calories.*

NOTE: *This recipe calls for toasted sliced almonds as a garnish. No problem. Simply spread sliced almonds in an ungreased pie pan, then set in a preheated 350°F oven for 5 to 7 minutes, until golden brown, stirring occasionally. Watch closely, however—nuts burn easily.*

*1 (8-ounce) container nonfat vanilla yogurt*

*¼ cup low-fat sour cream*

*2 tablespoons fresh lemon juice*

*1 tablespoon finely grated lemon zest*

*1 teaspoon vanilla extract*

*1 cup sliced, stemmed ripe strawberries*

*1 cup stemmed ripe blueberries*

*2 cups (8 ounces) ½-inch cubes homemade or store-bought angel food cake*

| PER SERVING |
| :---: |
| 289 calories |
| .... |
| 5 g fat (1 g saturated) |
| .... |
| 6 mg cholesterol |
| .... |
| 481 mg sodium |
| .... |

*¼ cup toasted sliced almonds (see Note)*

*4 sprigs fresh mint*

1. Combine yogurt, sour cream, lemon juice and zest, and vanilla in a small bowl.

2. Layer parfait in each of four (8-ounce) goblets this way: 1 tablespoon yogurt mixture, 2 tablespoons sliced strawberries, 2 tablespoons blueberries, ¼ cup cake cubes, 1 tablespoon yogurt mixture. Repeat sequence in each goblet.

3. Top each portion with 1 tablespoon toasted sliced almonds and a sprig of mint and serve.

RECIPE FROM

*Margee Striler-Berry; White Salmon, Washington*

Lynn is a doctoral candidate in math education and her husband teaches in high school. "As a teacher and a graduate student, we don't have much money to go out, so we entertain at home," she says. "We love to cook for our friends, but coming up with a meal to fit everybody's dietary needs can be a challenge. Plus, we don't want to spend the entire evening in the kitchen! This dish was created to meet all those needs. It's inexpensive, can be made ahead of time, it's a light way to finish a nice meal, and it satisfies the sweet tooth. Everybody's happy— including us. And no one feels like they've had to suffer through a 'diet' dessert!"

# *Balsamic Berries with Vanilla Cream*

*Makes 4 servings*

*You can toss this recipe together in no time, but you should let the berries macerate in the refrigerator for at least 4 hours before serving. Our taste-testers' verdict on this oh-so-easy dessert: "Truly delicious!"*

TIP: *Use highest-quality pure vanilla extract when making the Vanilla Cream, never perfumey imitation vanilla.*

### BERRIES

*1 cup fresh raspberries, washed and patted dry on*
   *paper toweling*

*1 cup fresh blackberries, washed and patted dry on*
   *paper toweling*

*1 pint fresh strawberries, washed, hulled, and sliced*
   *1/4 inch thick*

*2 tablespoons granulated sugar*

*1 tablespoon balsamic vinegar*

| PER SERVING |
| :---: |
| 157 calories |
| .... |
| 3 g fat (2 g saturated) |
| .... |
| 10 mg cholesterol |
| .... |
| 25 mg sodium |
| .... |

**VANILLA CREAM**

*½ cup low-fat sour cream*

*2 tablespoons dark brown sugar*

*3 teaspoons vanilla extract (see Note)*

1. *For berries:* Place all berries and sugar in large glass or porcelain bowl and toss lightly. Cover with plastic wrap and refrigerate for 4 hours, tossing occasionally.

2. *For vanilla cream:* Combine all ingredients in small glass or porcelain bowl, cover with plastic wrap, and refrigerate until ready to serve.

3. To serve, drizzle balsamic vinegar over berries and toss lightly. Divide berries and accumulated juices evenly among four dessert plates. Quickly whisk Vanilla Cream, then drift alongside berries, dividing amount evenly.

RECIPE FROM

*Lynn Geiger; Athens, Georgia*

# MICHELLE BLOCK

*San Jose, California*

Only eighteen, this talented young cook and restaurant waitress has already won both state and regional awards for her imaginative desserts and pastries. Her ideas often come suddenly, then take months to perfect. The inspiration for this recipe came while she was leafing through a magazine and saw a photograph of ordinary baked pears. "Using fillo dough for a crust just popped into my head," she recalls, "but it took me forever to create the fruit filling." She credits her mother, her father, and a culinary arts instructor with teaching her how to cook.

## *Amaretto-Baked Pears in Pastry*

*Makes 4 servings*

*Fillo, a Greek pastry as thin as onion skin, is marvelously versatile and a quick way to turn a simple dessert—this one, for example—into a show stopper. You'll find boxes of fillo in the frozen foods section of nearly every supermarket.*

NOTE: *To toast chopped almonds, spread in a small pie pan and bake uncovered at 350°F, shaking pan occasionally, until uniformly golden brown—4 to 5 minutes. But watch closely; nuts burn easily.*

2 tablespoons chopped dried apricots

1 tablespoon golden seedless raisins

1 tablespoon dried currants

2 tablespoons Amaretto (almond liqueur)

4 medium-size firm-ripe Bosc pears (about 2 pounds)

1½ ounces nonfat cream cheese, softened

1 tablespoon dark brown sugar

1 tablespoon lightly toasted, coarsely chopped almonds (see Note above)

1½ teaspoons apricot jam

12 (18 x 14-inch) frozen fillo leaves in single stack (from a 1-pound package)

| PER SERVING |
| :---: |
| 376 calories |
| .... |
| 6 g fat (1 g saturated) |
| .... |
| 0.9 mg cholesterol |
| .... |
| 337 mg sodium |
| .... |

*1 tablespoon granulated sugar mixed with 1 teaspoon ground cinnamon (cinnamon-sugar)*

*1 cup fresh raspberries, washed and patted dry on paper toweling*

1. Preheat oven to 350°F. Line jelly-roll pan with baking parchment and set aside.

2. Bring apricots, raisins, currants, and Amaretto slowly to a boil in small heavy saucepan over low heat, then transfer to small heatproof bowl and set aside.

3. Peel pears; then using apple corer, core from bottom, leaving stems intact. Level bottoms of pears as needed so they stand straight without wobbling.

4. Combine cream cheese, brown sugar, almonds, jam, and Amaretto–dried fruit mixture in small bowl, then stuff into cavities in cored pears.

5. Place fillo leaves on counter and cover with damp tea towel. Working quickly, coat each of 3 leaves with nonstick cooking spray (preferably butter-flavored) re-stack and center a pear on stack. Bundle four corners up over pear, then press ends together and twist slightly to enclose pear and secure. Spray fillo bundle with nonstick cooking spray and sprinkle with cinnamon-sugar. Wrap remaining 3 pears in fillo exactly the same way, spray, and sprinkle with cinnamon-sugar.

6. Place fillo bundles on prepared pan and bake until fillo browns lightly and seems to soften—about 30 minutes. Cool fillo bundles 15 to 20 minutes.

7. To serve, center fillo bundle on each of four dessert plates, then wreathe with raspberries, dividing total amount evenly.

RECIPE FROM
*Michelle Block; San Jose, California*

## PHIL HERRON

*Marietta, Georgia*

An account manager who was born in Alabama and learned to cook from his mother, Phil now lives on the outskirts of Atlanta with his wife Frances, a schoolteacher. He likes to enter recipe contests and has won an impressive twenty-three, including the prestigious Georgia Beef Cook-Off. He loves Mexican food and especially likes this recipe because it's easy to prepare and is built around tortillas and some of his favorite fruits—mangoes, kiwis, and raspberries.

# Sweet Nachos with Fresh Raspberry Salsa

*Makes 4 servings*

*A three-part recipe that's as glamorous as it is quick. You can, if you like, substitute blueberries for raspberries, even small quartered strawberries. Fresh fruit, it goes without saying, makes better salsa than frozen fruit, but if you can't wait until raspberry season, frozen berries will do.*

### SALSA
*1 pint fresh or frozen unsweetened raspberries, thawed*

*1¹/₂ cups diced mango (about 1 large mango;*
*for the easy way to pit, peel, and dice mango, see*
*Tips for Herbed Snapper with Warm Mango*
*Salsa, page 7)*

*1 ripe kiwifruit, peeled and cut into ¹/₂-inch dice*

### NACHOS
*4 (7-inch) low-fat flour tortillas*

*¹/₄ cup sugar mixed with ¹/₂ teaspoon ground cinnamon (cinnamon-sugar)*

### SAUCE
*¹/₂ (8-ounce) package low-fat cream cheese (Neufchâtel), softened*

*¹/₂ cup fresh orange juice*

*2 tablespoons honey*

| PER SERVING |
| :---: |
| 328 calories |
| .... |
| 8 g fat (4 g saturated) |
| .... |
| 20 mg cholesterol |
| .... |
| 345 mg sodium |
| .... |

1. Preheat oven to 500°F.  Line two large baking sheets with baking parchment and set aside.

2. *For salsa:* Combine all ingredients in medium-size glass or porcelain bowl, cover, and refrigerate until ready to serve.

3. *For nachos:* Stack tortillas and cut straight down into six wedges. Brush one side of each wedge with water and sprinkle with cinnamon sugar. Arrange sugared sides up on prepared baking sheets and bake until crisp—about 4 minutes. Remove from oven and cool.

4. *For sauce:* Pulse all ingredients in food processor until completely smooth—about 1 minute. Transfer to small heavy saucepan, set over low heat, and cook and stir until consistency of thin sauce—1 to 2 minutes.

5. *To serve:* Spoon salsa on four dessert plates, dividing total amount evenly, surround salsa on each plate with six warm nachos, and drizzle warm sauce over nachos.

RECIPE FROM

*Phil Herron; Marietta, Georgia*

## Houston, Texas

This travel consultant, born in England and brought up in Nyasaland, Africa, keeps her weight constant by limiting carbohydrates and running regularly. "I'm a devotee of baked Alaska," she told us, "but recognizing that the cake shell is a 'calorific' problem, I devised this alternative recipe, which substitutes crêpes while cutting down on the sugar in the crêpes, meringue, and ice cream." Nanette's husband, a physicist, commented, "It's not quite as sinful as a *loaded* baked Alaska, but it certainly comes a close second!"

# Crêpes Bombes Nanette

*Makes 4 servings*

*The scoops of ice cream you use for this recipe should be solidly frozen, so using a ¹⁄₂-cup ice cream scoop, drop four scoops onto four large squares plastic wrap and bundle each tightly, shaping as nearly as possible into balls. Secure bundles with twist ties, then set in freezer several hours or even a day or two ahead of time.*

CRÊPES
*3 large egg whites*

*1 teaspoon sugar*

*1¹⁄₂ tablespoons cornstarch*

*¹⁄₈ teaspoon salt*

MERINGUE
*4 large egg whites*

*¹⁄₄ cup sugar*

TO COMPLETE RECIPE
*4 solidly frozen ¹⁄₂-cup scoops low-fat chocolate ice cream
    (see headnote above)*

*1 cup thinly sliced ripe strawberries (about 12 small berries)*

PER SERVING

226 calories
....
2 g fat (1 g saturated)
....
3 mg cholesterol
....
221 mg sodium
....

1. Preheat oven to 450°F. Line large baking sheet with baking parchment and set aside.

2. *For crêpes:* With fork, whisk egg whites in small bowl until frothy but not stiff—about 2 minutes. Add sugar and whisk 1 minute more. Add cornstarch and salt and whisk 1 minute longer.

3. Spray 6-inch crêpe pan with nonstick cooking spray, set over moderate heat, and heat 1 minute. Spoon 2 tablespoons crêpe batter into pan, swirling to coat pan bottom evenly. Cook 45 seconds until lightly golden on bottom, turn, and brown flip side 30 seconds. Tip crêpe onto large plate, then cook three more crêpes the same way, recoating pan with nonstick cooking spray between crêpes.

4. *For meringue:* Beat egg whites at low electric mixer speed until frothy—about 1 minute. With mixer still at low speed, add sugar, 1 tablespoon at a time, and continue beating until meringue peaks stiffly but is not dry—about 3 minutes.

5. *To complete recipe:* Gently unwrap frozen scoops of ice cream, center one on each crêpe, then lift edges of crêpes over ice cream, pressing edges to seal. Place on prepared baking sheet, spacing far apart, then frost all with meringue, making sure crêpes are completely hidden.

6. Bake until meringue is golden brown—about 3 minutes.

7. To serve, center bombes on dessert plates and decorate with sliced strawberries.

RECIPE FROM

*Nanette Alsop; Houston, Texas*

*St. Clair Shores, Michigan*

"I enjoy making fruit mousse," writes this mother of two young daughters, "but when I decided to eliminate the egg yolks in order to make this recipe fat-free, I had to make it twice to determine the correct amount of gelatin and sugar to use. I added the meringue nests to give the dessert some crunch and the raspberry sauce to add color and flavor. My family loved the mousse and thought the meringue nests were a good touch!" Patricia, who says she taught herself to cook, likes preparing desserts best of all.

# Celestial Fruit Mousse in Meringue Nests with Raspberry Sauce

*Makes 6 servings*

*This recipe may seem a little fussy but the time you put into it will reap big rewards in the compliment department. Moreover, you could hardly ask for a prettier dessert. Or a more healthful one.*

NOTE: *In the good old days (before the Age of Salmonella), mousses were routinely made with raw egg whites. That's risky today so to play it safe, we use pasteurized liquid egg whites. You'll find them at your supermarket alongside the eggs.*

**MOUSSE**

¼ cup water

½ cup sugar

1 (¼-ounce) envelope plain gelatin

1 (10-ounce) package frozen unsweetened whole
   raspberries, thawed

½ cup pasteurized liquid egg whites (see Note above)

**Pinch salt**

**PER SERVING**

243 calories

····

0.3 fat (0 g saturated)

····

0 mg cholesterol

····

189 mg sodium

····

MERINGUE NESTS
*3 large egg whites*

*Pinch salt*

*⅔ cup sugar*

SAUCE
*¼ cup sugar*

*¼ cup water*

*1 (10-ounce) package frozen unsweetened whole raspberries, thawed*

*1 tablespoon fresh lemon juice*

1. Preheat oven to 400°F. Line baking sheet with baking parchment and set aside.

2. *For mousse:* Whisk water, ¼ cup sugar, and gelatin together in small heavy saucepan, set over moderate heat, and bring to a simmer, whisking constantly. As soon as gelatin dissolves completely, remove from heat and cool 5 minutes.

3. Meanwhile, purée raspberries by pulsing in food processor 1 minute. When gelatin mixture has cooled 5 minutes, drizzle down feed tube, pulsing all the while and taking care mixture does not splatter. When smooth—after about 1 minute—put through fine sieve and reserve.

4. Beat liquid egg whites with salt in large bowl at high electric mixer speed until frothy. With mixer still at high speed, add remaining ¼ cup sugar gradually and continue beating until mixture peaks stiffly—about 4 minutes. Gently fold in raspberry purée, cover, and refrigerate 4 hours.

5. *Meanwhile, prepare meringue nests:* Beat egg whites and salt in large bowl at high electric mixer speed until silvery. With mixer still at high speed, add sugar gradually and continue beating until meringue peaks stiffly—about 4 minutes.

6. Using ½-cup measure, scoop up meringue and drop into six mounds on prepared baking sheet, spacing far apart. Make hollows about 3 inches across in the center of each mound with large spoon. Set in oven, immediately turn oven off, and leave meringue nests in oven 4 hours.

7. *For sauce:* Bring sugar and water to a boil in small heavy saucepan over moderate heat. Remove from heat and cool 5 minutes. Meanwhile, purée raspberries by pulsing in food processor 1 minute. Drizzle cooled sugar syrup down feed tube, pulsing all the while. Put through fine sieve, mix in lemon juice, cover, and chill until ready to serve.

8. To serve, place meringue nest on each of six dessert plates, fill with mousse, and top with raspberry sauce.

RECIPE FROM

*Patricia Beels; St. Clair Shores, Michigan*

*Westlake Village, California*

"I had enjoyed this dessert for many years but had always thought it was decadent until I modified an old family recipe of my great-grandmother's," Kathy told us, explaining how she increased the number of egg whites in the original recipe, decreased the sugar, and used fresh fruit. "This terrific dessert is not only low in calories and fat," she added, "but it is fast and easy and will delight guests as a wonderful ending to your meal." As someone who's dieted on and off for years (Kathy's tried "every diet possible" and lost as many as eighty pounds only to keep them off "sometimes"), this San Francisco native and mother of a grown-up son and daughter now tries to limit her sweets to slimming ones like this.

# Simply Marvelous Meringues

*Makes 6 servings*

*Crisp, melt-in-your-mouth meringues mounded with a smooth, sin-free filling and freshly picked strawberries. There's a welcome play of flavors and textures—tart versus sweet, crunchy versus creamy.*

*4 large egg whites, at room temperature*

*1/8 teaspoon salt*

*1 cup sugar*

*1/2 teaspoon vanilla extract*

*6 tablespoons Skinny Whipped Topping (page 275)*

*1 cup thinly sliced fresh strawberries*

| PER SERVING |
| :---: |
| 177 calories |
| .... |
| 0 g fat (0 g saturated) |
| .... |
| 1 mg cholesterol |
| .... |
| 108 mg sodium |
| .... |

1. Preheat oven to 250°F. Line large baking sheet with baking parchment and set aside.

2. Beat egg whites and salt in large bowl of electric mixer at medium speed until frothy. With mixer still at medium speed add sugar, 1 tablespoon at a time, then continue beating until whites peak stiffly but are still moist and shiny—2 1/2 to 3 minutes. Fold in vanilla.

3. Spoon meringue onto prepared baking sheet in six mounds of equal size, spacing well apart.

4. Bake until pale golden and shells sound hollow when lightly tapped—about 1 hour. Remove meringues from oven and cool to room temperature.

5. To serve, cut tops off meringues, spoon 1 tablespoon Skinny Whipped Topping into each, cover with strawberries, dividing total amount evenly, then replace cut-off tops.

RECIPE FROM

*Kathy Figueiredo; Westlake Village, California*

"I love angel food cake, I love raspberries, and I love finger food. Taking these three factors and trying to create a new dimension for them led me to this recipe," Devon Delaney told us. This mother of three, married to an executive of a large brokerage house and herself a computer instructor, enters cooking contests as a hobby and has won or placed in a dozen or more. Such contests help her develop new and interesting menus for her husband and three children. "I based this low-fat dessert on full flavor and convenience while attempting to avoid excess butter and sugar," she says. "I wanted full taste and visual satisfaction and enjoyed discovering a new way to present an old favorite."

# *Angel Food Biscotti with Raspberry Coulis*

*Makes 6 servings*

*"Biscotti," explains Devon Delaney, who submitted this recipe, "means baked twice." Her angel food biscotti are first baked (as a cake), then browned in a skillet on top of the stove. For perfect biscotti, use homemade angel food cake instead of store-bought. P.S. You won't find a better one than Sara Moulton's on page 228. "Adults and kids love this dessert," Devon continues, "and served with the fantastic coulis and some fruit sorbet, it's fat-free, very elegant, and so easy!"*

$1/2$ *(10-inch) homemade or store-bought angel food cake, cut straight across into slices 1 inch thick*

*1 (10-ounce) package frozen unsweetened whole raspberries, partially thawed but not drained*

*2 tablespoons fat-free caramel sauce or topping*

*1 tablespoon mint jelly*

*6 ($1/4$-cup) scoops mango, lime, or lemon sorbet*

*6 mint sprigs*

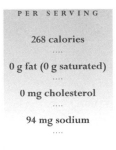

PER SERVING

268 calories

....

0 g fat (0 g saturated)

....

0 mg cholesterol

....

94 mg sodium

....

1. Place cake in ungreased large heavy nonstick skillet, set over moderate heat, and toast until crisp and brown—about $2^{1}/2$ minutes per side.

2. Remove cake from skillet, cut into biscotti-size strips about $2\frac{1}{2}$ inches long and 1 inch wide. Return to skillet and brown 2 to 3 minutes longer until all sides are crisp and brown. Remove from heat and set aside.

3. To make raspberry coulis, pulse raspberries, caramel sauce, and mint jelly in food processor or electric blender until blended but still a bit lumpy—about 10 seconds.

4. To serve, divide biscotti among six dessert plates, top each portion with scoop of sorbet, drizzle with raspberry coulis, and tuck in mint sprigs.

RECIPE FROM

*Devon Delaney; Princeton, New Jersey*

Mark and Colleen are young hospital pharmacists who met through their work, married, and are now expecting their first child. Among their shared interests are concert going, yard work, hiking, visiting antique fairs, and, when necessary, dieting. ("People tend to pick up weight when they get married," Mark observed, "so we decided that had to stop! We went on a diet together and each lost about ten pounds.") They collaborated on this recipe after an especially good blueberry harvest left them with an embarrassment of riches. "It satisfies your sweet tooth without the heavy crust," Mark promises.

# Blueberry Crisp

*Makes 8 servings*

*Oatmeal makes the crust crumbly and cinnamon and nutmeg make it spicy.*

NOTE: *You should prepare the topping crisp first. It's what Middle Easterners call* labna, *in truth nothing more than yogurt drained of most of its liquid. Use your finest sieve for the draining or a coarser one lined with a coffee filter. Classic* labna *is made with plain yogurt. We've used low-fat vanilla. To speed draining, cut through the yogurt with a knife in a crisscross pattern. Set the sieve over a small bowl and let it drip. The topping should be ready just in time for the crisp. To keep the blueberries from taking on a metallic taste, bake the crisp in an ovenproof glass pie plate.*

**TOPPING**
*1 (8-ounce) container nonfat vanilla yogurt*
  *(see Note above)*

**CRISP**
*2 cups fresh or solidly frozen blueberries, separated*

*2 teaspoons vanilla extract*

*1 teaspoon finely grated lemon zest*

*1/3 cup unsifted all-purpose flour*

**PER SERVING**

147 calories
....
5 g fat (3 g saturated)
....
12 mg cholesterol
....
25 mg sodium
....

$^1$⁄$_3$ cup old-fashioned rolled oats (not quick-cooking)

$^1$⁄$_4$ cup firmly packed dark brown sugar

3 tablespoons unsalted butter

1 tablespoon ground cinnamon

$^1$⁄$_2$ teaspoon ground nutmeg (freshly grated is even better)

1. Preheat oven to 350°F.

2. *For topping:* Dump yogurt into fine sieve set over small bowl, then slash with knife in crisscross pattern. Set in refrigerator and let drain 30 minutes.

3. *Meanwhile, prepare crisp:* Toss blueberries with vanilla and lemon zest in ungreased 9-inch ovenproof glass pie plate and set aside.

4. Using fingers or pastry blender, combine flour, rolled oats, sugar, butter, cinnamon, and nutmeg until uniformly crumbly. Scatter evenly over blueberries.

5. Bake uncovered until bubbly and golden brown—30 to 35 minutes.

6. Serve warm, topping each portion with $^1$⁄$_2$ tablespoon drained yogurt.

RECIPE FROM

*Mark and Colleen Barricklow; Fishers, Indiana*

# Emeril's Roasted Peach Soup with a Peach and Raspberry Sorbet

*Makes 6 servings*

*Emeril freezes his sorbet in an electric ice cream maker; if you have one, by all means use it as the manufacturer directs. For those who have no fancy ice cream makers, we show how the sorbet can be frozen in the freezing compartment of a refrigerator, then chunked and buzzed to silky smoothness in a food processor.*

NOTE: *Also see Emeril's Potato-Crusted Fish with a French Green Bean Relish (page 15).*

### SOUP
*2 pounds ripe peaches*

*1 teaspoon olive oil*

*$\frac{1}{8}$ teaspoon salt*

*$\frac{1}{8}$ teaspoon freshly ground black pepper*

*1 cup Sauternes (or other semisweet white wine)*

*1 cup water*

*3 tablespoons honey*

### SORBET
*2 pints fresh raspberries*

*1 cup sugar*

*$1\frac{1}{2}$ cups water*

*Pits and peels from peaches above*

### GARNISH
*6 sprigs mint*

| PER SERVING |
| :---: |
| 297 calories |
| .... |
| 2 g fat (0 g saturated) |
| .... |
| 0 mg cholesterol |
| .... |
| 300 mg sodium |
| .... |

1. *For soup:* **Preheat** oven to 450°F. Place whole unpeeled peaches in ungreased large shallow roasting pan, rub with olive oil, and sprinkle with salt and pepper. Set uncovered in oven and roast until very soft—about 20 minutes. Remove peaches from oven, cool to room temperature, then peel and pit, saving both the pits and peels.

2. Pulse peaches in food processor until completely smooth—about 3 minutes. Add Sauternes, water, and honey and pulse 1 minute more. Sieve purée directly into medium-size glass or porcelain bowl, cover, and refrigerate for at least 2 hours or until ready to serve.

3. *Meanwhile, prepare sorbet:* Bring raspberries, sugar, $1\frac{1}{2}$ cups water, and reserved peach pits and peels to a boil in a medium-size nonreactive saucepan over moderate heat, then boil uncovered for 10 minutes. Remove from heat and cool 20 minutes; discard pits.

4. Purée saucepan mixture by pulsing 3 minutes in food processor or electric blender, then put through fine sieve set over medium-size glass or porcelain bowl, and cool to room temperature.

5. Pour sorbet mixture into ungreased 13 x 9 x 2-inch pan and set in freezer for 3 hours. Remove from freezer, break sorbet into chunks, then churn 1 to 2 minutes in food processor until smooth.

6. To serve, divide cold peach soup among six dessert bowls, add $\frac{1}{2}$-cup scoop sorbet to each bowl, and garnish with mint.

RECIPE FROM

*Emeril Lagasse; New Orleans, Louisiana*

## SCOTT BREINING
### *Gaithersburg, Maryland*

This young medicinal chemist, a Ph.D. specializing in drug discovery, also likes to dream up new recipes. Because a food allergy prevents him from enjoying fresh, uncooked fruits, he decided to find a quick and easy cooking method that would retain as much natural flavor as possible. "Roasting the fruit in parchment fit the bill," he told us. "My wife, who is my primary taste-tester and also helps me finalize ideas, had a positive and encouraging reaction to this one. The only difficulty came in preparing the meringue—getting it brown without burning requires a close eye."

# *Heavenly Roasted Fruit*
### *Makes 4 servings*

*You can use almost any fresh fruits in season for this unusual recipe just as long as their flavors are compatible. For testing Scott Breining's recipe, we chose apples and pears, blueberries and strawberries—a lovely combination.*

NOTE: *As for the angel food cake on which the roasted fruits are served, use store-bought or homemade. You might even want to try the Spicy Whole-Wheat Angel Food Cake on page 230.*

**ROASTED FRUITS** (see headnote above)
*1 medium-size apple, peeled, cored, and cut into 12 wedges*

*1 medium-size pear, peeled, cored, and cut into 12 wedges*

*½ cup blueberries, stemmed*

*½ cup small strawberries, hulled*

*1 tablespoon honey*

*1 tablespoon dark brown sugar*

*1 tablespoon Grand Marnier or other orange liqueur*

*¼ teaspoon ground ginger*

**PER SERVING**

212 calories

····

0.7 g fat (0 g saturated)

····

0 mg cholesterol

····

243 mg sodium

····

*¼ teaspoon ground cinnamon*

*4 (2-inch) wedges angel food cake (see Note)*

MERINGUE
*2 large egg whites*

*⅛ teaspoon cream of tartar*

*¼ cup confectioners (10X) sugar*

1. Preheat oven to 400°F. Line one of two (17 x 11-inch) baking pans with baking parchment and set aside. Also tear off four 14-inch lengths of baking parchment.

2. *For roasted fruits:* Combine all fruits, honey, sugar, Grand Marnier, ginger, and cinnamon in large bowl. Place a full ½ cup fruit and juice in center of each of four lengths of parchment, bundle each up, and twist tops to secure. Place bundles on unlined baking pan and bake until fruit is tender but not mushy—15 to 20 minutes. Remove from oven and cool fruit in bundles. Also reduce oven temperature to 275°F.

3. *For meringue:* Beat egg whites and cream of tartar at high electric mixer speed until frothy—about 1 minute. With mixer still at high speed, add 10X sugar gradually and continue beating until meringue peaks stiffly but is not dry—3 to 4 minutes.

4. Using ¼-cup measure, scoop up meringue and drop into four mounds on parchment-lined baking sheet, spacing well apart and swirling into peaks.

5. Bake until meringues are golden—15 to 20 minutes.

6. To serve, place wedge of angel food cake on each of four dessert plates. Open bundles of fruit, one by one, letting contents spill onto cake. With spatula, carefully lift meringues from baking pan and set atop fruit.

RECIPE FROM
*Scott Breining; Gaithersburg, Maryland*

Ben's mother, a native of France, bequeathed to him a liking for complex recipes, although this one is deceptively simple. "Mom used to dip strawberries in sugar or jam, and always used different liquors in her cooking," Ben recalls, adding that this recipe is similar to one she made with wine and a sweet sauce. Born and brought up in New York City and today an engineer specializing in cellular design, Ben is married to a legal secretary and has a teenage daughter. One of his recipes was a prize winner in a recent chocolate festival held in Annapolis, Maryland.

# Amaretto Strawberry Dessert

*Makes 4 servings*

*Few desserts are prettier or easier than this one. And few are lower in fat and calories. We suggest crowning with dollops of Skinny Whipped Topping, then sprigging with mint, lemon geranium, or lemon verbena.*

2 pints red-ripe strawberries, hulled and quartered
  lengthwise

3 tablespoons seedless raspberry jam

2 tablespoons Amaretto

OPTIONAL TOPPING
*Skinny Whipped Topping (page 275)*

OPTIONAL GARNISH
*4 sprigs fresh mint, lemon geranium, or lemon verbena*

PER SERVING

100 calories
....
0.5 g fat (0 g saturated)
....
0 mg cholesterol
....
9 mg sodium
....

1. Place strawberries in small glass or porcelain bowl and set aside.

2. Heat jam in very small nonreactive saucepan or butter warmer over moderately high heat until melted—about 1 minute. Pour over strawberries, add Amaretto, and toss lightly.

3. To serve, divide berry mixture among four stemmed goblets, topping each portion, if you like, with a rounded tablespoon Skinny Whipped Topping and sprigging with mint.

RECIPE FROM

*Ben Levitan; Raleigh, North Carolina*

# . . . and a Bonus Recipe

## Skinny Whipped Topping

*Makes ¾ cup*

*Karen Pickus*, Good Morning America's *Chef/Food Stylist, developed this snowy top-ping, a fat-free "ringer" for whipped cream, and better, we think, than packaged whipped toppings. We use it throughout this book.*

3 tablespoons boiling water

¼ teaspoon plain gelatin

2 teaspoons sugar

3 tablespoons ice water

6 tablespoons nonfat dry milk powder

½ teaspoon vanilla

**PER TABLESPOON**

31 calories

....

0 g fat (0 g saturated)

....

1 mg cholesterol

....

40 mg sodium

....

1. Place boiling water in small bowl. Sprinkle gelatin evenly over water, then move bowl gently this way and that to help gelatin dissolve.

2. Add sugar, ice water, dry milk powder, and vanilla and beat with electric mixer at high speed until completely smooth—30 seconds to 1 minute.

3. Set mixture in refrigerator and chill until consistency of raw egg white—about 15 minutes.

4. Beat at high electric mixer speed until fluffy—about 1 minute—then chill until consistency of softly whipped cream—about 45 minutes. Use as a dessert topping.

**RECIPE FROM**

*Karen Pickus; New York, New York*

# APPENDIX

A CROSS-REFERENCE OF RECIPES BY CATEGORY

## ENTRÉES

### CASSEROLES, QUICHES, AND SAVORY PIES

Gazpacho Casserole

Coq au Vin

Chicken and Vegetable Enchiladas with Sour Cream and Scallions

Black Bean and Chicken Enchiladas with Green Chili Sauce

Spaghetti Squash with Parmesan-Turkey Balls

Tortilla Quiche

Portobello Que Bella

Mexican Black Bean and Quinoa Lasagne with Ancho Chili Sauce

Roasted Corn and Black Bean Enchiladas with Red Chili Sauce

Southport Seafood Pie

Shrimp and Asparagus Casserole

Dieter's Delight Casserole

Eggplant Pirogues

### ROASTS, POT ROASTS, MEAT LOAVES, AND OVEN-FRIES

Dill-Crusted Salmon

Baked King Salmon with Red Wine–Mustard Sauce

Oven-Fried Chicken with Andouille Sausage

Roasted Chicken with Black Bean Sauce

Feta-Stuffed Chicken with Cucumber-Dill Sauce

Chicken Parmesan
Curried Turkey Roulade with Ruby Sauce
Turkey Salsa Meat Loaf
Stuffed Turkey Cutlets
Oven-Fried Turkey Feathers with Jalapeño Pepper Mayonnaise
Ginger-Poached Filet of Beef with Vegetables and Horseradish Sauce
Some Kind of Wonderful Venison
Roast Pork Tenderloin with Garlic and Apples

## GRILLS AND SAUTÉS, STIR-FRIES, AND SKILLET DISHES

Emeril's Potato-Crusted Fish with a French Green Bean Relish
Cajun Cod Fillet with Melon Salsa
Grilled Halibut with Rum Sauce, Great Greens, and Olives
Poached Sea Bass with Shiitake-Soy Broth
Sea Bass with Curried Lentils and Rice
Herbed Snapper with Warm Mango Salsa
Fish Masala
Shrimp in Tasso Cream Sauce with Eggplant Medallions
Chicken Cutlets with Roasted Red Peppers, Clelia Style
Chicken Breasts and Fresh Tomatoes with Capers
Tasty Tangerine-Grilled Chicken
Low-Fat Tequila-Lime Chicken
Dijon Rosemary Chicken
Lean Caribbean Chicken with Rice
Oriental Chicken in a Garden
Curried Chicken
Broiled Marinated Lamb with Mediterranean Vegetables
Spicy Pork Lo Murro

## SOUPS AND STEWS

Stonington Clam Chowder
Cioppino
Teresina's Minestrone
Red Pepper Soup with Pan-Grilled Shrimp
Caramelized Onion Soup with Lemon-Corn Chutney
Hearty Broccoli-Potato Soup
Cabbage Soup with Turkey Sausage
Pasta e Fagioli (Pasta and Bean Soup)

Slickrock Mesa Chicken Stew
Romero Green Chili and Beans
Labladie's Lite Chili
Veal Stew in the Style of Ossobuco

## PASTA, RICE, AND OTHER GRAINS

Cajun Chicken Pasta
Fast and Easy Fusilli with Red Pepper Cream Sauce
Chipotle-Beer Shrimp with Pasta
Rebecca's Linguine with White Clam Sauce
Linguine with Crab and a Touch of Lemon
Penne Pasta with Eggplant, Tomatoes, and Olives
Sunny Penne Pasta with Seven Vegetables
Pasta di Cucina with Broccoli Rabe
Basil-Lemon Bowties
Creamy Shrimp with Rice
Dieter's Delight Casserole
Risotto-Stuffed Artichokes
Mexican Black Bean and Quinoa Lasagne with Ancho Chili Sauce

## SALADS AND SANDWICHES

Spicy Salmon Salad
Pecos Chicken-Cornbread Salad
Southwest Couscous Salad
Mushroom Veggie Burgers

## PIZZAS, WRAPS, AND ROLLS

Spicy Asian Pork Rolls
Smoked Sausage Tacos with Mango-*Chipotle* Sauce
Crab Enchiladas
Fajitas Richard
Sweet Potato Burritos
Black Bean–Mango Burritos
Quick Tortilla Pizzas

# DESERTS

### CAKES

Nonna's Raw Apple Cake
Plain and Fancy Tea Cake
It's My Chocolate Cake
Heavenly Chocolate Pudding Cake with Hot Fudge–Kahlúa Sauce
Chocoholic's Carob Cake with Orange Marmalade and Carob Frosting
Sara Moulton's Angel Food Cake with Mocha Sauce
Spicy Whole-Wheat Angel Food Cake
Dream Shares

### CHEESECAKES

Caramel Cheesecake with Praline Sauce
Paul's Chocolate Cheesecake
"Not" Cream Cheese Cake
Double Chocolate Hazelnut Cheesecake
Black Forest Cheesecake
Orange Cheesecake

### COOKIES

Caramel Apricot Brownies
Jennifer's Really Good Low-Fat Chocolate Chip Cookies
Peanut Butter–Chocolate Chip Cookies
Toffee Chip Cookies
Energy Cookies
Quick-as-a-Wink Lemon Balls
Lemon Meringue Cookies

### FROZEN DESSERTS

Emeril's Roasted Peach Soup with a Peach and Raspberry Sorbet
Crêpes Bombes Nanette

### FRUIT DESSERTS

Peach and Almond Custard Tart
Emeril's Roasted Peach Soup with a Peach and Raspberry Sorbet

Upside-Down Peach Pudding-Cake
Amaretto-Baked Pears in Pastry
Angel Food Biscotti with Raspberry Coulis
Sweet Nachos with Fresh Raspberry Salsa
Crêpes Bombes Nanette
Simply Marvelous Meringues
Celestial Fruit Mousse in Meringue Nests with Raspberry Sauce
Blueberry Crisp
Balsamic Berries with Vanilla Cream
Luscious Lemon-Berry Parfait
Heavenly Roasted Fruit
Amaretto Strawberry Dessert

## PIES AND TARTS

Italian Ricotta Pie
Peach and Almond Custard Tart
Lee's Low-Fat Peanut Butter Pie

## PUDDINGS

Carol's Tirami Sù
Bread Pudding
Low-Fat Chocolate-Banana Bread Pudding
Karen's Chocolate Pudding with Pralined Pecans
French Cream, Skinnied Down and Gussied Up
Lower-Calorie Rice Pudding
Date Pudding
Banana Flan with Exotic Sauce
Celestial Fruit Mousse in Meringue Nests with Raspberry Sauce
Blueberry Crisp
Upside-Down Peach Pudding-Cake

## TOPPING

Skinny Whipped Topping

# RECIPE CONTRIBUTORS

*(in alphabetical order)*

Ida Florence Alkire; Seiling, Oklahoma

Martha Allison; Amarillo, Texas

Nanette Alsop; Houston, Texas

Virginia C. Anthony; Jacksonville, Florida

Rebecca L. Balent; Exeter, Pennsylvania

Timothy G. Ball; West Seneca, New York

Mark and Colleen Barricklow; Fishers, Indiana

Patricia Beels; St. Clair Shores, Michigan

Karen R. Berner; Rhinebeck, New York

Michelle Block; San Jose, California

Page K. Booth; Richmond, Virginia

Karen Borch; Albuquerque, New Mexico

Alba Bragoli-Harding; Norfolk, Virginia

Scott Breining; Gaithersburg, Maryland

Rachel W. N. Brown; Mt. Sidney, Virginia

Chamein T. Canton; Amityville, New York

Patty Carson/Romero; New Castle, Colorado

Patricia Cassaro; Dallas, Texas

Gail S. Chammavanijakul; Dallas, Texas

Laurie Christopher; Portland, Oregon

Joan W. Churchill; Dover, New Hampshire

Nadine Clapp; Kansas City, Missouri

Sally Clark; Belding, Michigan

Kathy Cline; Rapid City, South Dakota

Edward Clukey; Terryville, Connecticut

Margaret Coalter; Eagar, Arizona

Barry Cohen; Cherry Hill, New Jersey

Erin Coopey; Mountain View, California

Leslie S. Couick; Rock Hill, South Carolina

Brigitte Cox; Hobe Sound, Florida

Jan Curry; Raleigh, North Carolina

Sharon A. Curry; Independence, Missouri

Darla J. Dalhover; Cincinnati, Ohio

Devon Delaney; Princeton, New Jersey

Alys R. Disterdick; Thousand Palms, California

Mary E. Ditto; Oak Park, Illinois

Stephanie Donovan; Mammoth Lakes, California

Emily Oaks Edens; Sanders, Kentucky

Clelia Graceffa Egan; Needham, Massachusetts

Betty Fauerbach; Clyde, North Carolina

Ellen Featherstone; Richmond, Virginia

Kathy Figueiredo; Westlake Village, California

Vincent V. Formisano; Weymouth, Massachusetts

Carl Franco; West Chester, Ohio

Doris Fridley; St. Louis, Missouri

Joanne M. Friedman; Newton, New Jersey

Sandy Fuller; Odessa, Florida

Nanette Gallagher; Coventry, Rhode Island

Jessica Gambino; Cañon City, Colorado

Joseph C. Gambino; Cañon City, Colorado

Lynn Geiger; Athens, Georgia

Kim A. Gilliland; Grove City, Pennsylvania

Beverly Goldberg; Stratford, Connecticut

Florence E. Goodman; Beverly, Massachusetts

Marsha D. Green; New York, New York

Sandy Greene; Wayne, Pennsylvania

Leanne Guido; Silver Spring, Maryland

Bobbie Lee Hatfield; Myrtle Beach, South Carolina

Phil Herron; Marietta, Georgia

Dawna Hoerner; Miamisburg, Ohio

Laura Hoover; Swisher, Iowa

Susan E. Hulburt; Sugar Land, Texas

Helen E. James; Rancho Mirage, California

Veronica Johnson; Seattle, Washington

Melissa Juarbe; Parsons, Kansas

Dianne Kaatz; Spokane, Washington

Mary Beth Kerekes; Boston, New York

Dru Kovacevich; Bakersfield, California

Poolsin Krisananuwatara; Houston, Texas

**Emeril Lagasse; New Orleans, Louisiana**

Ben Levitan; Raleigh, North Carolina

Mary Lu Lewis; Harrisonburg, Virginia

Arthur W. Lumsden; Cheyenne, Wyoming

Marcia Martin; Houston, Texas

Gayla J. McAlary; Jenks, Oklahoma

Wanda McHatton; Phoenix, Arizona

Meghan McVey; Bessemer, Michigan

Shawn Merkel; Owosso, Michigan

**Sara Moulton; New York, New York**

Joann Murro; Sewell, New Jersey

Vicki Niolet; Bay St. Louis, Mississippi

Debbie Paixão; Burlington, New Jersey

Shirley J. Panning; Ashburn, Virginia

Marolyn B. Patton; Yerington, Nevada

**Karen Pickus; New York, New York**

Shelly Platten; Amherst, Wisconsin

Paul Provenzano; Missouri City, Texas

Jennifer Regan-Mitchell; Tomahawk, Wisconsin

"John" Vernon Reid; Santa Monica, California

Kristin Renzema; Warren, Oregon

Dana Richardson; Durham, North Carolina

Richard Rizzio Jr.; Troy, Michigan

Carol Ross; Boyne City, Michigan

Richard Northcutt Saccaro; Watchung, New Jersey

Jenny Sacks; New Orleans, Louisiana

Carmel M. Salandra; Williamsville, New York

Ziva Santop; Agoura Hills, California

Keith Scardina; Baton Rouge, Louisiana

Joseph V. Schneider; North East, Pennsylvania

Diane Schofield; Penfield, New York

Kim Dayna Shafer; Barstow, California

Margaret Shelton; Chatham, Virginia

Arthur Sickle; Cheshire, Connecticut

Sherry Sirch; Kamloops, British Columbia, Canada

Celeste Skogerboe; Bemidji, Minnesota

Bruni Slinn; Aurora, Colorado

Angela Sommers; Lafayette, Louisiana

Suraiya Soofi; Southbridge, Massachusetts

Lisa Stift; Salem, New Hampshire

Margee Striler-Berry; White Salmon, Washington

Sarah Tackett; Springfield, Ohio

Donna Booth Turrisi; Pawcatuck, Connecticut

Marie Valenzuela; Westminster, Colorado

Amy L. Wasserman; Pelham, Massachusetts

Patricia Waterman; Flower Mound, Texas

Jo Anne C. White; Winnsboro, Texas

Robin Wilson; San Jose, California

DonnaMarie Zotter; Mechanicsburg, Pennsylvania

# Index

## A

Adobo, 102

Alkire, Ida Florence, 242–43

Allison, Martha, 102–3

Almond, Peach and, Custard Tart, 192–93

Alsop, Nanette, 258–59

Amaretto-Baked Pears in Pastry, 254–55

Ancho Chili Sauce, Mexican Black Bean and Quinoa Lasagne with, 166–68

Anderson, Jean, xv

Andouille Sausage, Oven-Fried Chicken with, 50–51

Angel Food Biscotti with Raspberry Coulis, 265–66

Angel food cake 271

Angel Food Cake, Sara Moulton's, with Mocha Sauce, 228–29

Angel Food Cake, Spicy Whole-Wheat, 230–31

Anthony, Virginia C., 62–63

Apple Cake, Nonna's Raw, 220–21

Apples, Roast Pork Tenderloin with Garlic and, 124–25

Arborio rice, 162

Artichokes, Risotto-Stuffed, 162–63

Asparagus, Shrimp and, Casserole, 35–36

Asparatame, 208, 224

## B

Baked King Salmon with Red Wine–Mustard Sauce, 18–19

Balent, Rebecca L., 37–38

Ball, Timothy G., 80

Balsamic Berries with Vanilla Cream, 252–53

Banana Flan with Exotic Sauce, 212–13

Barricklow, Colleen, 267–68

Barricklow, Mark, 267–68

Basil-Lemon Bowties, 160–61

Basmati rice, 13, 22, 91

Baumgart, Margo, xiii, xiv

Bayless, Rick, 102

Beans, Romero Green Chili and, 128–29

Beef, Ginger-Poached Filet of, with Vegetables and Horseradish Sauce, 108–10

Beels, Patricia, 260–62

Bell peppers, xvii, 62

Berner, Karen R., 11–12

Biscotti, Angel Food, with Raspberry Coulis, 265–66

Black Bean, Mexican, and Quinoa Lasagne with Ancho Chili Sauce, 166–68

Black Bean, Roasted Corn
and, Enchiladas with
Red Chili Sauce,
140–41
Black Bean and Chicken
Enchiladas with Green
Chili Sauce, 83–84
Black Bean–Mango Burritos,
138–39
Black Bean Sauce, Roasted
Chicken with, 72–73
Black Forest Cheesecake,
186–88
Black pepper, xvii
Block, Michelle, 254–55
Blueberry Crisp, 267–68
Booth, Page K., 140–41
Borch, Karen, 142–43
Bowties, Basil-Lemon,
160–61
Bragoli-Harding, Alba,
220–21
Bread Pudding, 204–5
Bread Pudding, Low-Fat
Chocolate-Banana,
202–3
Breining, Scott, 271–72
Broccoli-Potato Soup,
Hearty, 171–72
Broccoli Rabe, Pasta di
Cucina with, 156–57
Broiled Marinated Lamb
with Mediterranean
Vegetables, 119–21
Brown, Rachel W. N., 206–7
Brownies, Caramel Apricot,
234–35

Butter, xvii
Burritos, Black Bean–Mango,
138–39
Burritos, Sweet Potato,
136–37

*C*

Cabbage Soup with Turkey
Sausage, 104–5
Cajun Chicken Pasta, 64–65
Cajun Cod Fillet with Melon
Salsa, 9–10
Cake, Upside-Down Peach
Pudding, 214–15
Cakes and cookies, 217–47
Caramel Apricot
Brownies, 234–35
Chocoholic's Carob Cake
with Orange
Marmalade and Carob
Frosting, 226–27
Dream Shares, 232–33
Energy Cookies, 242–43
Heavenly Chocolate
Pudding Cake with Hot
Fudge–Kahlúa Sauce,
222–23
It's My Chocolate Cake,
224–25
Jennifer's Really Good
Low-Fat Chocolate
Chip Cookies, 236–37
Lemon Meringue
Cookies, 246–47

Nonna's Raw Apple Cake,
220–21
Peanut Butter–Chocolate
Chip Cookies, 238–39
Plain and Fancy Tea Cake,
218–19
Quick-As-A-Wink
Lemon Balls, 244–45
Sara Moulton's Angel Food
Cake with Mocha
Sauce, 228–29
Spicy Whole-Wheat Angel
Food Cake, 230–31
Toffee Chip Cookies,
240–41
Canton, Chamein T.,
186–88
Capers, Chicken Breasts and
Fresh Tomatoes with,
54–55
Caramel Apricot Brownies,
234–35
Caramel Cheesecake with
Praline Sauce, 178–79
Caramelized Onion Soup
with Lemon-Corn
Chutney, 173–74
Carob Cake, Chocoholic's,
with Orange
Marmalade and Carob
Frosting, 226–27
Carob Frosting, Chocoholic's
Carob Cake with
Orange Marmalade
and, 226–27
Carob powder, 226
Carol's Tirami Sù, 198–99

Carson/Romero, Patty,
128–29
Cassaro, Patricia, 45–46
Casserole, Dieter's Delight,
148–49
Casserole, Gazpacho,
114–15
Casserole, Shrimp and
Asparagus, 35–36
Celestial Fruit Mousse in
Meringue Nests with
Raspberry Sauce,
260–62
Chammavanijakul, Gail S.,
33–34
Chase, Sylvia, xiii
Cheesecakes, 177–90
Black Forest Cheesecake,
186–88
Caramel Cheesecake with
Praline Sauce, 178–79
Double Chocolate
Hazelnut Cheesecake,
182–83
"Not" Cream Cheese
Cake, 180–81
Orange Cheesecake,
189–90
Paul's Chocolate
Cheesecake, 184–85
Chicken, Black Bean, and
Enchiladas with Green
Chili Sauce, 83–84
Chicken, Curried, 76–77
Chicken, Dijon Rosemary,
68–69
Chicken, Feta-Stuffed, with

Cucumber-Dill Sauce,
60–61
Chicken, Lean Caribbean,
with Rice, 66–67
Chicken, Low-Fat
Tequila-Lime, 58–59
Chicken, Oriental, in a
Garden, 62–63
Chicken, Oven-Fried, with
Andouille Sausage,
50–51
Chicken, Roasted, with
Black Bean Sauce,
72–73
Chicken, Tasty Tangerine-
Grilled, 56–57
Chicken and Vegetable
Enchiladas with Sour
Cream and Scallions,
80–82
Chicken Breasts and Fresh
Tomatoes with Capers,
54–55
Chicken-Cornbread Salad,
Pecos, 85–86
Chicken Cutlets with
Roasted Red Peppers,
Clelia Style, 52–53
Chicken Parmesan, 70–71
Chicken Pasta, Cajun, 64–65
Chicken Stew, Slickrock
Mesa, 78–79
Chiffonade, 158, 160
Child, Julia, 108, 119, 164
Chili, Labladie's Lite, 98–99
Chili, Romero Green, and
Beans, 128–29

Chili peppers, 128
Chill
defined, xvi
Chipotle-Beer Shrimp with
Pasta, 31–32
Chipotles, 102
Chocoholic's Carob Cake
with Orange
Marmalade and Carob
Frosting, 226–27
Chocolate-Banana Bread
Pudding, Low-Fat,
202–3
Chocolate Cake, It's My,
224–25
Chocolate Cheesecake, Paul's
184–85
Chocolate Chip Cookies,
Jennifer's Really Good
Low-Fat, 236–37
Chocolate Chip Cookies,
Peanut Butter-,
238–39
Chocolate Hazelnut Cheese-
cake, Double, 182–83
Chocolate Pudding, Karen's,
with Pralined Pecans,
200–1
Chocolate Pudding Cake,
Heavenly, with Hot
Fudge-Kahlúa
Chocolate Sauce, 222–23
Christopher, Laurie, 146–47
Churchill, Joan W., 4–6
Chutney
lemon-corn, 174
Chutney, Lemon-Corn,

Caramelized Onion
   Soup with, 173–74
Cioppino, 43–44
Clam Chowder, Stonington,
   47–48
Clams
   little necks, 37
Clapp, Nadine, 68–69
Clark, Sally, 41–42
Cline, Kathy, 64–65
Clukey, Edward, 87
Coalter, Margaret, 164–65
Cod Fillet, Cajun, with
   Melon Salsa, 9–10
Cohen, Barry, 166–68
Cookies
   see Cakes and cookies
Cool
   defined, xvi
Coopey, Erin, 152–53
Coq au Vin, 74–75
Corn, Roasted, and Black
   Bean Enchiladas with
   Red Chili Sauce,
   140–41
Cornbread, 85
Cornbread, Pecos Chicken-,
   Salad, 85–86
Couick, Leslie S., 222–23
Couscous Salad, Southwest,
   164–65
Cox, Brigitte, 212–13
Crab, Linguine with, and a
   Touch of Lemon,
   39–40
Crab Enchiladas, 41–42
Crabmeat, 26

Cream Cheese Cake, "Not,"
   180–81
Creamy Shrimp with Rice,
   33–34
Cremini, 122
Crêpes Bombes Nanette,
   258–59
Crusts
   Cheesecakes, 178, 180,
      182, 184, 186, 189
   graham cracker, 196
   pie, 26, 192
Cucumber-Dill Sauce,
   Feta-Stuffed Chicken
   with, 60–61
Curried Chicken, 76–77
Curried Turkey Roulade
   with Ruby Sauce,
   91–93
Curry, Jan, xiv–xv, 178–79
Curry, Sharon A., 74–75
Custard Tart, Peach and
   Almond, 192–93
Cut the Calories Cook-Off,
   xiii–xv

D

Dalhover, Darla J., 76–77
Date pudding, 210–11
Delaney, Devon, 265–66
Desserts, 175–90
   fruit, 249–75
Dieter's Delight Casserole,
   148–49

Dijon Rosemary Chicken,
   68–69
Dill-Crusted Salmon, 20–21
Disterdick, Alys R., 210–11
Ditto, Mary E., 169–70
Donovan, Stephanie, 138–39
Double Chocolate Hazelnut
   Cheesecake, 182–83
Dream Shares, 232–33
Dressings, 4, 5, 24

E

Edens, Emily Oaks, 208–9
Egan, Clelia Graceffa, 52–53
Eggplant, Tomatoes, and
   Olives, Penne Pasta
   with, 152–53
Eggplant Medallions, Shrimp
   in Tasso Cream Sauce
   with, 29–30
Eggs, xvii
Emeril's Potato-Crusted Fish
   with a French Green
   Bean Relish, 15–17
Emeril's Roasted Peach Soup
   with a Peach and
   Raspberry Sorbet,
   269–70
Enchiladas, Black Bean and
   Chicken, with Green
   Chili Sauce, 83–84
Enchiladas, Chicken and
   Vegetable, with Sour
   Cream and Scallions,
   80–82

Enchiladas, Crab, 41–42
Enchiladas, Roasted Corn and Black Bean, with Red Chili Sauce, 140–41
Energy Cookies, 242–43
Entrées, 1–174
Exotic Sauce, Banana Flan with, 212–13

### F

Farfalle (pasta bowties), 160
Fast and Easy Fusilli with Red Pepper Cream Sauce, 158–59
Fauerbach, Betty, 35–36
Featherstone, Ellen, 96–97
Feta-Stuffed Chicken with Cucumber-Dill Sauce, 60–61
Figueiredo, Kathy, 263–64
Filling(s)
    cakes and cookies, 227
    cheesecakes, 180, 182–83, 184, 187, 189–90
    pies, 192–93, 198
Fillo, 254
Fish, Emeril's Potato-Crusted, with a French Green Bean Relish, 15–17
Fish Masala, 22–23
Flan, Banana, with Exotic Sauce, 212–13
Flour, xvii

Formisano, Vincent V., 132–33
Franco, Carl, 13–14
French Cream, Skinnied Down and Gussied Up, 206–7
French Green Bean Relish, Emeril's Potato-Crusted Fish with a, 15–17
Fridley, Doris, 114–15
Friedman, Joanne M., 156–57, 194–95
Frosting, 225, 227
Fruit desserts, 249–75
    Amaretto-Baked Pears in Pastry, 254–55
    Amaretto Strawberry Dessert, 273–74
    Angel Food Biscotti with Raspberry Coulis, 265–66
    Balsamic Berries with Vanilla Cream, 252–53
    Blueberry Crisp, 267–68
    Celestial Fruit Mousse in Meringue Nests with Raspberry Sauce, 260–62
    Crêpes Bombes Nanette, 258–59
    Emeril's Roasted Peach Soup with a Peach and Raspberry Sorbet, 269–70
    Heavenly Roasted Fruit, 271–72

Luscious Lemon-Berry Parfait, 250–51
    Simply Marvelous Meringues, 263–64
    Sweet Nachos with Fresh Raspberry Salsa, 256–57
Fruit Mousse, Celestial, in Meringue Nests with Raspberry Sauce, 260–62
Fruits, roasted, 271–72
Fuller, Sandy, 58–59
Fusilli, Fast and Easy, with Red Pepper Cream Sauce, 158–59

### G

Gaffney, Rickie, xv
Gallagher, Nanette, 154–55
Gambino, Jessica, 26–28
Gambino, Joseph C., 234–35
Garlic and Apples, Roast Pork Tenderloin with, 124–25
Garlic cloves, xvii
Garnish
    seafood, 8
Gazpacho Casserole, 114–15
Geiger, Lynn, 252–53
Gibson, Charlie, xiv
Gilliland, Kim A., 171–72
Ginger-Poached Filet of Beef with Vegetables and Horseradish Sauce, 108–10

Goldberg, Beverly, 144–45
Goodman, Florence E.,
    218–19
Graham cracker crusts, 196
Green, Marsha D., 160–61
Green Chili, Romero, and
    Beans, 128–29
Green Chili Sauce, Black
    Bean and Chicken
    Enchiladas with, 83–84
Greene, Sandy, xiv, 50–51
Grilled Halibut with Rum
    Sauce, Great Greens,
    and Olives, 4–6
Guido, Leanne, 70–71

### H

Halibut, Grilled, with Rum
    Sauce, Great Greens,
    and Olives, 4–6
Hatfield, Bobbie Lee,
    196–97
Hayes, Joanne Lamb, xv
Hazan, Marcella, 108
Hazelnut Cheesecake,
    Double Chocolate,
    182–83
Hearty Broccoli-Potato
    Soup, 171–72
Heavenly Chocolate Pudding
    Cake with Hot
    Fudge-Kahlúa Sauce,
    222–23
Heavenly Roasted Fruit,
    271–72

Herbed Snapper with Warm
    Mango Salsa, 7–8
Herron, Phil, 256–57
Hoerner, Dawna, 189–90
Hoover, Laura, 31–32
Horseradish Sauce,
    Ginger-Poached Filet of
    Beef with Vegetables
    and, 108–10
Hot Fudge–Kahlúa Sauce,
    Heavenly Chocolate
    Pudding Cake with, 222–23
Hulburt, Susan E., 54–55

### I

Ingredient substitution, xv
Isoldi, Kathy, xiv
Italian Ricotta Pie, 194–95
It's My Chocolate Cake,
    224–25

### J

Jalapeño Pepper Mayonnaise,
    Oven-Fried Turkey
    Feathers with, 89–90
James, Helen E., 244–45
Jennifer's Really Good
    Low-Fat Chocolate
    Chip Cookies, 236–37
Johnson, Veronica, 39–40
Juarbe, Melissa, 66–67
Juices, fresh, xvi

### K

Kaatz, Dianne, 214–15
Kerekes, Mary Beth, 130–31
Kovacevich, Dru, 173–74
Krisananuwatara, Poolsin,
    24–25
Kumin, Albert, 119

### L

Labladie's Lite Chili, 98–99
Labna, 267
Lagasse, Emeril, xiv, xv,
    15–17, 269–70
Lamb, Broiled Marinated,
    with Mediterranean
    Vegetables, 119–21
Lasagne, Mexican Black Bean
    and Quinoa, with
    Ancho Chili Sauce,
    166–68
Lean Caribbean Chicken
    with Rice, 66–67
Leeks, fresh, xvi
Lee's Low-Fat Peanut Butter
    Pie, 196–97
Lemon, Linguine with Crab
    and a Touch of, 39–40
Lemon Balls, Quick-As-A-
    Wink, 244–45
Lemon-Berry Parfait,
    Luscious, 250–51
Lemon-Corn Chutney,
    Caramelized Onion
    Soup with 173–74
Lemon zest, xvi

Lentils, Curried, and Rice, Sea Bass with, 13–14
Levitan, Ben, 273–74
Lewis, Mary Lu, 148–49
Linguine, Rebecca's, with White Clam Sauce, 37–38
Linguine with Crab and a Touch of Lemon, 39–40
Lomonaco, Michael, xiv
Low-Calorie Rice Pudding, 208–9
Low-Fat Chocolate-Banana Bread Pudding, 202–3
Low-Fat Tequila-Lime Chicken, 58–59
Lumsden, Arthur W., 230–31
Luscious Lemon-Berry Parfait, 250–51

## M

McAlary, Gayla J., 100–1
McFadden, Cynthia, xiii
McGrady, Phyllis, xv
McHatton, Wanda, 18–19
McVey, Meghan, 240–41
Mango, Black Bean-, Burritos, 138–39
Mango-Chipotle Sauce, Smoked Sausage Tacos with, 102–3
Mango Salsa, Herbed Snapper with Warm, 7–8

Mariani, John, 198
Marinades
  meat, 111, 120, 122
  seafood, 5, 13
  vegetable, 111
Martin, Marcia, 83
Masala, 22
Mayonnaise, 90
Meat, 107–33
  Broiled Marinated Lamb with Mediterranean Vegetables, 119–21
  Fajitas Richard, 111–13
  Gazpacho Casserole, 114–15
  Ginger-Poached Filet of Beef with Vegetables and Horseradish Sauce, 108–10
  Pasta e Fagioli (Pasta and Bean Soup), 132–33
  Romero Green Chili and Beans, 128–29
  Some Kind of Wonderful Venison, 122–23
  Spicy Asian Pork Rolls, 130–31
  Spicy Pork Lo Murro, 126–27
  Roast Pork Tenderloin with Garlic and Apples, 124–25
  Veal Stew in the Style of Ossobuco, 116–18
Meat Loaf, Turkey Salsa, 94–95

Meatless entrées, 135–74
  Basil-Lemon Bowties, 160–61
  Black Bean-Mango Burritos, 138–39
  Carmelized Onion Soup with Lemon-Corn Chutney, 173–74
  Dieter's Delight Casserole, 148–49
  Eggplant Pirogues, 150–51
  Fast and Easy Fusilli with Red Pepper Cream Sauce, 158–59
  Hearty Broccoli-Potato Soup, 171–72
  Mexican Black Bean and Quinoa Lasagne with Ancho Chili Sauce, 166–68
  Mushroom Veggie Burgers, 144–45
  Pasta di Cucina with Broccoli Rabe, 156–57
  Penne Pasta with Eggplant, Tomatoes, and Olives, 152–53
  Portobello Que Bella, 146–47
  Quick Tortilla Pizzas, 142–43
  Risotto-Stuffed Artichokes, 162–63
  Roasted Corn and Black Bean Enchiladas with

Red Chili Sauce,
140–41
Southwest Couscous
Salad, 164–65
Sunny Penne Pasta with
Seven Vegetables,
154–55
Sweet Potato Burritos,
136–37
Teresina's Minestrone,
169–70
Melon Salsa, Cajun Cod
Fillet with, 9–10
Meringue, 272
Meringue Nests, Celestial
Fruit Mousse in, with
Raspberry Sauce,
260–62
Meringues, Simply
Marvelous, 263–64
Merkel, Shawn, 162–63
Mesclun, 4
Mexican Black Bean and
Quinoa Lasagne with
Ancho Chili Sauce,
166–68
Minestrone, Teresina's,
169–70
Mocha Sauce, Sara Moulton's
Angel Food Cake with,
228–29
Moulton, Sara, 108–10,
124–25, 228–29
Mousse, Celestial Fruit, in
Meringue Nests with
Raspberry Sauce,
260–62

Murro, Joann, 126–27
Mushroom Veggie Burgers,
144–45
Mushrooms, xvii, 11, 144,
146

N

Nachos, Sweet, with Fresh
Raspberry Salsa,
256–57
Niolet, Vicki, 150–51
Nonna's Raw Apple Cake,
220–21
Nonreactive pan(s), xv, 4,
11, 18
Nonstick cooking spray, xvii
"Not" Cream Cheese Cake,
180–81
Nutrient counts, xvii

O

Olive Oil, xvii
Olives, Penne Pasta with
Eggplant, Tomatoes,
and, 152–53
Onion Soup, Caramelized,
with Lemon-Corn
Chutney, 173–74
Onions, xvii, 45
Orange Cheesecake, 189–90
Orange Marmalade,
Chocoholic's Carob
Cake with, and Carob

Frosting, 226–27
Oriental Chicken in a
Garden, 62–63
Ossobuco, Veal Stew in the
Style of, 116–18
Oven-Fried Chicken with
Andouille Sausage,
50–51
Oven-Fried Turkey Feathers
with Jalapeño Pepper
Mayonnaise, 89–90

P

Paixão, Debbie, 122–23
Pancetta, 132
Panning, Shirley J., 9–10
Parfait, Luscious
Lemon-Berry, 250–51
Parmesan-Turkey Balls,
Spaghetti Squash with,
96–97
Parmigiano reggiano, xvi
Pasta, Cajun Chicken, 64–65
Pasta, Chipotle-Beer Shrimp
with, 31–32
Pasta, Penne, with Eggplant,
Tomatoes, and Olives,
152–53
Pasta, Sunny Penne, with
Seven Vegetables,
154–55
Pasta bowties, 160
Pasta di Cucina with
Broccoli Rabe, 156–57

Pasta e Fagioli (Pasta and
Bean Soup), 132–33
Pastry, Amaretto-Baked
Pears in, 254–55
Patton, Marolyn B., 43–44
Paul's Chocolate
Cheesecake, 184–85
Peach and Almond Custard
Tart, 192–93
Peach Pudding Cake,
Upside-Down, 214–15
Peach Soup, Emeril's
Roasted, with a Peach
and Raspberry Sorbet,
269–70
Peanut Butter-Chocolate
Chip Cookies, 238–39
Peanut Butter Pie, Lee's
Low-Fat, 196–97
Pears, Amaretto-Baked, in
Pastry, 254–55
Pecans, Karen's Chocolate
Pudding with Pralined,
200–1
Pecos Chicken-Cornbread
Salad, 85–86
Penne Pasta with Eggplant,
Tomatoes, and Olives,
152–53
Pépin, Jacques, 108
Phan, Charles, 11
Pickus, Karen, xiv, xv, 102,
119–21, 200–1, 275
Pies and puddings, 191–215
Banana Flan with Exotic
Sauce, 212–13
Bread Pudding, 204–5

Carol's Tirami Sù, 198–99
Date Pudding, 210–11
French Cream, Skinnied
Down and Gussied Up,
206–7
Italian Ricotta Pie, 194–95
Karen's Chocolate
Pudding with Pralined
Pecans, 200–1
Lee's Low-Fat Peanut
Butter Pie, 196–97
Low-Calorie Rice
Pudding, 208–9
Low-Fat Chocolate-Banana
Bread Pudding, 202–3
Peach and Almond
Custard Tart, 192–93
Upside-Down Peach
Pudding Cake, 214–15
Pignoli (pine nuts), 52, 162
Pizzas, Quick Tortilla,
142–43
Plain and Fancy Tea Cake,
218–19
Platter, Shelly, 85
Poached Sea Bass with
Shiitake-Soy Broth,
11–12
Pork Lo Murro, Spicy,
126–27
Pork Rolls, Spicy Asian,
130–31
Pork Tenderloin, Roast, with
Garlic and Apples,
124–25
Portobello Que Bella,
146–47

Portobello mushrooms, 144
Potato Soup, Hearty
Broccoli-, 171–72
Potatoes, xvii
Poultry, 49–105
Black Bean and Chicken
Enchiladas with Green
Chili Sauce, 83–84
Cabbage Soup with Turkey
Sausage, 104–5
Cajun Chicken Pasta,
64–65
Chicken and Vegetable
Enchiladas with Sour
Cream and Scallions,
80–82
Chicken Breasts and Fresh
Tomatoes with Capers,
54–55
Chicken Cutlets with
Roasted Red Peppers,
Clelia Style, 52–53
Chicken Parmesan, 70–71
Coq au Vin, 74–75
Curried Chicken, 76–77
Curried Turkey Roulade
with Ruby Sauce,
91–93
Dijon Rosemary Chicken,
68–69
Feta-Stuffed Chicken with
Cucumber-Dill Sauce,
60–61
Labladie's Lite Chili,
98–99
Lean Caribbean Chicken
with Rice, 66–67

Low-Fat Tequila-Lime Chicken, 58–59
Oriental Chicken in a Garden, 62–63
Oven-Fried Chicken with Andouille Sausage, 50–51
Oven-Fried Turkey Feathers with Jalapeño Pepper Mayonnaise, 89–90
Pecos Chicken-Cornbread Salad, 85–86
Roasted Chicken with Black Bean Sauce, 72–73
Slickrock Mesa Chicken Stew, 78–79
Smoked Sausage Tacos with Mango-Chipotle Sauce, 102–3
Spaghetti Squash with Parmesan-Turkey Balls, 96–97
Stuffed Turkey Cutlets, 87–88
Tasty Tangerine-Grilled Chicken, 56–57
Tortilla Quiche, 100–1
Turkey Salsa Meat Loaf, 94–95
Praline Sauce, Caramel Cheesecake with, 178–79
Preheating, xvi
Provenzano, Paul, 184–85
Prudhomme, Paul, 15
Puck, Wolfgang, xiv

Puddings
    see Pies and puddings

Q

Quiche, Tortilla, 100–1
Quick-As-A-Wink Lemon Balls, 244–45
Quick Tortilla Pizzas, 142–43
Quinoa, Mexican Black Bean and, Lasagne with Ancho Chili Sauce, 166–68

R

Raspberry Coulis, Angel Food Biscotti with, 265–66
Raspberry Salsa, Sweet Nachos with Fresh, 256–57
Raspberry Sauce, Celestial Fruit Mousse in Meringue Nests with, 260–62
Rebecca's Linguine with White Clam Sauce, 37–38
Red Chili Sauce, Roasted Corn and Black Bean Enchiladas with, 140–41
Red Pepper Cream Sauce, Fast and Easy Fusilli with, 158–59

Red Pepper Soup with Pan-Grilled Shrimp, 45–46
Red Peppers, Roasted, Chicken Cutlets with, Clelia Style, 52–53
Red Wine-Mustard Sauce, Baked King Salmon with, 18–19
Regan-Mitchell, Jennifer, 236–37
Reid, "John" Vernon, 7–8
Relish, 16
Renzema, Kristin, 182–83
Rice
    leftover, 26, 66
    long-grain, 33
Rice, Creamy Shrimp with, 33–34
Rice, Lean Caribbean Chicken with, 66–67
Rice, Sea Bass with Curried Lentils and, 13–14
Rice Pudding, Low-Calorie, 208–9
Richardson, Dana, 136–37
Ricotta Pie, Italian, 194–95
Risotto-Stuffed Artichokes, 162–63
Rizzio, Richard, Jr., 89–90
Roast Pork Tenderloin with Garlic and Apples, 124–25
Roasted Chicken with Black Bean Sauce, 72–73
Roasted Corn and Black Bean Enchiladas with Red Chili Sauce, 140–41

Romero Green Chili and
    Beans, 128–29
Rosemary Chicken, Dijon,
    68–69
Ross, Carol, 198–99
Ruby Sauce, Curried Turkey
    Roulade with, 91–93
Rum Sauce, Great Greens,
    and Olives, Grilled
    Halibut with, 4–6


S

Saccaro, Richard Northcutt,
    111–13
Sacks, Jenny, 246–47
Salad, Pecos
    Chicken-Cornbread,
    85–86
Salad, Southwest Couscous,
    164–65
Salad, Spicy Salmon, 24–25
Salandra, Carmel M.,
    158–59
Salmon, Baked King, with
    Red Wine-Mustard
    Sauce, 18–19
Salmon, Dill-Crusted,
    20–21
Salmon Salad, Spicy, 24–25
Salsa, 94
    fruit desserts, 256
    seafood, 8, 10
Santop, Ziva, 202–3
Sara Moulton's Angel Food
    Cake with Mocha
    Sauce, 228–29

Sauce(s)
    Ancho Chili, 166–67
    Cucumber-Dill, 61
    for desserts, 206, 212–13,
        256, 261
    Horseradish Sauce, 109
    Mango-Chipotle, 102
    for meat, 123
    mocha, 228
    for poultry, 50–51
    raspberry, 261
    Red Chili Sauce, 140
    Ruby Sauce, 92
Sauce, Black Bean, Roasted
    Chicken with, 72–73
Sauce, Black Bean and
    Chicken Enchilidas with
    Green Chili, 83–84
Sauce, Fast and Easy Fusilli
    with Red Pepper
    Cream, 158–59
Sawyer, Diane, xiv, xv
Scallions, Chicken and
    Vegetable Enchiladas
    with Sour Cream and,
    80–82
Scardina, Keith, 104–5
Schneider, Joseph V., 20–21
Schofield, Diane, 204–5
Sea Bass, Poached, with
    Shiitake-Soy Broth, 11–12
Sea Bass with Curried
    Lentils and Rice, 13–14
Seafood, 3–48
    Baked King Salmon with
    Red Wine-Mustard
    Sauce, 18–19
    Cajun Cod Fillet with

Melon Salsa, 9–10
Chipotle-Beer Shrimp
    with Pasta, 31–32
Cioppino, 43–44
Crab Enchiladas, 41–42
Creamy Shrimp with Rice,
    33–34
Dill-Crusted Salmon,
    20–21
Emeril's Potato-Crusted
    Fish with a French
    Green Bean Relish,
    15–17
Fish Masala, 22–23
Grilled Halibut with Rum
    Sauce, Great Greens,
    and Olives, 4–6
Herbed Snapper with
    Warm Mango Salsa,
    7–8
Linguine with Crab and a
    Touch of Lemon,
    39–40
Poached Sea Bass with
    Shiitake-Soy Broth,
    11–12
Rebecca's Linguine with
    White Clam Sauce,
    37–38
Red Pepper Soup with
    Pan-Grilled Shrimp,
    45–46
Sea Bass with Curried
    Lentils and Rice, 13–14
Shrimp and Asparagus
    Casserole, 35–36
Shrimp in Tasso Cream
    Sauce with Eggplant

Medallions, 29–30

Southport Seafood Pie,
26–28

Spicy Salmon Salad,
24–25

Stonington Clam
Chowder, 47–48

Seafood Pie, Southport,
26–28

Shafer, Kim Dayna, 56–57

Shelton, Margaret, 224–25

Shiitake-Soy Broth, Poached
Sea Bass with, 11–12

Shrimp, Chipotle-Beer, with
Pasta, 31–32

Shrimp, Creamy, with Rice,
33–34

Shrimp, Pan-Grilled, Red
Pepper Soup with,
45–46

Shrimp and Asparagus
Casserole, 35–36

Shrimp in Tasso Cream Sauce
with Eggplant
Medallions, 29–30

Sickle, Arthur, 116–18

Simply Marvelous
Meringues, 263–64

Sirch, Sherry, 180–81

Skinny Whipped Topping,
275

Skogerboe, Celeste, 192–93

Slickrock Mesa Chicken
Stew, 78–79

Slinn, Bruni, 238–39

Smoked Sausage Tacos with
Mango-Chipotle Sauce,
102–3

Snapper, Herbed, with Warm
Mango Salsa, 7–8

Sodium content, 43, 47, 70,
89

Some Kind of Wonderful
Venison, 122–23

Sommers, Angela, 29–30

Soofi, Suraiya, 22–23

Sorbet, Peach and
Raspberry, Emeril's
Roasted Peach Soup
with a, 269–70

Soup, Cabbage, with Turkey
Sausage, 104–5

Soup, Caramelized Onion,
with Lemon-Corn
Chutney, 173–74

Soup, Hearty
Broccoli-Potato,
171–72

Soup, Pasta and Bean (Pasta
e Fagioli), 132–33

Soup, Red Pepper, with
Pan-Grilled Shrimp,
45–46

Sour Cream and Scallions,
Chicken and Vegetable
Enchiladas with,
80–82

Southport Seafood Pie,
26–28

Southwest Couscous Salad,
164–65

Spaghetti Squash with
Parmesan-Turkey Balls,
96–97

Spicy Asian Pork Rolls,
130–31

Spicy Pork Lo Murro,
126–27

Spicy Salmon Salad, 24–25

Spicy Whole-Wheat Angel
Food Cake, 230–31

Squash, Spaghetti, with
Parmesan-Turkey Balls,
96–97

Stew, Slickrock Mesa
Chicken, 78–79

Stew, Veal, in the Style of
Ossobuco, 116–18

Stift, Lisa, 60–61

Stonington Clam Chowder,
47–48

Stratta, Alessandro, 108

Strawberry, Amaretto,
Dessert, 273–74

Striler–Berry, Margee,
250–51

Stuffed Turkey Cutlets,
87–88

Sunny Penne Pasta with
Seven Vegetables,
154–55

Sweet Nachos with Fresh
Raspberry Salsa,
256–57

Sweet Potato Burritos,
136–37

Swiss Chard, 169

## T

Tackett, Sarah, 94–95

Tacos, Smoked Sausage, with
Mango-Chipotle Sauce,
102–3

Tangerine-Grilled Chicken, Tasty, 56–57

Tart, Peach and Almond Custard, 192–93

Tasso Cream Sauce, Shrimp in, with Eggplant Medallions, 29–30

Tasty Tangerine-Grilled Chicken, 56–57

Tequila-Lime Chicken, Low-Fat, 58–59

Teresina's Minestrone, 169–70

Tirami Sù, Carol's, 198–99

Toasted cheese-bread crumbs, 162

Toffee Chip Cookies, 240–41

Tomatoes, Fresh, Chicken Breasts and, with Capers, 54–55

Tomatoes and Olives, Penne Pasta with Eggplant and, 152–53

Topping(s)
   cakes and cookies, 219, 223
   cheesecakes, 180, 183, 185, 187, 190
   desserts, 215, 267
   meatless entrées, 151
   pies and puddings, 193, 199, 200
   poultry, 81, 97
   seafood, 27, 32, 46

Tortilla Pizzas, Quick, 142–43

Tortilla Quiche, 100–1

Tortillas, low-fat, 58

Turkey Balls, Parmesan-, Spaghetti Squash with, 96–97

Turkey Cutlets, Stuffed, 87–88

Turkey Feathers, Oven-Fried, with Jalapeño Pepper Mayonnaise, 89–90

Turkey Roulade, Curried, with Ruby Sauce, 91–93

Turkey Salsa Meat Loaf, 94–95

Turkey Sausage, Cabbage Soup with, 104–5

Turrisi, Donna Booth, 47–48

## U

Upside-Down Peach Pudding Cake, 214–15

## V

Valenzuela, Marie, 78–79

Vanilla Cream, Balsamic Berries with, 252–53

Vanilla extract, xvi

Veal Stew in the Style of Ossobuco, 116–18

Vegetable, Chicken and, Enchiladas with Sour Cream and Scallions, 80–82

Vegetables, Broiled Marinated Lamb with Mediterranean, 119–21

Vegetables, Ginger-Poached Filet of Beef with, and Horseradish Sauce, 108–10

Vegetables, Sunny Penne Pasta with Seven, 154–55

Venison, Some Kind of Wonderful, 122–23

## W

Wasserman, Amy L., 226–27

Waterman, Patricia, 232–33

Whipped topping, 186, 196, 210

Whipped Topping, Skinny, 275

White, Jo Anne C., 98–99

White Clam Sauce, Rebecca's Linguine with, 37–38

White fish, 4, 9, 11

Wilson, Robin, 91–93

## Z

Zotter, Donnamarie, 72–73